D1453328

Twilight on the Zambezi

Twilight on the Zambezi: Late Colonialism in Central Africa

Eugenia W. Herbert

Our approach to African history should allow us to number district commissioners among the dancing dead—along with our usual cast of chiefs and witchdoctors, warriors and herders, peasant men and women.

—John Lonsdale

palgrave
macmillan

TWILIGHT ON THE ZAMBEZI: LATE COLONIALISM IN CENTRAL AFRICA
© Eugenia W. Herbert, 2002

First published 2002 by
PALGRAVE MACMILLAN
Houndmills, Basingstoke, Hampshire RG21 6XS and
175 Fifth Avenue, New York, N.Y. 10010
Companies and representatives throughout the world

PALGRAVE MACMILLAN is the global academic imprint of the Palgrave Macmillan division of St. Martin's Press, LLC and of Palgrave Macmillan Ltd. Macmillan® is a registered trademark in the United States, United Kingdom and other countries. Palgrave is a registered trademark in the European Union and other countries.

ISBN 0–312–29431–X hardback

Library of Congress Cataloging-in-Publication Data

Herbert, Eugenia W.
    Twilight on the Zambezi: late colonialism in Central Africa/
    by Eugenia W. Herbert
        p. cm.
    Includes bibliographical references and index.
    ISBN 0–312–29431–X
        1. Zambia—History—1953–1964. 2. Zambia—Colonial influence.
3. Western Province (Zambia)—History—20th century. 4. Kalabo District
(Zambia)— History—20th century. I.Title.

DT3108.H47 2002
968.9403—dc21   2002020076

A catalogue record for this book is available from the British Library.

Design by Newgen Imaging Systems (P) Ltd., Chennai, India

First edition: July, 2002
10 9 8 7 6 5 4 3 2 1

Printed in the United States of America.

To the memory of Kawayawaya and Peter
Musyala fo

CONTENTS

ILLUSTRATIONS

Cover: Zambezi Sunset (John Herniman)

1. Lewanika in England, 1902
   (Caplan, *Elites,* between pp. 94–95)
2. Kalabo *boma* from the air
   (Murray Armor)
3. DC's house, Kalabo
   (John Herniman)
4. Touring camp
   (John Herniman)
5. Prisoners dancing as Christmas trees
   (John Herniman)
6. Grace Hart at Hart's store, Kalabo
   (John Herniman)
7. DC: Ndoka Canal
   (John Herniman)
8. The DC leaves Kalabo, May 1960
   (Murray Armor)
9. H.R.H. The Queen Mother, *litunga* Mwanawina III, and
   Gervas Clay, Resident Commissioner, 1960
   (Murray Armor)
10. The installation of the *mulena mbowanjikana*
    (Murray Armor)
11. Queen Mokwae—Slaves bringing her food
    (Coillard, *Threshold,* facing p. 213)

MAPS AND TABLES

Maps

Tables

GLOSSARY

ANC: African National Congress

baloi (sing. *muloi*):   witches

boma: a colonial district headquarters; in Swahili, originally an enclosure for animals

BSA (BSAC):   British South Africa Company

Bulozi: the Lozi heartland; the floodplain

bush: uncultivated land

cadet: a probationary colonial officer

Devonshire Course: the year-long course most newly appointed officials took at Oxford or Cambridge before setting out for their first assignment

district commissioner (DC):   the senior colonial official in a district

district officer (DO):   a colonial official junior to the DC

induna: an official of the Native Authority

ishee: the husband of a *mulena*

kapasu: chief's messenger

Katengo: a council of commoners, given increased authority during the late 1940s

kopje: a small hill rising abruptly out of a plain

kuomboka: the annual move to higher ground during the Zambezi flood, lit. "to get out of the water"

kuta: a court or assembly of notables; also, the district headquarters of the Barotse Native Authority

line of rail: the settlements flanking the railroad in Northern Rhodesia

litunga: the ruler of the Lozi nation, lit. "the earth"

makishi: costumed and masked dancers

maoma: royal drums

Mau Mau: a largely Kikuyu-led armed uprising against British rule in Kenya. Attacks against white settlers and collaborating chiefs began in 1952. The movement was suppressed by 1955, although large numbers of insurgents were detained for "re-education" and "rehabilitation."

Mboo: legendary ancestor of the Lozi ruling family

messengers: men employed by the *boma* to carry out a range of duties

moyoo: the senior wife of the *litunga*

mukolo: a canoe

mulena mbowanjikana: the female ruler of Libonda

mulena mukwae: the female ruler of the southern part of Bulozi

mosquito boot: a boot worn in the evenings. Women's were usually white, men's black

nalikwanda: a royal barge

ng'aka: witchdoctor, i.e., someone who identifies and combats witches

ngambela: the prime minister, lit. "speak for me"

natamoyo: the chief judicial officer, lit. "master or mother of life"

Rand: the richest gold mining area of South Africa (short for Witwatersrand)

resident commissioner: the chief administrative officer of Barotseland Province; elsewhere the term "provincial commissioner" was used

showelela: the salute reserved for high-ranking people

silalo (pl. *lilalo*):   a territorial administrative unit in Barotseland

sishanjo: rich peat soil on the margins of streams and ponds

sitapa: the zone of alluvial soil in the floodplain

sleeping dictionary: an African mistress

sundowner: a drink taken at 6 P.M. and thereafter

UNIP: United National Independence Party

Wenela: the Witwatersrand Native Labour Association; the main recruiting agency for migrant labor in Barotseland

Wiko: immigrants from Angola, lit. "people from the west"

ZANC: Zambian African National Congress

TIME CHART

Sixteenth–Sevententh c. Gradual movement of Lozi into Bulozi Plain, establishing rule first in Kalabo area. Breakaway royals extend Lozi influence southward throughout the floodplain

Development of Lozi system of political and social organization

Eighteenth c. Lozi ruler dominates floodplain and begins to extend sway to bush areas beyond the floodplain as well as raiding and exacting tribute farther afield

1840s Conquest of most of Lozi areas by Kololo invaders from south; retreat of royal family up Kabompo River to Lukwakwa, i.e. Mbunda country

1851; 1853 Livingstone visits Kololo capital at Linyanti, then ventures north before heading west to Luanda

1864 Restoration of Lozi monarchy under Sipopa

1871 Arrival of trader George Westbeech from south; promise of abundant guns to ward off Ndebele threat

1874 Sipopa moves capital south to Sesheke in search of new power base

1876 Revolt against Sipopa's ruthlessness leads to his assassination, followed by brief rule of Mwanawina

1878 Mwanawina deposed, Lubosi gains kingship and establishes capital at Lealui

1882–4 Missionary Arnot in Barotseland; leaves in anticipation of civil war

1884	Lubosi overthrown but restored a year later, taking name Lewanika, "to join"
1886	Coillard returns to Barotseland after having been tarnished by association with the usurper
1889	Ware Concession: right of Kimberley Co. to prospect for gold. Sold to British South Africa Company
1890	Lochner Concession (BSAC): sole rights to all minerals in Barotseland, defined by Lozi to include all of what became North-Western Rhodesia, in return for protection, education, and annual payment of £2000 to king. None of these forthcoming
1897	Robert Coryndon arrives as first BSAC administrator of Barotseland-North-Western Rhodesia
1900	Lewanika Concession: guaranteed central Bulozi as reserve for Lozi, free of white settlement or prospecting, but confirmed hegemony of BSAC, not Crown over Barotseland
1902	Death of Rhodes. Broken Hill mine discovered
	Lewanika in London for coronation of Edward VII
1904	Railroad from Bulawayo reaches Victoria Falls
1905	Settlement of border dispute with Portugal: much of Lozi-claimed territory west of Zambezi awarded to Portugal, along with parts of Luvale and Lunda country to north
1906	Railroad reaches Broken Hill
	Barotse National School founded
	British proclaim emancipation of slaves
1907	Codrington, administrator of North-Western Rhodesia, downgrades Lozi king to paramount chief
1909	Railroad reaches Katanga
1911	Unification of Northern Rhodesia (North-Eastern and North-Western) with Livingstone as capital. About 1,500 Europeans in the country
	Bwana Mkubwa only copper mine in operation
1915–16	Pleuro-pneumonia epidemic wipes out most Lozi cattle
1916	Death of Lewanika. Succeeded by son, Yeta III, head of mostly Christianized and literate new elite
1924	End of Chartered Company rule. New constitution reaffirms special status of Barotseland

1925   Royal tribute abolished in Barotseland; replaced by lump payment

1926   Successful prospecting at Roan Antelope marks beginning of exploitation of Copperbelt proper.

1935   System of Native Authority extended to Barotseland (1929 elsewhere in Northern Rhodesia)

1938   Yeta III attends coronation of George VI in England

1946   Death of Yeta III. Succeeded by Imwiko

1947   Local Government Despatch aims to reform local government in the colonies

1948   Death of Imwiko. Mwanawina III, another son of Lewanika, becomes paramount chief

       African National Congress (ANC) formed

       African Mine Workers' Union formed

1951   Victoria Falls Conference on federation stalemated because of African objections

       (Oct.) Tory victory in Britain leads to resumption of federation talks

1953   Central African Federation established over African opposition

       Mwanawina III goes to London for coronation of Elizabeth II

       Kaunda becomes secretary general of ANC under Nkumbula

1957   Kaunda visits UK for first time as guest of Labour Party to attend socialist conference

1958   (Oct.) Zambian African National Congress (ZANC) breaks away from ANC

       (Dec.) Kaunda and Nkumbula attend All African Peoples' Conference in Ghana

1959   Queen confers knighthood on Mwanawina III in New Year's Honours

       Kaunda and others in domestic exile and prison

       Elections under Benson Constitution; boycotted by ZANC

       Devlin Commission underscores African discontent with Federation and other grievances in wake of Nyasaland uprising

1960   Kaunda released from detention. United National Independence Party (UNIP) actively campaigns for self-government and independence

(Jan.–Feb.) Macmillan visits Central and South Africa

(May) Queen Mother visits southern Africa, including Barotseland. Throws switch at Kariba Dam

(Oct.) Monckton Commission Report recognizes impossibility of Federation in present form. Recommends increase in African representation and right of secession

(Dec.) Federal review conference in London a fiasco

1961   Mwanawina III visits London to argue for preservation of special status; threatens secession

Increasing unrest and violence in Northern Rhodesia during summer

1962   New constitution for Northern Rhodesia with expanded franchise

(Oct.) Elections inconclusive; later by-elections

(Dec.) UNIP and ANC form coalition government

1964   (Jan.) UNIP sweeps elections under new constitution. Kaunda elected prime minister

(April) Barotseland Agreement signed by Mwanawina III and Kaunda in London

(Oct.) Independence. Northern Rhodesia becomes Zambia

PROLOGUE

History is not truth. History is in the telling.

—Robert Penn Warren

I have always been fascinated by the Japanese film *Rashomon*. Made in 1950 by Akira Kurosawa, *Rashomon* tells the story of a medieval noblewoman who is traveling through the forest with her Samurai husband when they are attacked by a brigand. The story seems straightforward enough. As it is recounted by each of the eyewitnesses in a series of flashbacks, however, the viewer becomes less and less sure of what actually happened. How did the Samurai die? Was his wife raped or did she submit willingly, even eagerly? Did the Samurai and the brigand fight heroically or were they both cowards? Each account seems credible in its turn, but since the accounts are contradictory at key points, they cannot all be true. But are they all lies?

Rashomon is a beautiful film. It is also a salutary model for historians, for there is, in reality, no master narrative. One does not have to be a postmodernist to realize that each actor in a historical drama has a different perspective, both enriched and limited by his or her vantage point. One of the most difficult tasks for the chronicler is to respect that vantage point without falling into the arrogance of hindsight or latterday righteousness. It requires an act of imagination to transport oneself back into that other country of the past, discarding for a moment at least the omniscience that is the historian's preferred cloak. It is not so much, as the priest exclaims in *Rashomon*, that none of the stories makes sense, but that all of them do. The reader, then, can draw conclusions and make judgments from the material presented as well as I can.

Suggestive as the *Rashomon* model is, it only takes us so far. My canvas stretches much more broadly than a single forest and a small cast of characters. It embraces four disparate, indeed far-flung, settings and a multitude of players: Kalabo, district headquarters of the British colonial administration in what was then Barotseland, Northern Rhodesia; Libonda, the site of the neighboring and parallel Native Authority, also in Barotseland; Salisbury (Southern Rhodesia), the capital of the Federation of Rhodesia and Nyasaland, of which Northern Rhodesia was a part; and, finally, Whitehall, the nerve center of British colonial and foreign policy in London.

Life at the *boma,* the district headquarters, was lived very much in the circumscribed here and the bounded now. Its inaccessibility isolated it even from the Northern Rhodesian capital of Lusaka (635 miles away), to say nothing of the Federation capital of Salisbury (1,100 miles) or of Whitehall in distant London. The same was true of Libonda, even more isolated and insulated, whose primary compass points were Kalabo and Lealui, not Lusaka, Salisbury or London, its calendar dominated by the rise and fall of the Zambezi River. The stories of both Kalabo and Libonda lend themselves to the "ethnographic present," as if change in Africa really did move at the pace of the ox, as was often said.

And yet this sense of isolation and timelessness was illusory. There was no escaping the history being shaped for them in those distant cities nor the reciprocal impact of events on the local level. To cite one example, on August 29, 1959, a spectacular regatta took place at Liyoyelo, where the Luanginga River meets the Zambezi. It was organized by the District Commissioner Kalabo under the patronage of the Paramount Chief of Barotseland, Sir Mwanawina Lewanika, K. B. E. It was intended to demonstrate the harmonious relations between colonials and subjects in a full roster of contests, games, and demonstrations—and to give everyone a day of rip-roaring fun. That night, however, a murder took place. The victim was Akashambatwa, son of the late paramount chief and nephew of the incumbent ruler, Mwanawina. By early the following year, rumors were in full spate that the prince had been killed on orders from Mwanawina himself. The case fell to the colonial authorities to investigate, since murder was not part of the package of legal affairs left to the Native Authority. But so tangled was the web of local politics that it was impossible to uncover the true story.

This might have remained a purely regional matter, overshadowed by events affecting a far larger segment of the Empire. In fact, however, it had implications for the Federation government and for Whitehall itself. Both had been assiduously wooing Chief Mwanawina to support the

Federation against growing African hostility—hence the knighthood conferred in the New Year's Honors List of 1959. The incident revealed not only fissures within the royal family but also a public ready to accept the rumors of Mwanawina's complicity in the murder with unseemly eagerness. And yet this same public exhibited a fierce attachment to its regional and ethnic identity. This exalted sense of Barotse exceptionalism complicated nationalist strategies just as much as it complicated federal and colonial strategies. At the time, no one could tell how these interwoven strands would play out; only in retrospect do they form a larger pattern that could not have been visible from the limited perspective of any one of our four vantage points.

I have adopted and adapted the *Rashomon* approach to my story of late colonialism in the Upper Zambezi Valley for several reasons. First, as a teacher I had been frustrated for a long time by my inability to convey the ordinary realities of colonialism to undergraduates in the classroom, to bring them beyond the reified notion of an impersonal and monolithic leviathan. I was acutely aware of how difficult it is for students— indeed, for any of us—to imagine other worlds, even those of the relatively recent past and to resist the temptation simply to see "colonialism" and "nationalism" as so many abstractions, rather than the day-to-day actions of a variety of individuals, each operating in an imperfectly understood tangle of relationships and possibilities. It is much easier to divide the actors willy-nilly into good guys and bad guys and move on. Everyone acknowledges that our own lives are a lot more complicated than that, but we often fail to grant the same complexity to the past.

Second, I stumbled into an area that seemed tailor-made for my *Rashomon* experiment. My earlier work had taken me to Africa on a number of occasions to interview metalworkers and to document the dying technologies of brasscasting and iron smelting. Now I found myself interviewing former colonial officers and others about the vanished world they had once been part of. The difference was that their voices could be matched with those of a host of contemporaries, in person or through the printed record. It seemed possible to recover not the single choral line I had previously aimed for but an antiphony, even a cacophony, of voices, all of them eager to tell *their* version of what happened in the forest. To be sure, memories recounted forty years on are colored by a lifetime of reflection and experience (to say nothing of a knowledge of how things turned out), but there are letters, journals, photographs, and reports from the same period. All of these provide both an anchor and a filter for recreating life as it was lived in Kalabo District in 1959. Kalabo then serves as the springboard for the other tellings of the story.

I have chosen to focus on 1959—actually, what might be called a "long" 1959 (like the "long" nineteenth century, beloved of historians) since it stretches from late 1958 to May 1960—for a very particular purpose. This is the last moment, I believe, when British colonialism still seemed, both to the man-on-the-spot and to the policymakers at home, to have a future in the Upper Zambezi, the area in question. That is, it still seemed possible to make a difference, to devise and carry out political and economic development projects that would at last justify Great Britain's declared goal of benefiting the people it had taken under its wing almost seventy years earlier. After the impediments of two world wars and a great depression, the way at last seemed clear to go beyond the mere establishment of law and order to prepare the subject races of Northern Rhodesia to govern themselves one day and to take their place in the club of civilized people. There was "indefinite time ahead," to use the mantra of the period. It is therefore a moment when one gets a last glimpse of the particularities of colonialism, what it was like on the ground to the administrators and the administered, and a reminder of just how unpredictable history is when one is living it.

For we now know that there was, in fact, no time left; by early 1960 the sands in the hourglass had run out. But even in Salisbury and Whitehall, where decisions were being taken that would radically affect even the most remote corners of Barotseland, there was little sense of how fragile the existing world was. Just as no one foresaw the momentous changes of 1989—the collapse of the Soviet Union and the Communist regimes in Eastern Europe, the end of apartheid in South Africa—so even in 1959 and early 1960 no one foresaw the headlong rush to independence in Northern Rhodesia that began the very next year until all were caught up in the maelstrom. It was too late for a leisurely, controlled devolution to self-government, and the belated commitment to development fell victim to an obsession with security.

The reader will note that the changes in perspective are matched by changes in voice, just as changes in time are matched by changes in tense. I have employed the present tense when the lens focuses on the events of 1959, the past tense for earlier periods and for the epilogue. Because it is based so much on the personal testimony of those on the spot (much of it contemporary), chapter one has a particular immediacy that gradually fades as we move out in concentric circles from the district headquarters. The chapters on Salisbury and Whitehall therefore fill in more of the historical background to colonial policy-making and rely more on the published record, including both secondary works and memoirs of such leading figures as Sir Roy Welensky, Kenneth Kaunda, and Harold Macmillan. By definition these subsume the personal under the political; to label them works of self-justification is simply to state the obvious, but it does not detract from their importance.

Until very recently, colonial history has been out of fashion. Understandably so. It was imperative to right the balance and restore African history as first and foremost the history of Africans in their own continent, something that was only begun seriously about 1960. Earlier, if African history was studied at all, it was primarily the history of European activity in Africa, beginning with the "Discoveries" of the fifteenth century, the voyages of Portuguese explorers along the African coast. Soon, a host of other nationalities followed in their wake, seeking first gold and ivory, then slaves: English, French, Danes, Swedes, Brandenburgers, the whole lot. This was not colonization but trade; foreigners might meddle in local affairs but rarely did they control territory outside their small enclaves. With the exception of the Cape Peninsula in South Africa, few European came to settle; instead, they tried to make as much money as they could in as short a time as possible so that they could leave before being carried off by tropical diseases. The colonial period proper lasted in most areas of Africa south of the Sahara Desert for barely a single lifetime, from the late nineteenth or early twentieth century until the early 1960s. The brevity of colonialism is easily forgotten.

The first generation of African historians, inspired by the independence movements of the late 1950s and 1960s, felt compelled above all to rescue Africans "from the intolerable condescension of imperial history written by our seniors, in which African history was conceived as the story of how energetic white men had stirred up a stagnant continent," in the words of John Lonsdale, a prominent member of this founding generation. But Lonsdale himself recognizes that this approach, necessary as it was at the time, was "simply reversing the colour bar."[1] It is now time that colonial history become an integral part of African history as one attempts to piece together the intricate patterns of continuity and change. Time, too, to acknowledge that colonial officers must be numbered among "the dancing dead," in Wole Soyinka's phrase, along with the cast of African actors in the colonial drama. Few in number and distant from the centers of power and policy-making, individual officers could in fact have considerable impact on local affairs in their districts. Lonsdale has dubbed them "schoolmasters in modernity" and notes that they answered more to a "ruling culture of self-control, a habit of command disciplined by the opinion of one's peers and the likely reaction of subject notables"[2] than to a tight chain of command.

They were not, most emphatically, faceless or interchangeable bureaucrats. The particular character, even idiosyncracies, of the "man on the spot" counted for a lot. In Kalabo District, for example, the district commissioner (DC) serving in 1959 was as different in personality as night is from day from the man who preceded and succeeded him (the same man), and their day-to-day administration reflected these differences. Often these qualities of individual personality were shrewdly summed up in a pithy African nickname bestowed by the local people. For example, the DC Kalabo who is the focus of chapter one was nicknamed Kawayawaya, "little man who goes around in circles"—a reference to the frenetic energy with which he pursued his many projects. His predecessor had been given the sobriquet Kamilatu, "bringer of tears;" to some of his British colleagues he was known less eloquently as the "Barotse bastard." Needless to say, there was no love lost between the two men.

By the same token, the other roles in the drama cannot be compressed into stereotypes or "isms." They are, again to quote Lonsdale, "real people," who have too often been "flattened under our academic juggernaut," buried "under a sesquipedalian heap of theorization about such processes as modernization, the advance of capitalism, or underdevelopment."[3] The paramount chief, *litunga* Mwanawina, was quite different from his father, Lewanika, or from *mulena mbowanjikana* Makwibi; just as Roy Welensky was different from Godfrey Huggins and Stewart Gore-Browne, Kenneth Kaunda from Harry Nkumbula, Alan Lennox-Boyd from Iain Macleod. Clerks and messengers, missionaries and healers, recruiters and migrant laborers--each tells a unique story. Each, too, left distinctive tracks on the sands of Central Africa, but none could be sure where those tracks were leading.

If this story has a moral, it is a familiar one: Men—and women—make their own history, but not in conditions of their own choosing nor to the ends they may have had in mind. Like Soyinka's Dirge-Singer, we must therefore beg the living to "leave the dead some room to dance."[4]

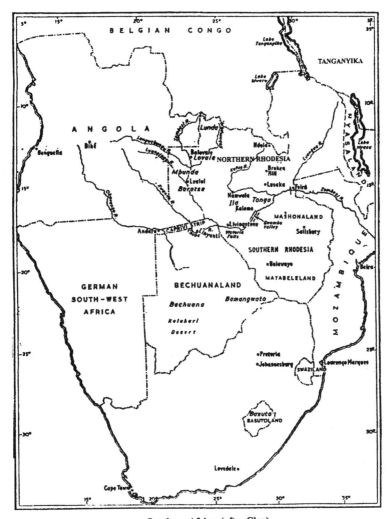

Southern Africa (after Clay)

Map 1 Southern Africa

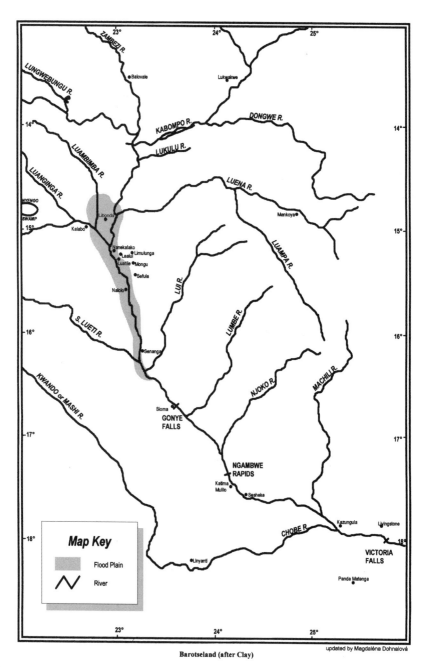

Barotseland (after Clay)

updated by Magdaléna Dohnalová

Map 2 Barotseland

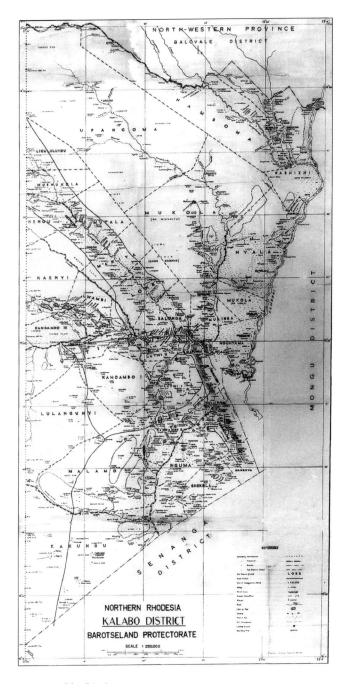

Map 3 Kalabo District

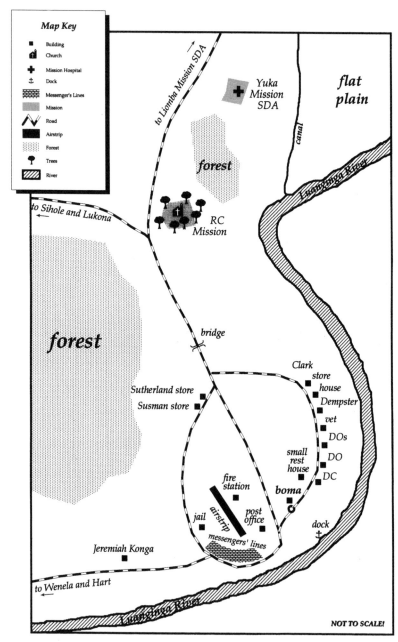

Map Key

- ■ Building
- ⌂ Church
- ✚ Mission Hospital
- ⚓ Dock
- ▦ Messenger's Lines
- ▨ Mission
- 〰 Road
- ▬ Airstrip
- ⣿ Forest
- 🌳 Trees
- ▨ River

to Liomba Mission SDA

✚ Yuka Mission SDA

flat plain

canal

Luanzinga River

forest

to Sihole and Lukona

⌂ RC Mission

forest

bridge

Clark
store
house
Dempster
vet
DOs
DO
DC

Sutherland store
Susman store

small rest house

fire station

boma

jail
airstrip
post office

dock
⚓

messengers' lines

Jeremiah Konga

to Wenela and Hart

Luanginga River

NOT TO SCALE!

Kalabo Boma 1959 (Magdaléna Dohnalová)

Map 4 Kalabo *Boma*

INTRODUCTION

Barotseland

The soil [in the Barotse floodplain] is extremely fertile, and the people are never in want of grain, for, by taking advantage of the moisture of the inundation, they can take two crops a year. The Barotse are strongly attached to this fertile valley; they say, "Here hunger is not known." There are so many things besides corn which a man can find in it for food, that it is no wonder they desert from Linyanti to return to this place...

It is covered with coarse succulent grasses, which afford ample pasturage for large herds of cattle; these thrive wonderfully, and give milk copiously to their owners. When the valley is flooded, the cattle are compelled to leave it and go to the higher lands, where they fall off in condition; their return is a time of joy.

—David Livingstone, missionary (1853)

The river itself is always beautiful with the monsters that sport in its depths, the clouds of water-fowl that animate its sandy shores, its verdant isles, its rapids and cataracts, its banks, here bare and irregular, there bordered with wooded hills.... At certain places, I could have believed myself on Lake Como or Maggiore.

—François Coillard, missionary (1885)

The Leeambye [Zambezi]! Nobody knows
Whence it comes and whither it goes.

—Zambezi boatmen's song

The Zambezi bubbles up as a small trickle of water in the far north-western corner of Zambia, not far from the origin of that other mighty river of Central Africa, the Congo. Where the Congo flows north and finally west into the Atlantic, the Zambezi heads south. At first it assumes a leisurely pace, then it gradually becomes a torrent as it rushes over rocks and gathers branches from east and west before it arcs at The Victoria Falls and makes its circuitous way east to the Indian Ocean.

A few hundred miles south of its source as the crow flies, but much farther as the river meanders, the Zambezi opens up into the floodplain that is the heart of Barotseland, the subject of this narrative (map 2). The diamond-shaped floodplain is roughly a hundred miles long and twenty to thirty miles wide, dotted with mounds, both natural and artificial, that stand out when the annual flood reaches its peak in February and March and covers the rest of the plain, forming a vast shallow lake. Some years, even the mounds disappear under the flood. Beyond the plain on the low escarpment that hems in the river is the bush, out of reach of the river and its rising waters. On the west, it extends with little relief toward the Angolan border, much of it infertile and uninhabited wasteland. On the east, the land rises very gently to the Rhodesian plateau. When the weather is unusually clear (paradoxically the clearest days come during the rainy season), one can see all the way across the valley from Mongu to Kalabo District.

There are few trees on the plain. Those that do exist have been brought from the bush to shade royal graves or have been planted by missionaries. Otherwise, the plain is a sea of grass, changing color and height with the changing seasons. At the end of the dry season, it is set on fire so that the whole plain turns black. Then green sprouts appear, growing rapidly with the rains and flood. Sometimes it is swallowed up by the blue of an unusually high flood; in other years the green tips stand out above the rising waters. As the flood recedes, the plain turns golden brown under the scorching sun. Once it abounded with game. It is still home to ducks and geese when the flood is up, to teeming quantities of fish, and to clouds of insects that are the scourge of man and beast. The flies, wrote one visitor, are "not single spies, but in battalions."[1] Malaria is endemic.

Most of Barotseland is covered with a mantle of Kalahari sands that do not hold water but are also not prone to erosion. The most fertile areas are those where the Zambezi has deposited layers of alluvial soil. In some of the long narrow valleys, too, sandy soils give way to peat that is fertile but must be drained if it is not to become waterlogged. The bush fringing the floodplain was once heavily wooded with Rhodesian teak and other hardwoods; now, severely deforested by the demands of sawmills in the south and the ever-increasing need for agricultural land, it is mostly scrub and secondary growth.

To a large extent, the river defines the world of the Lozi and the many other groups that inhabit what came to be known in colonial times as Barotseland or Bulozi, "the land of the Lozi." The Zambezi and its main tributaries are navigable the length of the heartland, as far south as the Ngonye Falls, the constriction that creates the floodplain behind it when the river swells from the rains at its source. Here one must portage along the rocky riverbank. Between Ngonye and Victoria Falls there is a series of rapids extending some 80 miles, with clear stretches between. The rapids can be very dangerous; one bears the sinister name of Noshu (Death). The Lozi were renowned for their skills as paddlers, often astonishing travelers with both their endurance and their speed, to say nothing of their fearlessness in negotiating rock-strewn channels infested with hippopotamus and crocodile. It is no wonder that the central Lozi ritual remains the annual move from the floodplain to higher ground, led by the paramount chief in the royal barge, accompanied by hundreds of other canoes.

By the eighteenth century, the Lozi were the dominant peoples of the floodplain. They tell two different stories about how they came to live in the valley of the Upper Zambezi. The first is essentially a myth of origin: They were created by the supreme god, Nyambe, and given the good things of the valley from the beginning of time. The second recounts a gradual movement southward from the Lunda-speaking areas of modern-day Angola and Congo, beginning perhaps as early as the late seventeenth century and leading them to settle first in the Kalabo area. They intermarried with many of the peoples they encountered and in time consolidated their rule over the entire plain. Culturally and linguistically, however, the process was reciprocal between the various groups, so that distinctions between Lozi and non-Lozi became increasingly blurred. This was less the case as the ruling dynasty extended its sway over groups living away from the river whom they periodically raided for cattle and from whom they demanded tribute in goods and people.

Like many African monarchies, that of the Lozi was inherently unstable. While any claimant to the throne had to be a male member of the ruling family, there were always plenty of candidates in a society where rulers prided themselves on the large number of wives they acquired. Civil strife was frequent, exacerbated by long-standing divisions between northern and southern sectors of the river valley and by rival centers of spiritual power. This no doubt made it easier for the Kololo, an invading group from the south, to overthrow the Lozi rulers about 1840. Remnants of the Lozi royal family fled to the north while the Kololo established themselves in the south. Their rule lasted scarcely more than a generation. Then they were overthrown in their turn and Lozi rule re-imposed. Most of the Kololo men were killed as insurance against a future resurgence, but the women and children were absorbed by the conquerors. As a result, the Kololo interlude, brief though it was, left a curious heritage: The primary language spoken in the Valley for the next generation was essentially Kololo. Even now SiLozi, the language of the Lozi, is a blend of Kololo and the Luyana spoken before the invasion. The earlier language survives above all in terms for certain political and social institutions and in songs and ritual invocations.

The restored monarchy faced the same problems as its predecessors: constant rivalries among royals, separatist tendencies between north and south, and restive peoples of the bush who felt little loyalty to their would-be masters in the floodplain. Only by ruthless extermination of fellow princes and alliances with strong families of commoners could a king hope to hang onto power for very long.

Even before the restoration, however, winds of change were blowing that would prove to be decisive before the end of the nineteenth century. Europeans began straggling into the Zambezi Valley, first from Portuguese Angola to the west, then from South Africa. David Livingstone formed close ties with the Kololo ruler, Sebitwane, arriving at his capital, Linyanti, in 1851. Linyanti lay south of the floodplain in an area so pestilential that travelers remarked on the sallow, fever-ravaged countenances of the populace. Cattle, too, could not survive long here because of the tsetse fly, which was not found farther north beyond the rapids. As the missionary-explorer followed the river northward, he was amazed and delighted with its almost Eden-like fertility and abundance of good things.

In Livingstone's wake came traders, hunters, and missionaries of all denominations, forerunners of "the encroaching tide of European immigration," in the prophetic words of one of them.[2] The most influential of the hunter-traders was George Westbeech, the "man with the toothbrush in his hat" (it was, he said, his only link with civilization) and a wife in every village along the Upper Zambezi, or so legend had it. Westbeech spoke the local languages like a native and became virtually indigenized among the Lozi. Hard-drinking but extraordinarily generous and compassionate, he was respected by everyone who ever met him, African or European, as a man of integrity. Sipopa, the Lozi king, filled his wagons with ivory and wept openly when Westbeech left after his first extended visit in 1871–72. On his return, he was made a member of the Barotse council of state. But the drinking and philandering were just too much for his Afrikaner wife who left him after only a few years of marriage.

It was through Westbeech's good offices and the trust that Sipopa's successor, Lewanika, placed in him that François Coillard of the Paris Missionary Society was allowed to establish missions in Barotseland, although Coillard never acknowledged as much (Westbeech was often bitter about the ingratitude of missionaries). Traders' motives and behavior were easy to understand. Lozi rulers quickly saw the benefits gained by the exchange of ivory for prestige goods to maintain their elaborate networks of clientship and guns to protect against rivals. Traders were few enough, too, that they had to abide by whatever restrictions rulers might impose. For the most part, the Lozi resisted pressures by Portuguese and Mambari merchants to sell slaves, largely because they needed all the labor they could muster for their complex agricultural and pastoral economy, and for the extensive system of canals that facilitated both drainage and communication within the Valley.

Unlike traders, missionaries were something of an enigma. Why were they so eager to leave their homes and to settle among the alien corn? Why were they so intolerant of indispensable rituals such as the consultation of royal graves? Why did they insist that men should have only one wife? Why did they refuse to trade or even to share their stocks of goods? On the other hand, they clearly had desirable skills to offer: carpentry, masonry, medicine. The Barotse ruler Lewanika loved to tinker with his hands and was so fascinated with building and architecture that he had the Paris Mission carpenter build him a house in his capital. He delighted in making miniature houses in his backyard as models for the carpenter to copy for others. But above all the missionaries held the secret of literacy. It is impossible to overstate the awe inspired by the printed word among non-literate peoples or the Africans' own equally awe-inspiring ability to get the mail through to Europeans in the most remote outposts, brandishing the familiar cleft stick like an icon of invincibility. Once, Westbeech received a large packet of letters while camped at the N'gambwe Cataract on the Zambezi—"Was it not a strange post office?", he asked rhetorically in his diary. As he smiled at anything amusing in the letters, his African companions remarked quietly to one another, "Look, he's laughing again. How wonderful! What can he see in that thing that he's looking at that causes such pleasure? For he does not speak, neither does it."[3] Then there was the matter of the Bible: It might be incomprehensible, but there was no doubt to outside observers as to its centrality in Christian belief and ritual. Did the Bible possibly have magical powers, given how tenaciously Europeans clung to it?

Many African rulers realized early on that missionaries might also prove useful in everyday dealings with the European concession seekers who began appearing in the region in ever greater numbers in the late 1880s and 1890s. King Lewanika, who had managed to regain the Lozi throne late in 1885 after being overthrown almost two years earlier, was in touch with his fellow monarch Khama to the south in Bechuanaland (present-day Botswana). Khama had converted to Christianity and found a *modus vivendi* with both traders and missionaries that seemed to offer mutual advantages. In 1885 he went a step farther, requesting and receiving protectorate status under the British Crown, a move that pre-empted attempts to annex his territories to the Boer Republic of the Transvaal. Khama's strategy was all the more impressive when compared with the alternative followed by Lobengula, ruler of the neighboring Ndebele, Lewanika's enemy and rival for domination of groups south and east of the Zambezi. Lobengula had been tricked into signing concessions that ceded much of his land to speculators from South Africa. When settlers and prospectors swarmed over the country, Lobengula at last resorted to armed resistance, but his armies were no match for the mounted troops and Maxim guns of the Europeans. Lobengula was defeated and killed. His country was taken over by Cecil Rhodes and his British South Africa Company, which parceled out the prime agricultural lands and mineral resources to white settlers who then exploited them with African labor.

Since Westbeech had died several years earlier, Lewanika was forced to rely on Coillard in his negotiations with the European concession seekers between 1889 and 1900. Khama had avoided being swallowed up by Rhodes's imperial steamroller, but he had been forced to agree to the alienation of some of his more fertile lands to white speculators from the Cape and Transvaal. Lewanika managed to avoid both conquest and land alienation, and like Khama ended up with a protectorate. However, his "protector" was not Queen Victoria, as he had at first supposed, but the British South Africa Company which, in return for the exclusive right to prospect for minerals in Barotseland, undertook to provide protection, an annual subsidy, educational facilities, and a resident commissioner.

None of these materialized until 1897 when the first Company administrator for Barotseland and North-Western Rhodesia took up residence in Kalomo, some distance east of the Valley. The long postponed annual subsidy was much less than the £2,000 initially promised, and the Company never provided for education or training in practical crafts. Nevertheless the final Concession of 1900 did guarantee that central Bulozi would remain free of white settlement or prospecting (actually there were no minerals in the region), all the while confirming the rule of the British South Africa Company rather than the Crown. Since by now all of Northern Rhodesia had a similar status, Barotseland found itself in the curious position of being a protectorate within a protectorate, something that would come back to haunt the country right down to the present. Lewanika preferred to think of Queen Victoria as his sovereign and pointedly displayed the large painting of her in his dining room, a peace offering laboriously brought out to him in 1897 by the British resident commissioner. When news of her death in 1901 reached Barotseland, he and virtually all his important *indunas* attended the memorial service held at the mission station.

Education did come by other means. Already in the early 1880s, the missionary Frederick Arnot had started a short-lived school. Coillard and other missionaries followed suit. Dissatisfied with the limited curriculum of these schools, Lewanika looked to other agents for a more secular, practically oriented educational system. When these failed to materialize, he backed the creation of the Barotse National School in 1906. For many years the only non-mission school in Northern Rhodesia, the Barotse National School was funded by the percentage of the colonial hut tax earmarked for the king, with no contribution at all from the Company. Its students were primarily the elites of Barotseland—the sons of the ruler and of leading chiefs and headmen—but, combined with mission schools, it produced a population with far higher levels of literacy than in the rest of the country.

1915. François Coillard and his wife lay buried in the little hilltop churchyard at Sefula, the first permanent mission in Barotseland. Rhodes had predeceased them and had chosen a far grander spot to await eternity: a rocky summit of the Matopos Hills in then-Southern Rhodesia, fittingly called the "top of the world." Westbeech, who had never much cared for missionaries, rested in the cemetery of the Jesuit mission at Vleeschfontein in the Transvaal, free at last from the fevers to which he had grown so accustomed that he never felt quite right without them. Livingstone's internal organs had been buried near where he died at Chitambo's village on the southern shore of Lake Bangweulu in what would become Zambia; his mummified body was carried to the coast by his African companions in one of the most extraordinary journeys in the

annals of African travel, and he was ultimately laid to rest in the august
precincts of Westminster Abbey.

Now ordinary Lozi and their neighbors were dying as soldiers and
porters in a world war between the colonial powers, a war that was fought
not only in Flanders and on the Somme but in Togo and Cameroon, South
West and East Africa. When World War I broke out, Lewanika had volun-
teered to send his warriors to join the armies of Britain. He also hoped that
Germany's early defeat in the Caprivi Strip would restore that strange sliver
of map-making fantasy to Barotseland, a hope that was soon disappointed.

But 1915 also marked two calamities that even the shrewdest statesman was powerless to forestall. First, the annual flood failed entirely, with
serious repercussions for crops and pasturage. The aging Lewanika
remembered such a failure only once before, in his youth. Next an
epidemic of bovine pleuro-pneumonia broke out, decimating cattle
throughout Barotseland. There was no known cure in either the Lozi or
the European pharmacopoeia. Ironically, cattle in most of the region had
escaped the devastation of the rinderpest epidemic that had wiped out
so many animals over much of southern Africa in the 1890s. Now, they
succumbed to a disease that had been introduced by oxen teams brought
in by a Portuguese Boundary Commission. Where once great cattle
drives had followed the Zambezi corridor to the markets to north and
south, for the next 30 years not a single beast could be legally exported
from the region.

Early the following year, King Lewanika died. He had learned first to
survive the deadly game of Lozi royal politics, then the even more baf-
fling challenge of European imperialism. In 1902, the year of Rhodes's
death, he had gone to London to attend the coronation of King Edward
VII (just as his son Yeta would attend the coronation of George VI
in 1938, and another son the coronation of Elizabeth II in 1953); in
England it was hard to miss his resemblance to Benjamin Disraeli,
Queen Victoria's favorite prime minister (see figure 1). Five years later
a colonial administrator summarily downgraded Lewanika from king
to paramount chief. To his subjects, however, he remained the *litunga,*
literally the "earth."

Lewanika had bridged two worlds and done so with more success
than most of his contemporaries. Four paddlers carried the news of his
death the 370 miles from Lealui to Livingstone in the unbelievable time
of four days. His body was placed in a canoe that proceeded stern first,
as was the custom, to the burial place at Nanikelako, the mound he had
chosen as his final resting place, with all of his favorite possessions except
the ambassador's uniform he had worn at the coronation that became

a much-prized uniform of his successors (see figure 9). Over the enormous burial chamber, skilled reed-workers wove an elaborate roof of thatch. Baskets of aromatic barks were scattered in the grave, their perfume making "a cloud of rose-coloured sweet-smelling dust" that lingered in the air.[4] The chief mourner was Mawana Amatende, the wife who had accompanied him into exile more than 30 years before. Thousands of Lozi were joined by the local British administrator (who himself would shortly be dead) and European traders and missionaries. The missionaries were allowed to hold a brief service at the graveside just before sunset. The next day a large number of cattle were slaughtered and Lewanika's royal barges were sunk in the Zambezi. Nanikelako now joined the other tree-shaded royal graves as a sacred place where future kings would come to consult their ancestors.

CHAPTER ONE

Kalabo: The View from the Boma

They were young men recruited in London, mainly from the public schools and older universities, and sent out to rule over vast areas of bush, forest, plain and desert, in the name of their Sovereign, as best they could. After a short apprenticeship as a cadet, they were sent as assistants to a District Commissioner who, perhaps himself not much above thirty, might have a region as large as half of England under his care. In Africa they went to a station known as the Boma, where there might also be a policeman, possibly a Public Works engineer or a Veterinary Officer if it was large enough, but very often just the D.C. They would spend, in those days, more than half their time on safari, camping by African villages and learning how the people lived and thought and acted, their languages, their needs. The villagers did not resent their presence in those bygone days. Quite the contrary. As a rule they accepted these white men cheerfully and without rancour as a kind of natural phenomenon from another world, and possessors of immensely potent forms of magic. Those peculiar strangers also collected taxes, which no one ever likes, gave judgements which the loser resented, and orders which might offend against deeply held customs and ways. So they were not uncritically accepted, but accepted they were, and respected and obeyed, especially if they had a sense of humour which bridged many cultural gaps. They were the chiefs, indeed superchiefs, and the peasants had not yet learnt to call themselves slaves. It was all very old-fashioned, Sanders-of-the-River-like, and today seems either incredible or absurd.

—Elspeth Huxley, writer

It is a terrible thing to be an Englishman, and worse still to be an Empire-builder. No man has the right to be such a nuisance to his fellows. I sometimes stand back and look at myself, and think how pleasant it would be to live in a hut in a mealie patch and mind nobody's business but my own until my dying day. Think of having no clothes but a loin-cloth and a blanket, and no possessions but one mat, a pot, a carved pipe, and three long spears!

—Kenneth Bradley, district officer

You know, Africa is an old bitch; it gets you in the end.

—unidentified asst. district officer

1959. Noontime. The district commissioner comes home for lunch. A bachelor, he always lunches alone, served by Dick, who is immaculate in white gloves and a white steward's jacket. Dick runs the household and is a stickler for form—hasn't he been to England twice with his regiment, the King's African Rifles, and slept in Hyde Park? Hasn't he bestowed on his sons names of British aristocrats?

He has set the place, with a book on the stand by the table. Currently, it is a book on bees, for DC Armor is an avid bee-keeper, the fifth generation of his family to be absorbed in apiculture. This is not as out of place in Kalabo as it might seem. On a recent visit across the border to Portuguese Angola, he was fascinated by an ambitious government-sponsored plan to expand beeswax production in that colony and hopes to experiment with a hive of stingless indigenous honey bees in Kalabo. Honey had been one of the traditional gifts sent in tribute to the *litunga* by subject peoples in the precolonial period and was served up to the court in the form of honeybeer. Livingstone once encountered a honey guide, what he called "this wonderful bird,"[1] northwest of Kalabo. Singing her *chichi-chat-chirr* song, she led him about a quarter of a mile to a hive in the hollow of a tree. Perhaps more could be done to develop the honey and beeswax industry in the district in these post-war days when development is very much on the colonial agenda.

As colonial outstations go, Kalabo in the late fifties is more "civilized" than those of bygone decades (see figure 2). The DC no longer lives in a thatched hut in an isolated village, days by foot from any other

Europeans save perhaps for the occasional trader or hunter who has "gone bush" and settled down with African women, happy to shed the customs of his homeland. In the early days of Company rule even many of the officials kept African women (referred to euphemistically as "sleeping dictionaries"[2]). This so horrified the wife of one provincial administrator that she insisted he draft regulations forbidding such ménages. These had to be rescinded immediately or he would have lost 75 percent of his staff. In the 1950s such liaisons are not only frowned upon, they simply do not occur. The present DC lives in a comfortable bungalow with a neatly manicured lawn sweeping down to the river (see figure 3). He has been able to indulge his love of construction by supervising the building of a brand new brick house for two of his junior officers, one of whom brought his fiancée out for Christmas in hopes she will join him for good in his new quarters. (She will not.) He has also rigged up a system that intermittently supplies water to the *boma,* when the tank isn't leaking or the pump out of order.

The word "*boma*" is Swahili for "enclosure," specifically a thorn enclosure to protect livestock from marauding beasts. It was first used in East Africa when posts were literally fenced in. The word only gradually and grudgingly came into official use to designate the administrative capital of a district in British Central Africa. When at full strength, the Kalabo *boma* consists of the district commissioner, a district officer, and a cadet or two, young men in their first year of training. What with leaves and transfers, however, there are often only three officers. From their offices in the whitewashed brick building located up from the port and shaded by a magnificent jacaranda tree, they oversee a territory of some 10,000 square

Table 1.1   Colonial administration of Barotseland

H. M. The Queen
|
Secretary of State for the Colonies
|
H. E. The Governor
|
Secretary for Native Affairs
|
Resident Commissioner
|
District Commissioners
|
Cadets

miles and 74,000 souls. This is in line with the provincial administration as a whole where 27 officers are assigned to all of Barotseland, a territory roughly the size of Wales. This administration does not number a great many more officers than it did at the time of Lewanika's death forty-plus years earlier. The main difference is that they are now assisted by more professional and technical staff: agricultural and veterinary, educational, medical, forestry, and public works.

In Kalabo, the administrative officers are very young. The cadets are just down from Cambridge, while the DC is the old man at the venerable age of 30. Only one of them has a wife and baby, both living with him on the post. The normal term of service is two and a half years, then home via the much cherished Union Castle steamship line for six months "long" leave. Subsequently, they may be transferred around the region or to another part of the colony altogether (which means learning another language). Cadets serve a probationary year; if they like the life, they can then stay on as district officers. For all officers, advancement depends not only on how well their superiors deem they do the job but also on passing examinations in the local language. For married men, there is an attractive bonus attached to their wives' linguistic achievements.

Within the district the DC's word is law and his authority unquestioned. That he and his few subordinates, the "thin white line"[3] of European officers, succeed in administering so large a territory is due in large measure, however, to the much thicker "black line" that complements it. The "eyes and ears of the *boma*"[4] are the messengers. They come from good families and know everyone in the district and everything that is going on. Some speak English, others don't; it is not a prerequisite. Each post has about two dozen messengers, and many have served for decades as translators, policemen (although they are usually unarmed), road builders, indeed as guides, philosophers, and friends to the foreign rulers, as one DC put it. They are the indispensable link between the *boma* and the villagers, on call 24 hours a day, and have been so for more than half a century. They have memories, it has been said, which are worth books of records and files. All officers depend on messengers but junior officers most of all. Fortunate the newly arrived cadet who has a savvy senior messenger as mentor on his first tour. The head messenger is Njekwa. He is tall and imposing but inclined to be taciturn. His second in command is small, with something of the old soldier about him. Both inspire great respect among the villagers and other messengers.

Originally messengers used the traditional Lozi salute of vigorously raising and lowering the right arm and fist, accompanied by the greeting "*more*" (short for "*morena,*" a term of respect similar to "sir"), but this has fallen out of favor since a messenger badly frightened an uninitiated nursing sister at the local hospital. Rather like federal marshals, they have the power to arrest. A messenger thinks nothing of walking a hundred miles off into the bush to apprehend someone who has fled a crime—or simply gone berserk (something that tends to happen at the new moon)—and bring him in. At night he ties his prisoner to a tree via an extremely sensitive part of his anatomy and resumes his walk to the *boma* the next day.

The messenger's uniform is distinctive: blue shirt and shorts, boots, and puttees. In some places, the red fez has been replaced by a blue slouch hat, but not for important occasions in Kalabo. Red stripes on their chests signify their rank: The head messenger has three or four stripes. While the uniform provides the messenger with considerable prestige and assures him universal access to the population, it is a somewhat misbegotten piece of clothing. The bucket-like boots and baggy trousers don't do much for the wearer, while the leather puttees that swath the lower legs may be handy against snakes but are otherwise an abomination in the hot climate. If a messenger doesn't already have a bicycle, he is given a loan to buy one. Bicycles are often of dubious practicality in this sandy region, but that doesn't prevent them from being a symbol of status and modernity.

In the late fifties, there are no truly all-weather roads in the district. When the B148 was completed south to Senanga district last year, it was supposed to be passable at all seasons. That was probably a vain hope; in any event its extension in the neighboring district floods every year so Kalabo remains isolated from the rest of the territory much of the time. The road east to the provincial capital at Mongu has only been open for four months this year and even in that short time managed to break the chassis of a new Land Rover bringing the minister to visit. Indeed, with 70 percent of the district flooded at least part of the year, the only reliable communication is by air, via the sturdy little Beaver planes of Central African Airways that alight on the landing strip near the *boma* ten times a week and still can't keep up with demand. The airstrip dates back to 1932, when it was built for the princely sum of 4 shillings. Local prisoners supplied the labor, while the 4s went to replace DC Oliver's wife's panties, which served as windsock. There is fire equipment of a sort that is hauled out every time a plane is due, but it is probably just as well it has never been needed. During one fire drill, the equipment shot out a cloud of angry hornets that had taken up residence in the hose instead of the expected foam; during another, the hose turned out to be blocked and blew up with an enormous explosion, scattering people in all directions. The airstrip now has a small terminal with a multi-racial tea bar. The Swedish wife of Cadet Herniman runs the booking office. The few vehicles in the district consist of the *boma* Land Rover and two two-ton Bedford flats, the livestock officer's vanette, and the trucks belonging to Wenela, the agency responsible for recruiting local labor for the mines of South Africa. Nevertheless, the DC in a moment of whimsy has constructed a one-way roundabout in front of the *boma*. He has even embellished it with a fountain in the middle and has ambitions of illuminating it for the up-coming visit of the resident commissioner. Since there is no reliable plumbing, the fountain is activated by a man hidden in the bushes who pumps vigorously from a tank whenever anyone approaches. This installation no doubt satisfies the DC's love of order. His motto, it is said, could easily be "If it doesn't move, whitewash it." A sign nearby provides Kalabo's coordinates (latitude, longitude, and height above sea level), as well as directions to the main points of call: *boma,* post office, airfield, Clark's store, Yuka. Should hordes of tourists descend, Kalabo is ready.

Kalabo itself is situated on the Luanginga, a tributary of the Zambezi. The *boma* fleet consists of six boats of various sizes. The DC has his own motor launch, christened *Mutinglati* (kingfisher), which is his pride and joy, and can make the run to Mongu in two-and-a-half hours when the water is up. It compares to all other crafts, he boasts, as a Land Rover does to a lorry. A local trader has optimistically brought in a seven-ton freighter, a "Clyde puffer," but the Luanginga needs more clearing and straightening before barges can use it economically to haul goods in and out. The Lozi and their fellows travel among the maze of waterways in shallow canoes poled standing up, a bit like punting back in England. To non-Lozi these vessels always seem perilously close to capsizing. "I do not think that in 20 odd years at sea I was ever more nervous," commented a DO of a terrifying trip down the Luanginga.[5] One of the DC's pet projects is a boat-building school he has set up at the *boma* in hopes of teaching local carpenters to build large canoes capable of carrying up to a ton of grains and legumes from the forest villages down to the plains and exporting dried fish and other goods. These boats substitute planks for the traditional dugouts from Angola or the north, which have become scarce as the supply of large trees dwindles.

Mostly, however, in this land of water and sand, one gets around on shank's mare. Even in the late fifties, touring remains the quintessential duty of the British colonial officer and the ideal is still touring on foot, spending the night "under canvas." When one hapless officer makes use of the Beaver to fly to a mission station in his touring area, thereby avoiding the tedium of a barge moving up the Zambezi at the stately pace of one mile an hour, he is sternly rebuked by the resident commissioner: "Has he no hobbies; no interest in the people; no interest in increasing his efficiency in the language, and no interest in the country through which he passes?"[6] Boats, bicycles, and horses, yes, Land Rovers only to get to the area, planes not at all. The purpose of touring, he declares, is not to save time but to get to know the Africans and to investigate their concerns.

The more days spent on tour and under canvas, the more the DC can gloat in his annual report. There is also an extra allowance for touring that is welcome since colonial salaries are low. In 1958 the three officers stationed in Kalabo spent 322 days on tour, 188 of them under canvas, not a bad showing given the severe problems of food shortages and the aftermath of the outbreak of witchcraft in the district. One year later, with more normal conditions and an additional officer, the DC hopes to tour the entire district, visiting every last village, most of it on foot, the rest by canoe, something that has never been done before and that will be difficult since most touring must be squeezed into the short period when the flood is down. In a curious way, touring totals are apt to be higher in districts where most of the officers are bachelors since touring offers a welcome relief from spending lonely weekends at the station.

Touring, it must be said, is both an art and a ritual. In practical terms, it is the way the administrator keeps in touch with what's going on in the far corners of his domain. At the ideological level, it reminds people that they are part of a global empire, subject to a distant queen, however fuzzy that concept may be. It doesn't matter so much what you do on tour, one DC confessed, as long as you are simply there to be seen and spoken to. A single European officer, even a cadet, sets out at the break of day with 20–30 carriers, several *boma* messengers, the local chief and several local *indunas* (representatives of the Native Authority), a cook, the court messenger, and a retinue of camp followers. There may be as many as 50 or 60 people, strung out in a caravan several hundred feet long. The caravan is a "very efficient little machine," as the DC puts it. It is also a mobile statement of hierarchy: The number of carriers allotted depends on the rank of the officer, and the same is true for the chief, the messengers, the clerks, and so forth. Some of the porters carry maize (corn) meal to be swapped for other food at villages. Others carry the tax registers, the deed boxes, the theodolite (for surveying), the medicine trunk, and the district messengers' kits. The DC's kit includes a portable table and chair, camp bed, canvas bathtub and folding tray for a washbasin. After years of experience, he has his "crash box" down to one man's load containing everything he could ever need or want: pens, pencils, folding telescope, matches, candles, whiskey, medicines, jelly, cartridges of all sizes. A unique assortment, he thinks, unmatched among his fellow officers. Unlike one of his predecessors, however, he does not travel with a chest of drawers and an aspidistra in a pot to lend a homey touch to the rigors of camp life.

When the touring procession approaches a village, it is greeted by the headman and by dancing and ululating women who fall into step with the caravan, singing all the while. They are dressed in colorful print dresses and often have babies on their backs. A century earlier women turned out to greet Livingstone in the same way during his travels in Barotseland: "Their shrill voices to which they give a tremulous sound by a quick motion of the tongue, peal forth, 'Great lion!' 'Great chief!' "[7] he noted in his journal. The visit of the officer is one of the big events of the year and will immediately be memorialized in popular songs about the tour, the messengers, the new development center at Namushakende, the Seventh Day Adventists—whatever is topical at the moment.

Once arrived at their destination, the DC expects camp to be set up and everything unpacked within ten minutes; otherwise they must pack up again and move on to another site and start over. Discipline is discipline. This is rarely necessary, however, since the system has been honed to perfection. The DC has a tent but prefers to sleep in the open when possible. More commonly, officers stay in temporary straw huts that have been built for them within reed palisades—"a green leaf shelter put up the day before" is the ideal because it's cool and the ticks haven't had time to settle in.[8] The flag is planted just outside the enclosure; cooking and washing equipment are set up in inside (see figure 4). At the back is a small straw latrine. For the fastidious, colonial outfitters supply pierced toilet seats with folding legs. Some officers prefer a large tin bath tub, rather than the canvas variety, because it can be packed full of more fragile items and carried between two poles.

In the evening, the DC may chat with local officials over the fire, but he does not invite them to share a meal or a drink; they in turn do not expect him to join local beer parties. Before retiring for the night, the head messenger gives a very precise accounting of everyone and everything from the day just past. Sometimes the stillness of the night is broken by Africans singing nearby. On one occasion an officer finds himself listening to a solitary man somewhere nearby singing Adventist hymns half the night. On another, he comes across a cheerful blind man playing an instrument of his own design: a length of bamboo on the end of which is a calabash in the shape of a trumpet. In his youth he learned to play with the Salvation Army, but now he remembers a single tune that sounds like a cavalry charge or possibly "Come to the cook house door, boys."

Sometimes the night will be filled with dancing. On the whole, though, the DC reflects that there is less singing and dancing here than at his previous postings in Kenya. How different from the magical scenes described by a young colonial veterinarian traveling in Barotseland earlier in the century. He would hide in the trees to watch so that the Africans would not be inhibited by his presence, entranced by the dancing which would go on far into the night. The dancers would form two lines, then begin a sort of humming while swaying and clapping their hands. As they gradually warmed up, one or two would jump into the middle and perform fantastic movements. Then they would withdraw and others would take their place. Excitement mounted, women twisted and turned with tiny babies on their backs. They would keep up the pace until everyone dropped with fatigue. "It was," he commented, "a gripping and strangely emotional sight."[9]

The first order of business on any present-day tour is updating the population census and checking off the tax register. This the DC does with the local *kuta* president, his two *indunas,* and the court clerk, but everyone from the entire *silalo,* or subdistrict, is expected to turn out. Since the *silalo* may have a population of more than 4,000 people spread thinly over a wide area, many come a long way. Chairs or stools of some description are set up for the dignitaries under a tall tree or, if it is wet, in a little open-sided thatched hut at the center of the village. The proceedings begin with greetings. Everyone is expected to get down on their knees and give the *showelela* salute, the same one they would give to a senior member of the Barotse Native Authority. The DC crouches down and returns the salute. There is more to this ritual than a simple show of respect: It is a way for the DO to spot the idiots and the blind. Those who do not salute because they are handicapped or retarded do not have to pay taxes—a way of making sure that the community will not do away with them, as the administrators assume they might if someone had to come up with their taxes. The same is true of twins who have an ambivalent status: They are feared as well as cherished. All in all, the palaver provides a great deal of drama as well as farce since people's names frequently change from year to year, family matters are tangled by a high rate of divorce, and much imagination goes into trying to evade taxes.

When taxes have been disposed of, the officer listens to complaints, answers questions, and offers advice. Negotiations proceed for the exchange of local grain for seed grain. He inspects the village, the crops, and especially the famine garden that each locality is required to plant.

In general, the Lozi are very provident, but the men whose job it is to build fences around the gardens to keep out the wild pigs don't really like the bother. A long palaver follows about who should shoot the marauding pigs; by now this has become almost a set piece. Occasionally the officer hears a court case with the local *indunas* and an interpreter. The hearing is held al fresco and since both the DO and the *indunas* must always be in the shade, they keep moving as the sun moves and everyone else along with them. Before long, it all begins to look, he muses, like the Mad Hatter's Tea Party.

Although there are separate education officers who make their own tours, every district officer visits all the schools along his route and comments on the state of the buildings, the energy of the teachers and local school council, and the appearance of the children. One cadet is "mildly surprised" to be greeted during a school visit by a song that sounds very much like "The Red Flag" ("Bandeira Rossa"). He is even more surprised to find a pin-up of a very attractive young lady on the wall. She is a "visual aid," the teacher explains.[10] The DC warns the cadet that "his own severely formal education should not prejudice him against progressive schools;" in any case since it is a Catholic school, "no doubt action will be taken."[11] Provincial headquarters is more agitated about "The Red Flag" than the pin-up, fearful that Communists have somehow infiltrated the local schools. It is, after all, the height of the Cold War, and who knows how far the Kremlin's tentacles may reach. Helpfully, the cadet supplies musical notation for both the original tune of "The Red Flag" and the version he heard, but whether his superiors can read music is unclear.

If a hospital assistant has come along, he makes his services available to the villagers. If not, people simply flock to the DO since medical treatment is one of the most popular parts of an official visit. "My aim," writes another flustered cadet, besieged on his first tour by a steady stream of patients, "is to do no harm."[12] Hippocrates could ask no more. Sometimes the touring officer hears court cases, but usually these come to the *boma* or are handled by the traveling *indunas* if they involve "customary," that is, indigenous, law. When business is over, everything is packed up again and the caravan moves on, danced along by the local women until they are relieved by women of the next village.

Nowadays there is a political education component to touring. Colonial policy aims to expand grassroots participation in government by reviving the Katengo Council, an indigenous institution that had been dormant for a half-century before its revival in 1947. Candidates are represented by colors or by symbols: axe, canoe, bird, fish. Voters, both male and female, file past the pictures and point to the one chosen by the candidate of their choice. This is fine for illiterate voters, but some officers feel it is time to move on to written ballots for the literate. Initially, the idea of such elections was so alien that they had to be orchestrated entirely by the *boma,* but the emphasis these days is on training local *indunas* to conduct them. The system receives its first real test in the elections of 1958. From the *boma* standpoint the results are disappointing. The candidates are not of great ability and while voter turnout is quite high, almost everyone votes for their home candidate so that the nominee of the sub-district with largest population naturally wins. But how to alter the system "to make the results less of a foregone conclusion"?[13] In 1959 such preoccupations with a leisurely introduction to the electoral system are superseded by the sudden need to register voters for the upcoming territorial election. Initially the paramount chief refuses to allow registration at all, then belatedly changes his mind so that officers must scramble to sign up voters in time for the election.

The average tour lasts two or three weeks but may go on even longer. Touring is the acid test for the officer in the bush station—if you don't like it, you had better find a desk job in the capital. Officers are not entirely cut off since messengers bring them mail from time to time. Still, it can be very dreary in the rain. They endure heat and insects and the frosty nights of winter. During the flood the water often comes up over their Wellingtons (blest be the name of the good Duke, none the less). One DO remembers that toward the end of a long hot day's walking, the messengers gleefully pointed out the rock on which a previous DC had sat the year before with his head between his knees, saying he simply couldn't go on. He did, of course, but it was ten minutes before he painfully got to his feet again. The food is monotonous, with a steady diet of rice and bananas. Once a tin is opened, its contents reappear meal after meal until it is all gone since there is no refrigeration to preserve it. Hunting is therefore both a diversion and a necessity—to provide meat for the collective pot. The DC is a keen hunter but the same is not true of all of his officers.

In spite of everything, there is a mystique of living "under canvas," and bush officers tend to look down on their desk-bound colleagues, although it is an unfortunate fact that the path to advancement in the Service inevitably lies in the paperpushing routines of the Secretariat. And even those who love going on tour, as many do, acknowledge that one of its greatest pleasures is coming home to the luxury of a house, a hot bath in a proper tub, clean clothes, and a drink. But the wise man, an officer observed many years earlier, pours himself "one, long decent-sized sundowner, then has the bottle and the soda safely packed away."[14]

What has brought these young men to such a remote spot? What possessed them to join the Colonial Service? The classic answer is that, unlike the Indian Civil and Political Service or the Sudan Political Service, the British Colonial Service doesn't require passing an exam. What it does require is a good university degree, usually from Oxford or Cambridge but also possibly from University College, London, or Trinity College, Dublin. It helps, too, to have demonstrated athletic prowess. It is not necessary to have won a "first," a degree with the highest distinction; in fact, such candidates are discouraged. Ralph Furse and the small group around him in London who have selected colonial service officers for almost 40 years justify their personalized methods of recruitment via letters of recommendation and interviews on the grounds that it takes a very special type to live in "unfamiliar scenes and strange conditions."[15] While still in his twenties an officer may find himself in charge of an expanse of Africa as big as Yorkshire and quite possibly alone. Academic excellence itself is no predictor of success but athletics are, since one must not only be in good physical condition but also enjoy strenuous exertion to survive the rigors of outstation life. A classical education is undoubtedly a plus: "A man who has read 'Greats' can tackle anything."[16] Furse remains an idealist as far as empire is concerned, but he regrets that the Victorian empire was modeled so much on the Roman with its emphasis on engineering feats, rather than on the Greek ideal of a spiritual and cultural alliance between ruler and subject peoples as personified in Alexander the Great's rapprochement with the Persians. Poor Furse is more often thought of as "the man who keeps the white man's grave filled."[17]

For young men eager to see the world, to exercise an unusual amount of responsibility at a very young age, to escape or postpone the unwelcome routine of a nine-to-five desk job, to prove themselves in the face of hardship, danger, and disease—and possibly to do some good in the world—the lure can be irresistible. As one colonial secretary reminded a group of young officers about to set out on their first postings: "In what other task can you have so much power so early? You can at the age of 25 be the father of your people: you can drive the road, bridge the river, and water the desert; you can be the arm of justice and hand of mercy to millions. You can, in fact, serve England."[18] The classically trained may recognize that they have been cast in the role of Plato's guardians, "men nurtured to serve the state and their fellows, just, detached, uncorruptible."[19] And independent. However severely superiors may minute the reports of their officers in the field, the truth is that their very remoteness guarantees a wide freedom of action.

Contrary to the common image of the colonial officer as a younger son of the nobility, most are quintessentially middle class in origin, as often as not from professional families with a heavy sprinkling of teachers and clergymen in the ancestral line. They genuinely believe in the solid values of their class and country: in decency, service, authority exercised with restraint—in the virtues that to their thinking have made Britain great and can in turn be instilled in subject peoples so that one day they can take their place among the "civilized" nations. It is not quite Kipling's "White Man's Burden" that has impelled them to go off to the four corners of the earth but a less flamboyant, often unspoken faith that they are making a genuine contribution to the well-being of the less fortunate races. They see colonialism as "a venture in applied philanthropy—not as an enterprise designed to maximize metropolitan profits."[20] In the 1950s, many of the recruits are ex-servicemen, like the DC Kalabo (who came directly from the Army without having gone to university, something that makes him exceptional), or transfers from the Indian or Sudan Service, both of which have by this time become extinct. Earlier they could expect advancement through the ranks and finally a comfortable but hardly munificent retirement, but by 1959 a lifetime career in the Service is looking more and more problematical. The British Empire may not go on forever after all.

Before taking up their first appointments, recruits participate in the year-long Devonshire Course at Oxford or Cambridge that is supposed to prepare them for what is to come. "To this end," one officer remembers, "our mentors sought to instill in us the Elizabethan ethos of a love of learning combined with a life of action."[21] Such is not the unanimous view. There has been much debate about how much can be taught and how much can be learned only on the job, which is perhaps to be expected given the high level of discomfort that theory often provokes among the British. Get them out in the field, then send them back for courses say some; no, before they go, they need to know the rudiments of colonial history, anthropology, law, tropical agriculture (almost all remaining British colonies are in the tropics). Courses are taught by regular faculty but also by Service officers, an odd mixture of the academic and the practical. Since World War II, the program has been more systematic, thanks especially to the influence of Margery Perham with her redoubtable combination of scholarly and practical background in colonial administration (see chapter 4). In some cases Africans are available to provide language training, especially for more common languages such as Hausa and Swahili, but these are of no use in Northern Rhodesia. There is a provision for a Second Course, a sort of sabbatical year, after officers have been in the field for a while, although this is more hit or miss because officers can rarely be spared from the field to teach or attend. In retrospect, some recruits feel the Devonshire Course is useful, while for others it is "a bit of a dog's dinner"—with something missing.[22] But all enjoyed the year at Oxbridge.

There is of course a pecking order among the colonies. India and Sudan had been one and two, but they were not part of the Colonial Service at all. Those that are within its purview range from Barbados to Hong Kong, the Falklands to Fiji. Within the fourteen territories in tropical Africa the most prestigious are Kenya, northern Nigeria and the Gold Coast; they constitute the "colonial Ivy League." Northern Rhodesia is not very high on the list. It is some consolation that Barotseland is considered the plum assignment in the colony. The DC served in Kenya for his first six years but became more and more entangled in the Mau Mau Emergency. He is glad to be far away from all that now and able to concentrate on development rather than insurgency and the "re-education" of forest fighters.

The Colonial Service is a man's world. The only women recruited are in nursing and education, and these activities are still mostly in mission hands in 1959. Officers are allowed to bring out wives and families, but it is a lonely and boring life for those who come. Their husbands are often out on tour, servants run the household and do all the work (and may begrudge the presence of wives as interlopers in a comfortable ménage), children must sooner or later be sent away to school, there is a lot of heavy drinking. Transfers from one remote area to another are frequent. "It is a fact," one service wife noted ruefully, "that out there men can get along without us. It was the rule rather than the exception in years gone by, and the rule still runs that there is little we do that cannot be done after a fashion by somebody else."[23] Indeed, there are still some die-hards who resent the presence of women in the colonies at all. They argue that when men are mostly on their own, they settle more deeply into the life of the district, make friends among its people, go hunting and drinking with the chiefs, with no one to complain about long absences or overdoing the booze.

Wives can be a positive influence, however, in at least two spheres: food and gardens. They quickly learn to order all their European food in bulk: sugar, flour, rice, tinned goods, since shipments are few and far between. It is best to cultivate a taste for local foods as much as possible since they are cheaper, more varied, and more readily available if one learns the rhythm of the seasons. Chicken (rather scrawny), eggs (check for freshness), fish, venison, and beef can generally be bought locally; and of course fruits: oranges, mangoes, bananas, pawpaws, pineapples, and various wild fruits. When a wave of longing for English cuisine sweeps over, it is lamb that is usually missed the most. Everyone has vegetable gardens—they order seeds from catalogs—and swaps what they have in abundance. Butter, cheese, and bacon are shipped in, packed in salt. There are also dried fruits and dehydrated vegetables, billtong, and spicy South African sausages, *boerewors,* from the Caprivi Strip. Of course, almost anything can be flown in, but that is beyond the budget of most households. By this time officers' quarters are usually supplied with kerosene refrigerators, which smoke a lot and often break down.

Realistically, wives know that the meat is apt to be tough or suspiciously high and the general diet monotonous. The remedy is the indispensable bottle of Lea & Perrins Worcestershire sauce, itself an import from colonial India. On her way out to Central Africa, one wife was offered Worcestershire sauce with lunch on board ship. When she refused, her tablemate warned, "You had better get a taste for that or you'll never be able to eat anything out here."[24] The trader Westbeech had discovered that secret of survival decades before, and tried never to be without it. To avoid running low, most people buy it by the case, when available. Like any addiction, however, one tends to get used to Lea & Perrins over time and to crave something stronger. The answer is home brew. Take an old bottle, add a few chilies, fill it up with gin and serve. As the level drops, top it off with more gin. Or, make it in quantity using a whole row of bottles, a basket of extra strong chilies, and a crate of gin. Then lay the bottles down like fine wine to mature. The chilies can be removed from time to time and replaced, and so on. The advantage of home brew is that one can always invite unsuspecting newcomers to "try the sauce" and watch them cough and splutter and gasp for air. Some connoisseurs consider gin to be vulgar, preferring to add a good dash of sherry. On the occasion of Queen Elizabeth's visit to Nigeria in 1956 a lunch was arranged for 180 people at the University of Ibadan. When the African catering officer was informed by the planning committee that he could not have Worcestershire sauce on the table, he broke down and wept. What was courtesy if not a handy bottle of Lea & Perrins? Civilization can be a confusing thing.

Gardens are so crucial to survival in outstations that a manual for prospective colonial brides includes a whole chapter on them. While tropical flowers can be made to grow in abundance, there is a great yearning to grow plants from home. "Your great triumphs," the chapter begins, "will always be when you have induced some ordinary English flower ... to make itself at home in an unlikely clime, as you will be doing with yourself."[25] Indeed, one DC's wife was so determined to have roses that she got caught up in an unseemly fight over the limited amount of manure available from the *boma* horses. It has become proverbial in the Service, however, that planting roses is sure to lead to a transfer—one will be gone before the effort bears fruit. The spring flowers, snowdrops, crocuses, narcissi, and daffodils, are what one misses the most, and no amount of manure can make them grow in Barotseland gardens. Sometimes it is a triumph even to have a proper lawn. On the other hand, there is no lack of help—boys to fetch water or pull the weeds or turn the soil of a new flower bed so that white ants do not settle in—and every European house has its gardens filled with hibiscus, bougainvillea, frangipani, poinsettias, lantana, and fruit trees. After the rains they run riot; during the long dry season they wait.

But for some women, *boma* life remains a hardship. The lone officer's wife at Kalabo was met on her arrival by a snake in the outside lavatory. It was hardly reassuring that its head was lopped off when the door was opened. Perhaps because she is Swedish, she finds herself wondering, too, about the whole enterprise of colonialism in a way that her fellow Brits do not. What do the Africans think of having alien rulers in what is after all their country? Do they resent the fact that the Europeans live so much better than they do, with servants they can hire for a pittance? The gulf between African and Europeans standards of living makes her uncomfortable and at the same time worried, however much she acknowledges the achievements of colonial administrators and the jobs they have provided for the local populace.

Since childhood, she has been afraid of the dark, and Kalabo is unbelievably dark on the long moonless nights, surrounded by the strange noises of the African bush. During the rainy season, violent thunder storms seem to shake the earth to its core. When her husband is away on tour, the nights become unbearably frightening alone in the house with small children, no electricity and no telephone. So frightening that on one occasion she packs up the children and takes them along on tour. Paul, a little over a year and a half, is carried seated in a wooden *machila* with a folded pram packed up next to him; his sister Denise, only a few months old, is stashed securely in the "meat safe," a box slung between two poles with wire gauze sides and "curtains" to keep out the sun. After eight days, however, touring has lost much of its romance, and she is throwing crockery at her husband and Nelson, the cook, out of pure frustration.

Some wives, however, adore bush posts—the wilder the better. Far from seeing touring as the lesser of two evils, they jump at the chance to bundle up their offspring and set out. Such was Betty Clay (who had no doubts at all about the ultimate blessings of the colonial enterprise): "I wasn't going to be deprived of the fun of going on tour just because I had babies!"[26] But, then, Betty is the daughter of Sir Robert Baden-Powell, founder of the Boy Scouts, and had of course been a Girl Guide, which is more than she can say for her husband in spite of the fact that he has risen to be resident commissioner for Barotseland in 1959.

The *boma* dominates life in Kalabo but does not define it. Ironically, the administrative officers are its most transient population. The current DC is actually in place for the theoretical two years before going on long leave, but more commonly there is a game of musical chairs of officers and cadets coming and going as the Service tries vainly to meet its needs. The same is true of technical staff such as livestock officers. But there is a more permanent population of both Africans and Europeans. The *boma* messengers and their families live close by in housing provided for them, the messengers' "lines." Add to them the army of clerks, medical dispensers, mechanics, cooks, gardeners, and house servants. All of them are male, even the cooks and house servants, since no self-respecting man would allow his wife to work for the *boma* or for other Europeans. Many of the men live in the surrounding African villages and return there at night.

All told, the African workforce in Kalabo numbers in the hundreds. In addition, the ten-to-twenty odd prisoners housed in the jail adjacent to the landing strip perform all sorts of daily chores such as fetching water and wood to heat it, emptying nightsoil from European "thunderboxes," and tending the *boma* grounds. They are mainly in for drunkenness and fighting. By law, they can only be kept in the *boma* prison for sentences of less than nine months; since the prisoners provide such useful services, there is considerable incentive to keep sentences within the limit. They move about freely and escapes are virtually unheard of. In fact, when the warden has had too much to drink, the prisoners carefully lock themselves up at night. Their most bizarre penalty may be having to dance as Christmas trees during the holiday season with leafy branches stuck in the back of their shorts (see figure 5)—what can the Europeans be thinking of? Except for the witchcraft troubles several years earlier (which didn't affect the European population in any case), serious crime is so rare that houses are never kept locked. Most Europeans don't even know where the doorkey is. Once the witchcraft outbreak subsided, there haven't been any murders in the district.

The long-term European residents are traders, labor recruiters, and missionaries. Some trading firms have had ties with Barotseland since the very beginning of the century. This is the case with Susman's, founded by an immigrant Jew from Lithuania. (Jews played a surprisingly important part in the early commercial history of Northern Rhodesia.) Several other traders are more recent. One of the most remarkable is Mrs. Dempster. Mrs. Dempster comes from a family of Swiss hoteliers. As a young girl she trained at the best schools in London, St. Petersburg, and New York. Then she abruptly decided the hotel trade was not for her, joined the Paris Missionary Society, and came out to Lukona Mission near the original site of the *boma* before it was moved to Kalabo. There she met Billy Dempster, a trader who had moved up from Bulawayo to Lukona, then followed the *boma* to Kalabo. Between them, they built a thriving trade in otter skins. Mrs. Dempster was the first passenger when air service came to Kalabo. By the late 1920s they were shipping out nine parcels a week of skins in the mail bag. Dempster was much older than his wife and died shortly after their marriage. The then-DC put on the death certificate that he died of alcohol deprivation. As a consequence, Mrs. Dempster refused to have anything to do with the administration until now when she gets on very well with the present DC.

After her husband's death, she continued the export of hides and has proved to have a very good head for business. Once she decided she wanted to take a holiday and see "God's wonderful sea." Although well on in years, she walked all the way from Kalabo to Lobito, on the coast of Angola, and back, a distance of over a thousand miles, accompanied only by her houseboy and gardener with headloads of skins. At the time—this was in the early fifties—Angola was very unsettled, having just gotten over the Mbunda wars, and her black companions were foreigners to the Angolans. Mrs. Dempster is famous not only as a traveler but also as a *cordon bleu* cook, and her invitations to lunch are coveted. One arrives promptly at noon and only leaves the table at 4:00. In between she serves the best sherries and wines and food imaginable. But Mrs. D. never sits down with her guests—she is busy in the kitchen. When lunch is finally over, she does at last join them, always sitting up ramrod stiff in a straight-backed chair.

Another trader, Rob Hart, is the son of a Livingstone blacksmith. He flew combat missions for the South African Air Force in World War II and eventually came up to Barotseland with his second wife, Grace, a nurse (see figure 6). He persuaded the paramount chief to make him head crocodile hunter in exchange for a trading concession and the commission to construct the ruler's ceremonial barge, *Nalikwanda*. Hart has an extraordinary knowledge of local birds so that it is not surprising that one of his sons has also been fascinated with birds since childhood.

He was schooled first at home, then in Mongu, but his parents have discovered that he has been corresponding with ornithologists at a university who have no idea that he is only 12. Since Livingstone's time, Northern Rhodesia has been renowned for its prodigious variety of birds, especially in the Zambezi Valley.

The Japps are also passionate collectors of local fauna. Dick Japp is the recruiter for Wenela, the Witwatersrand Native Labour Association. He and his son Mike both collect specimens for an American biologist, Mel Trailor, who has come out to Kalabo several times (and is consequently well aware that Mike is only a young boy). Trailor's wife is an ornithologist. Between them they have named a new species of snake and bird after Dick's wife, Hazel. At an early age Mike learned to prepare specimens for shipment to Trailor and to an expert in the Northern Rhodesian government. Dick Japp is especially fond of snakes and has a large pit outside for live ones. The house is also full of them, which can be unnerving for guests. Once a rather timid missionary was visiting and a snake got loose in the house. When the missionary got up in the night to go to the loo, he saw a snake in the passageway. He let out a cry of horror. Dick came out, looked the snake over, said, "No, that's not the one," and went back to bed.

In addition to the snake pit, the Japps have a very large enclosed area in which they keep an extensive and changing array of animals. They are known to buy orphaned animal babies, so that there is a steady stream of Africans at the door offering small animals for sale. Unfortunately, the Japps probably provide an incentive for producing orphans. Their favorite animals are a hyena, Mungilo, and an otter, Moses. The hyena is so tame that when they later give it to the Livingstone Zoo, it is allowed to walk around freely among the startled visitors. For now, the otter lives in the house. It gets so excited to be released from its cage in the morning that it makes a flying leap into the large water dish used by the dogs, then, dripping wet, makes the rounds of all the beds in the family to wake everyone up.

Mike's life is more like that of an African child than a European. His everyday language is SiLozi, his playmates, African boys of his age. His closest companion is the son of Mubita, a renowned herbalist. They constantly evade their parents' admonitions and slip off to play in the crocodile-infested river. The worst fate Mike can imagine is to have to wear shoes. For now his mother teaches him and his sister at home, along with their fellows, but the day will come when he has to go across to Mongu for schooling along with other European children, boarding with local families there.

Wenela has a large presence in Kalabo, with its trucks and provisions and staff of 40–50 workers. It also maintains a smaller post at Sikongo, out by the Angolan border. It is only about 40 miles away, but it takes all day to get there. It is even more isolated than Kalabo. Squire Davis ("Squire" is his Christian name) has manned the station for some 20 years, repatriating workers and looking after their wages. Davis is unmarried, his visitors are few, and he is deathly afraid of going bush. Each day he shaves and puts on immaculately washed and ironed clothes. He is a great connoisseur of Christmas puddings, which he orders direct from Harrods and Fortnum & Mason. In fact he eats one every day, but saves the choicest for guests. On such occasions there is much discussion about which to choose from his "cellar" until, like a fine wine, they may settle on a seventeen-year-old Harrod's—"That's a good one." Aside from fine food, he also likes his whiskey.

Squire Davis is very large, not to say corpulent. However, he has thoughtfully provided his outhouse with Russian-doll type seats, running from small to very large, so that children won't fall in. (This cannot quite match the flush toilet installed in a baobab tree by a magistrate in Katima Mulilo to the south.) Though Davis likes good living, he has also learned to be self-sufficient: When necessary he pulls out his own teeth with a pair of pliers. A practical man, he has had a coffin made, just in case.

One who *has* gone bush is Ellis, an Afrikaner from the Transvaal whose original name was probably Els. Ellis is one of the last of the "barefoot trekboers." As a small boy in Pretoria, he used to exchange greetings with President Kruger of the Transvaal Republic every day on his way to school. He trekked with his family, taking immense herds of cattle north to the Belgian Congo through Bechuanaland, South West Africa, and Angola, then returning by the route that later became the line of rail in Northern Rhodesia—a formidable journey but not unique in the early years of the century. One year he came down the Zambezi and just stayed in Barotseland instead of going back to South Africa, living largely outside the law raising cattle and the best oranges in the district. Now he is a very old man, almost at death's door and in great poverty. When the South African attaché in the North Rhodesian capital learned from the DC that they had a real trekboer out in Kalabo, he got very excited and proposed to make a big fuss over him—that is, until he discovered that Ellis has a seraglio of African wives and a bevy of mixed-race children. After that he was no longer willing to spend a cent on him. Ironically, whatever his living arrangements, Ellis's racist views about Africans would go down as well in apartheid South Africa as in the old Transvaal Republic. He expresses these views freely in front of his wife and children, which may be one reason his son Patrick regularly beats the old man. Or did until the DC put a end to it.

The missionaries are quite a different story. Once settled in Lukona, the Paris Missionary Society was loath to move when the capital shifted to Kalabo in case the British should decide to move again. The Roman Catholic Mission, staffed by Irish fathers, is 30 miles out at Sihole. To get there by car takes a good three hours sitting on top of a boiling hot engine. Father Connor, who is a Latin scholar, remains in charge at Sihole, but this year a new mission has opened in Kalabo, a pretty, white-arched church and convent with red trim. It is home to three priests: Father Bruno, Father Anton, and Brother Joe. Father Bruno is a genial Northern Irelander with a luxuriant black beard. He supervises a number of Catholic schools in the District, spending much of his time on tour much like the district officers. Brother Joe is very shy and almost never says anything, even to children. There are also four Irish teaching sisters. The new mission is just over a mile from the *boma*. This is no accident since everything within a mile must conform to rather strict building regulations. Although most of the administrative officers are Anglican, they get on best with the Catholics whose devotion and effectiveness they admire. Because the fathers never get leave, they are very much part of the local scene and know the people and the language well. During the DC's canal building campaign, he occasionally comes upon odd bits of canal already dug here and there. They turn out to be penances meted out to parishioners: For adultery the priest demands 40 Hail Marys and 20 yards of canal. The priests are also good company and eagerly welcome guests—it is the only time they are permitted to have a drink.

The Seventh Day Adventists, too, are very much a part of life in the District. They have built an impressive hospital at Yuka, several miles outside of Kalabo on a bluff overlooking the river, complete with electricity and running water. Dr. Birkenstock and his wife are very good doctors and altogether worthy people but somewhat suspect because they don't touch tea or coffee or alcohol, only Postum. Meals at the Mission are always preceded by long prayers focusing on "the sinner in our midst." The prayers seem especially pointed when the DC visits, but he has taken his revenge: When he is asked to say grace, he inserts a very long prayer for the reconversion of the lapsed, which Father Connor has translated from Latin for him. This has put an end to such prayers altogether, at least when he is around.

Although the hospital is well stocked and well staffed, many patients prefer to go to the clinic at the *boma*. There the hospital assistant, Daniel Muliwana, may not be as well trained as Dr. Birkenstock, but he is a far better psychologist. Where Birkenstock tends to hem and haw about what may be wrong and how best to treat it, Muliwana diagnoses every ailment instantly and decisively, and assures the patient that he has exactly the right medicine for it. Needless to say, the patient feels better before his foot is out the door. On tour to remote corners of the district without any dispensaries of their own, he treats a never-ending flow of patients—766 on one tour, working late into the night by the light of a large fire and a hurricane lamp.

Dr. Birkenstock has tangled with the administration from time to time over medical and educational priorities. He prefers to be guided by the will of God rather than local regulations and agreements. In fact the DC often finds it trying to deal not only with the Adventists but with the various sets of competing Christian missionaries. If one of them wants to build a new mission or school or hospital, it involves a lengthy palaver with the Native Authority as well as the *boma*. It is very hard to get them all to sit down together and work out rival claims; they prefer to write letters to the DC. In a fit of desperation he calls them to a meeting to sort out their differences once and for all. Several of the missionaries and *indunas* arrive drunk, and the proceedings get so cantankerous that the DC announces the meeting will adjourn to a nearby tree. He and the drunken parties climb up into the trees to continue the discussions while some of the sober ones, notably the Seventh Day Adventists, stay on the ground.

There are some 23 Europeans in Kalabo, including children. But the *boma* is to some extent a world apart from the more permanent population. The Japps and Harts, for example, live next to each other but at the opposite end of Kalabo from the *boma*, a long slog if one is forced to cover the two-three miles on foot through the sand (see map 4). Just as the DC is the heart and soul of the *boma*, Hazel Japp and Grace Hart are the heart and soul of this other world. No problem or crisis seems to faze them. They have one leg in the European world and one in the African, but Africa is "home," not England. They expect to live out their lives here and are very happy do so. When someone asks Hazel Japp if she would like to take her children to visit England, she replies in horror, "But it's so dangerous!"

Still, at this moment there are exceptionally cordial contacts between official and non-official populations. There is much more socializing than under previous administrations—somehow, the chemistry is better. The DC plays poker every Saturday night with Rob Hart and often goes hunting with Hart and Japp. At Christmas, the European contingent gets together for a seemingly endless round of festivities: Christmas Eve,

Christmas Day, Boxing Day, the whole English repertoire. Even Father Bruno joins in the games with gusto, passing the orange from under his bushy black beard to beneath the chin of a lissome lass on a holiday visit. But the adults find the hoola-hoop competition impossible; best left to the children. The Seventh Day Adventists unknowingly eat some sherry trifle and find it delicious. Grace Hart judiciously doesn't mention the key ingredient when pressed for the recipe. Best of all, a shipment of potatoes miraculously arrives in time for the holidays. But just as in England, many are heartily glad when the Christmas season is finally over. It can be wearing to see the same set of people at party after party.

Relations between Africans and Europeans in Kalabo are also friendly but more distant since they are usually those of employer and employee. This changes in the bush, whether on tour or hunting. Here the African is on home turf, Europeans are his guests. He knows very well how dependent they are on him once away from the *boma,* so much so that the paternalism inherent in colonial relations is turned on its head. "In the bush," reminisced one DO, "the white man was a wayward, irresponsible child who would get hurt if you didn't keep sharp things out of his messy little hands." One could wander off after the day's work to look for birds or other things, secure in the knowledge that the messenger would always be looking out to "see what the silly bugger is up to now."[27] For once, race and rank dissolve in the camaraderie of life in the wild.

Other relationships also transcend race. The Japps have grown close to Mubita, the herbalist, who has a superb knowledge of medicinal plants that they often use. Mubita is also one of the few who knows how to find the secret fountain in the Liuwa Plain across the Luanginga, a spring that can only be used by the paramount chief. He has taken Mike there several times. On the *boma* side, the young cadet is an avid footballer and plays with the local African team. His daily lessons in English and arith-metic have turned out to be a huge success for younger and older students since so few Africans can come up with the money to continue their education beyond Standard VI (which corresponds to about age 11 in England).

In contrast to other parts of East Africa, there are no Indian store-keepers in Kalabo, but there are a number of African petty traders and hawkers, and one proper storekeeper. Jeremiah Konga is a Luvale from the Northwestern Province and the first African in Kalabo to own a Land Rover. Stories about his mishaps with it are legend, which is not surprising given the road conditions.

In spite of its remoteness, Kalabo does get an occasional visitor. In the main they are officials representing various arms of the provincial government, but this year, G. R. Oliver, he of the windsock fame, has come back to see the *boma* he administered a quarter of a century earlier. More surprising has been the visit of an American filmmaker, Reid H. Ray. Ray is in search of "primitive" ironworking for a film commissioned by the National Machine Tool Builders Association in the United States. His query went first to the high commissioner in Salisbury, then worked its way down to Lusaka and finally to Kalabo. The DC wrote to the American Consul saying that there were indeed local ironworkers in the district and enclosing a sample spearhead. Nothing more was heard until about a year later when he received the draft of a film script in which Kalabo was referred to as the "Pittsburgh of Barotseland." It was forwarded to him by the resident commissioner who thought it would be a good thing if the local administration could give as much help as possible to the filmmaker. The next thing they knew, Ray was on their doorstep. Nothing daunted, the DC put him in touch with a group of Luchazi ironworkers, led by a delightful old man named Chilundu. Chilundu had been born into a family of smiths in Angola and moved down to the Simunyange Plain in 1928, at a time of mass exodus from Angola. He worked the local iron deposits on the Plain until 1948 when the rising water table flooded his ore pits, forcing him to go up the Luanginga where he and his team found both ore and a profitable market for his hoes, axes, and spearheads.

Because of the various prohibitions surrounding iron smelting, Chilundu and his men need a secluded spot and have found it in the *boma* orchard. Ray is delighted to find them working so well and comes back several months later with a film crew. He captures the whole process from gathering the ore, transporting it to the furnace by canoe, smelting it, and finally forging a hoe from the iron produced. The film is entitled *One Hoe for Kalabo,* but in fact the Kalabo sequence only shows up in a short scene at the beginning intended to underscore the contrast between the primitive techniques of the African smith and the sophisticated know-how of the American machine tool industry. Nevertheless Ray's footage is very valuable for researchers, and the DC and one of his officers have found the experience so intriguing they are publishing an article on indigenous iron working in the *Northern Rhodesia Journal*. True, they have eliminated all references to Pittsburgh but do describe in detail one of the last surviving examples of a major African technology.

1959 is a moment of calm at Kalabo after several years of disasters, natural and otherwise. First there was the outbreak of witchcraft and witchcraft accusations that began in Kalabo in late 1956 when one of the

Catholic fathers at Sihole Mission informed the DC of rumors that two old women had recently been murdered and that their deaths were somehow related to witchcraft. The DC investigated and soon found the corpses of the victims. He also found the perpetrators who had killed them at close range with short-barreled homemade muzzle-loading rifles, known locally as "*kaliloze* night guns." From Kalabo, the epidemic of the so-called "Kaliloze gunmen"—witches who used crudely shaped guns, sticks, and needles to kill people in particularly nasty ways—spread quickly but unevenly throughout the Protectorate. Soon poison also became part of the witches' arsenal. At the peak of the scare, hundreds of people, many of them "elderly and of benign aspect" filled the jails to overflowing, while colonial officials were "deluged with charms and potions surrendered by self-accusing witches and wizards" to quote the 1957 *Annual Report*.[28] It was particularly difficult to deal with the outbreak because victims and witnesses were often too frightened to talk. More fundamentally, it was beyond the range of European understanding: Why the sudden burst of witchcraft killings? What motivated witches and how did they choose their victims? Most officers had little experience to guide them.

Witchcraft is not a new phenomenon in Barotseland. When the missionary Frederick Arnot arrived in Lealui, the Lozi capital, in 1882, witchcraft trials were in full swing. The accused were forced to plunge their hands into a pot of boiling water five times in order to remove five stones. If they came through unscathed, they were exonerated; if not, they were burned alive. Whether out of bravado or ignorance, Coillard chose the mound on which the witches were burnt as the site for his mission station at the capital.

Lewanika declared that there was no such thing as witchcraft and abolished witchcraft ordeals. The colonial Witchcraft Ordinance is more ambiguous. While it shares Lewanika's view that witchcraft does not exist, it goes into great detail about what constitutes witchcraft and how it is to be punished. This puts the authorities in the awkward position of seeming to believe in the existence and malevolent powers of witches. Nevertheless, during the spate of witchcraft accusations in 1956–57, the *boma* courts found that it was almost impossible to fit verbal accusations into a form that would meet the accepted rules of evidence. The result was that people so accused were almost never charged but were released, to the consternation of their neighbors. Why, they asked, does the government let people out of prison when it knows they are witches? Cases brought to trial had to rely instead on objects associated with witchcraft that were actually found in people's possession: not just *kaliloze* guns and red beads but divination baskets, charms and figurines, needles, utensils for necrophagy, and so forth. Ironically, these are the tools of the trade for diviners as well—those responsible for smoking out witches—but since the Ordinance prohibits divining as a means of identifying witches, the net gathered up witch and witchfinder willy-nilly.

In 1957 the then DC at Kalabo heard 162 witchcraft cases. He did not resort to boiling water. Instead he obtained information and confessions by ordering a messenger to take men and women out and torture them with *serui* ants: The men were forced to drop their trousers and the women to lift their skirts, whereupon the ants were turned loose on their private parts. They attack like tigers, in the words of one writer, and eat the flesh right down to the bone. After 30 seconds of this, most people were ready to talk, and the DC had earned a new sobriquet: Mulena Kamilatu, charitably translated as "the scourge of the Baloi" [witches] or more generally as "bringer of tears."

Whether because of administrative severity or because it had simply run its course, the outbreak died down almost as quickly as it had begun. The present DC is relieved to report that there have been no cases at all in 1959.

What continues to be troubling, however, is the increasing frequency of disastrous floods. Two years of unprecedented high water have had a catastrophic effect on local agriculture. Two-thirds of Kalabo District disappeared under water in the 1957–58 season. The government has had to organize mammoth relief efforts, importing cassava from the Lunda regions to the north and maize meal from the "line of rail" to the east—in all more than £30,000 of food had to be imported. Whole plains now bubble up like giant springs in January and February. Elsewhere, pans have flooded for the first time in memory with the water rising steadily during the dry season. Thousands of acres are now so waterlogged that they no longer support crops or cattle. Much of the floodplain has become like a sponge that won't dry out. Even in normal years Barotseland is no longer able to feed itself. How has it come to this in a land that Livingstone described as one of the most bountiful he had ever seen?

The height of the annual flood depends on both local rainfall and rainfall at the source of the Zambezi and its tributaries. Rainfall tends to be cyclical and the floods of the period 1956–58 may represent the peak of a cycle. There may also be subtle subterranean effects of volcanic action elsewhere in Africa, and the persistence of standing water may itself affect rainfall patterns. But the DC and others see more than natural forces at work. The most crucial may be the neglect of channels and canals that used to be cleared artificially. Further, large patches of forest in the district have been cut down to accommodate the agricultural practices of Wiko immigrants from Angola over the last four decades. When this land is abandoned and allowed to regenerate, it can support only scruffy bush. The increasing use of fish traps and dams in the middle and upper stretches of the watershed also hinders run-off. Even the wholesale slaughter of hippos in recent times has probably contributed to the abnormally high water table: Hippos grazing and slogging through channels act as four-footed roto-rooters, keeping them from becoming choked with papyrus and grasses.

Without regiments of hippos to do the job, the DC is determined to mobilize large numbers of human workers throughout the district to restore the canals to their earlier effectiveness. With his accustomed energy, he attacks the problem on all fronts. While urging specialists to study the hydrology and human ecology of the province more comprehensively than has ever been done in the past, he has made canals his top priority. (As one *induna* explains to his people, "O.K. It was witches last year, this year canals are the big thing."[29]) Teams of men have been organized under *kapitãos* who have been to a canal school at the *boma* where they were trained not only in the techniques of the job but also in the public relations aspects and the water conservation regulations of the Barotse Native Government (BNG). Working with local *indunas*, the DC has prepared films, slides, posters, and tapes to spread the word about the importance of drainage. Leaflets have been dropped by plane and a profusely illustrated book on the District's canals prepared for use as a school reader. Parallel canal courses and conferences have been held for officials of the BNG. Local woodcarvers have been enlisted in a competition to create a statue that will commemorate the completion of the Ndoka Canal, one of the most ambitious projects (see figure 7).[30] The films are the biggest draw (just as Livingstone's and Coillard's magic lantern shows were in earlier days). They are shown three times a week to eager audiences. The 16 mm projector is powered by a small boy pedaling a bicycle with his back to the screen while someone provides a running commentary. If the boy gets too engrossed craning his neck to see the film and forgets to pedal, the DO puts a tea cozy over his head.

The actual digging and clearing of canals is done by both volunteer and paid labor. Paid workers receive 2 shillings per day or 2 shillings 8½ pence for foremen. All told, some 1,600 people are employed at the peak period. The day begins with drummers summoning the workers to their sites. Since they have a fixed quota of yards to be dug, hard workers may finish as early as 10 A.M. The district officers are very much engaged in the canal projects, learning on the job along with the *kapitãos* and messengers and, like them, often walking as much as 18 miles a day. The work is complex: Not only must channels be dug but bridges also need to be constructed over them. One day a hippo in the upper reaches of a canal holds up the work, a problem never faced by James Brindley, the great English canal builder, as one of the cadets notes in a letter home. Two and a half tons of hippo meat are hard to turn down (they would have been equally welcome in eighteenth-century England) and the locals are all for shooting him, but the DC stands firm on retaining his services as canal cleaner.

Results so far are impressive. A 25-foot wide channel has been completed to Sikongo, Squire Davis's base near the Angola border, at a cost of £6,400. The canal incorporates a section of the Lueti River and now makes it possible for Wenela barges to make the run from Kalabo in ten hours (against the current) or seven and a half hours on the return. Other canals drain the Simunyange Plain. Discipline has finally been imposed even on the Luanginga, that obstinate river that "performs many amazing contortions in its attempts to evade its ultimate responsibility of reaching Kalabo boma."[31] Blockages have been cleared and some of the more intricate bends by-passed, with the result that 30-ton Zambezi River Transport barges can reach the *boma* part of the year, and shallower barges can navigate all the way to Mutala and the Angolan border, 300 tortuous miles from the river's confluence with the Zambezi. Maize is now being grown on land that was permanently under water from 1948 to 1958. All in all, 400 square miles of land have been reclaimed for agriculture. But the DC notes ruefully that digging is the easy part. More important is to create a "canal consciousness" among all the villagers of the District, to instill in them the idea of regular voluntary maintenance of the system. This is the purpose of the intensive public relations campaign and the involvement of so many officials, and it may be bearing some fruit: In Salunda *kuta* to the northwest of Kalabo, women greet the touring officer with a song that exhorts their men to "take up their shovels and go to work clearing the canal on Monday, Tuesday, Wednesday, and Thursday and to rest the remaining three days of the week."[32] It is a start.

There is a suspicion, however, that some canals may have been laid out all wrong. In the Simunyange Plain, villagers complain that the canal has actually damaged farms around Namatindi and this seems to be the case. The touring officer concludes that the canal "not only does not work but has never worked, and that it has remained a rather bad joke to the local villagers for quite a long time."[33] The problem is that it has apparently been designed on the European principle of the transverse drain, quite contrary to the indigenous practice of digging in a way to assist the natural flow of water, as was done with the old canal from Lewanika's time. Perhaps it is time to acknowledge that "these villages understand their business a great deal better than they are credited with doing."[34]

Colonial policy currently trumpets the importance of economic development, not just the maintenance of law and order, and in 1955 the provincial administration promulgated its first short-term plan with year-by-year objectives. The nerve center of the plan is the Barotse Development Centre, a cluster of buildings at Namushakende, just south of the old mission station at Sefula. Some £100,000 has been spent on the Centre to build a model farm and offer adult education courses to train craftsmen, court clerks, hygiene assistants, and even chiefs. The idea is that extension agents will fan out from here carrying the gospel of drainage canals, agricultural uplift, and better utilization of land. The agents will, for example, distribute improved strains of rice, maize, groundnuts, and so forth at subsidized prices, hoping to arrest the decline in agricultural production. They are particularly keen on expanding rice cultivation throughout the floodplain, but it is an uphill battle. Rice takes much more work than millet or maize, it is tempting to birds, and the market price is not attractive enough to provide an incentive. Besides, it washed away along with everything else during the terrible flood years. "The trouble is," lamented a touring officer, "that people here do not like rice, and until they learn to do so I do not think they will grow it readily."[35]

A booklet published in 1955 explained that policy would be directed first "towards the production of sufficient food, and the right kind of food, with emphasis on proper land utilization and maintenance of soil fertility. Once subsistence level is gradually being reached, the emphasis is placed upon cash crops to be fitted into the agricultural pattern, so as to broaden the present exchange economy."[36] The public relations unit backs the agents up with speeches, improvised plays, slides, films, posters, and songs, all with appropriate messages:

> Spray your huts against insects.
> Drain your valley-soils and grow more food.
> Move your villages to healthy, dry sites.
> Send your daughters to school. Even girls need
> education these days.[37]

Periodically the resident commissioner comes by to deliver his own pep talk. "Our way is slower than the Russian way," the Namushakende DO admits. "Old Stalin breaks down resistance by terror and hopes that sooner or later his subjects, or their children, will see that he's right." British ways may be slower, but possibly more efficient in the long run, and certainly more humane. "Anyway," he adds, "we don't have a choice. Our temperament and our traditions don't equip us for the Stalin way. Nor our legal system. I can't say I regret it."[38]

Unfortunately by 1959 the Centre has largely gone to rack and ruin; many of its large houses stand empty. Barotseland has not been a high priority for development funding. One of the Centre's few triumphs has been to create the song that now tops Kalabo's hit parade: "One man and his shovel went to dig a canal," sung in SiLozi to the tune of "One man and his dog." With more capable management, the Centre may yet function more effectively. Still, development seems an elusive will o' the wisp as far as Barotseland is concerned. Small wonder that Namushakende is known locally as a "place of great mystery." What is the point of expanding agricultural production or the size of cattle herds if there is no way to reach distant markets? The boat-building school is a small step in that direction, but cheap and reliable transport whether by land or river requires far more investment than is available.

For a born entrepreneur/builder such as the DC, this is all very frustrating. He has had to content himself with overseeing the construction of a market at Kalabo to facilitate regional trade, of modest amounts of housing for the African population as well as the new officers' quarters, and of an experimental nursery for gum seedlings behind the jail that is intended to produce some 1,600 trees to be planted throughout the District to counter deforestation. For his subordinates, all this activity is both admirable and exhausting. They secretly breathe a sigh of relief when he is off on a visit to Angola or Mongu or Livingstone and a welcome haze of peace settles over the *boma* for a short spell.

Days at the *boma* follow each other in a fixed routine. At dawn (which comes relatively late in these latitudes with only a little variation from season to season), the flag is raised and everyone soon gets down to whatever business is at hand. Unfortunately there seems to be an ever-expanding mountain of paperwork even in rural outstations. As one exasperated DC puts it, one is forever expected to be counting things— people, goats, prisoners, bags of grain, rifles and ammunition, the list is endless—and then making lists of what one has counted. There may be court cases to hear, although the officers are not lawyers. True, law has found its way into the Devonshire Course, along with a fortnight's secondment to a London court and a week with the security forces. But in Barotseland the presiding officer is both judge and jury. Furthermore, he must mediate conflicts between three different legal systems: customary law, statute law, and British Common Law, all the while heeding the proviso that any ruling not be "repugnant to natural law and justice."

Always, always the need to pinch pennies, to manage on a shoestring. Next year's budget must be submitted without really knowing how many messengers' uniforms will be necessary or what the price of cassava will be. It is not just the bottom line that has to balance but every single category of expenditure; switching money from one account to another is strictly taboo. There is no provision for inflation. And as sure as sure can be, when the budget is sent to Lusaka, it will come back heavily marked with blue pencil and cut. Still, each *boma* has its "goat" bag (known in some districts as "bull" bag)—a bit of cash teased here, a bit there, and hidden from the prying eyes of Secretariat accountants. The name comes from the practice of buying a goat, cow, or other animal to feed the men while on tour. When it has been eaten, some villager usually comes along and offers to buy the animal's skin. The officer makes sure not to enter the sum in his account book but to put it aside for a rainy day—for building a squash court, for example, or some other project that might not seem as indispensable to the governor as to the local DC.

During the day, the officers wear shorts, open shirts, and knee socks. When work ends about 4, they change to athletic attire. Life without games would be unimaginable in a British colony. Kalabo has a surprisingly good tennis court, a football field (mostly used by Africans), and a recently built swimming pool for the Europeans: a wire cage lowered into the Luanginga to keep crocodiles and swimmers separate. Tennis is one of the few activities at which the DC does not excel, but he has trained Dick's sons, Duke of Clarence and Prince Charles, to act as referees so that his shots are always in and his opponent's out. He really prefers squash, but a proper squash court will have to wait for a later posting.

Darkness puts an abrupt end to games soon after 6. Time for a bath, a change to "longs," and the indispensable sundowner. In principle one does not touch alcohol until the sun goes down. Mosquito boots, soft leather boots coming up to just below the knee, used to be *de rigueur* evening wear for both men and women to protect against mosquitoes' particular fondness for ankles. They have mostly fallen out of favor, going the way of the cholera belt and the old coffin-shaped spine pads that buttoned onto cotton shirts and dangled so conspicuously down David Livingstone's back (they were supposed to protect the spine from the sun). Tropical outfitters still try to push both mosquito boots and spine pads on cadets headed for their first encounter with Africa, but few actually wear them any more. The same is true of the impressive array of heavy pith helmets that were once obligatory colonial wear—headgear with exotic names like Cawnpore Helmets, Bombay Bowlers, and Double Terai Hats. With her customary eye for the absurd, Margery Perham observed that there is "something difficult as well as unaesthetic about swimming in a helmet."[39] Indeed, it has long been suspected that the only thing more dangerous than going out in the noonday sun *without* a helmet is going out *with* one—and broiling under its suffocating weight. Evening dress is becoming less formal too. It used to be that at proper dinner parties, no matter how hot it was, men could not remove their jackets until after dinner and then only if they were not wearing suspenders. Women wore long skirts, for reasons of style and defense against mosquitoes. Mostly, though, evenings are spent catching up on work and correspondence, reading, or playing chess, all by the light of Tilley lamps (kerosene-burning pressure lamps).

Inevitably, a lot of the social life revolves around heavy drinking. Sometimes, when the officers have had just a bit too much to drink, they fantasize that if the bombs drop—for the outside world is obsessed in 1959 with the threat of nuclear annihilation—and only Barotseland is spared because of the oddities of Africa's climate patterns, they will marry into the Barotse royal family, stage a palace coup, and rule here forever.

Some of the officers find hunting a welcome antidote to loneliness and routine. Margery Perham once wrote of the great imperial proconsul, Frederick Lugard: "He found some solace in shooting. How many beautiful African creatures must have been offered up in sacrifice to appease the broken hearts of white men!"[40] But there are, in fact, less romantic reasons to hunt. Without game, one lives on a diet of scrawny chickens and tinned meat. Hunting also feeds fantasies of another sort. Canadian Club whiskey has been running ads about exciting moments and seems especially keen on exciting photographs involving wild animals. The DC, Rob Hart, and Dick Japp have decided to arrange a shot of a lion in mid-leap, which should be a sure winner. They dig a trap with a door for a lion and two nearby holes. When the lion falls into the trap, Japp will let him out, Hart will shoot, and the DC will photograph. Each can fall back into his respective hole for safety. They catch the lion all right, but when he is let out, he sits down like a contented house cat. Japp starts chasing him around the trap, but the other two are laughing so hard they can't photograph or shoot. Gone are dreams of Canadian Club glory. Sometimes it is easier to bag lions when you aren't looking for them. One day the DC and DO stop for a brief rest under a large tree, not noticing a lion resting over their heads until it climbs down and saunters on its way. The DC grabs his rifle and kills it.

Lions are a very real threat in the District. One lion kills 7 people and more than 90 cattle before it is chased back to Angola. The DC and his messenger track down and shoot another marauder that has been terrorizing the District. Elephants sometimes destroy villagers' crops and must be hunted as well. Although less dangerous to humans, they are also harder to kill. The Africans prefer to hunt with spears, but the Europeans carry rifles. It is the custom, also, to have a big hunt at Christmas time to provide meat for the villagers. The distribution turns out to be incredibly complicated. One can't just hand out equal pieces to each person. There is a protocol for who gets what that is embedded in social structures and largely beyond the comprehension of outsiders. It must be acknowledged, too, that game is becoming increasingly scarce; within a few years the District will be shot out. Rare is the animal that does not already have shotgun pellets under its hide. The ban on shooting lechwe antelope is universally ignored. The only area where game is still abundant is the Liuwa Reserve, the private hunting ground of the paramount chief. It is an enormous tract of some 2,500 square miles that has just been surveyed for the first time. Here large herds of oribi, wildebeest, tsessebe, zebra, roan antelope, and buffalo still roam the plains, as they once did throughout all of Barotseland.

Against all odds, the DC has managed to keep two horses at the *boma*, training the staff how to keep them well groomed and tick-free. His 14-year-old mare, Amber, has won the Protectorate Plate in Mongu. Horse races are a great novelty for the local population because the animals are not indigenous to the region. Once the DC raced a government pilot taking off at the airstrip. The badly shaken pilot was still sputtering about it when he landed in Mwinilunga, far to the north.

Since the Lozi are water people and most of the *boma* staff rowed at university, the DC decides to crown the year's activities with a regatta at Liyoyelo, where the Luanginga joins the Zambezi. What started out as a local affair has mushroomed and now involves the entire protectorate. A proper printed program explains how to get to the regatta and announces the schedule of events with precise and probably chimerical starting times: races of all sorts (canoes, barges, motor boats—the DC is a good bet to win this—oxen, horses), football matches, *makishi* dancers, a shooting contest for ex-messengers, policemen, and servicemen, and a film show in the evening. In some cases there are separate competitions for men and women, Africans and Europeans, and a tug of war for the school children. As with any proper fete, all the events carry prizes, donated by local merchants: The "survivor" of the crocodile spearing contest, for example, will receive a bicycle. The DC is eager for the cadet to play on the *boma* football team: As the only European and one of only two members who will be wearing shoes, he is sure to be a big draw. Programs are numbered and the lucky winner of the drawing at the end of the afternoon will receive a free airline ticket anywhere the trusty Beaver flies.

To cap it off, the paramount chief has been enlisted as patron. He arrives with suitable pomp in the royal barge, *Nalikwanda,* usually reserved for the annual move to high ground as the floodwaters rise. The regatta provides a chance to show off traditional Lozi river skills, the skills that so impressed Livingstone as he made his way up the Zambezi a hundred years earlier. It is also an occasion for the many thousands of enthusiastic spectators to salute their chief. The only mishap occurs when the overworked cadet trips and spills seven bottles of mineral water all over the chief and the resident commissioner. In spite of this, and like so many of the DC's pet projects, the regatta has combined fun with the more serious purpose of cementing national unity. He hopes that it will become an annual August event.

In May 1960, just before the DC leaves Kalabo for the last time (see figure 8), a still greater symbol of national, indeed imperial unity, visits Barotseland. Elizabeth, Queen Mother of England, has been invited to throw the switch starting the giant turbines of the newly built Kariba Dam on the Zambezi. At the end of her tour of Central and Southern Africa, she has a few days to spend wherever she wants, and she has chosen Barotseland. The Lozi have always been favorites of British royals, perhaps because they are monarchists at heart and know how to put on a good show. She met the paramount chief and his consort at a state banquet in Lusaka two years earlier, the first occasion on which a Lozi queen, the *moyoo,* had ever left her home territory.

The Queen Mother is scheduled to fly to the provincial capital at Mongu, and for weeks the little town has been bustling with preparations. A whole new wing must be built onto the Residency, with the lavatory done up in powder blue. One of the local DOs has been teaching the British women there how to curtsy properly (it is harder than it looks). When the Queen Mother's little red plane appears as a speck on the horizon, all the ladies lined up along the airstrip burst into tears. The DO has anticipated this and passes out hankies. Together with the resident commissioner in full ceremonial attire (said to date from the Crimean War) and the paramount chief decked out just as smartly in his ambassador's uniform (given to his father by Edward VII during his visit to England in 1902), she walks along the neatly manicured street to the cheers of the assembled throng (see figure 9). "No visitor to Barotseland had ever received such a great and spontaneous welcome," enthused the chronicler of the *Annual Report* for 1960.[41]

She has a full schedule. She spends a morning at the winter capital of Limulunga, a short ways from Mongu, as a guest of the paramount chief. She delivers a message from Queen Elizabeth to the council and assembled throng. In response, the entire court drops to its knees, clapping solemnly and intoning the royal salute. The paramount chief presents her with an ivory-handled fly whisk of zebra hair. A performance of "tribal" dancing follows. Later she returns to Mongu for a garden party attended by 450, half Europeans, half Africans. All this is only the prelude to the climax of the visit, the meeting of the royals on the river. The river swarms with boats of all sizes and descriptions, carrying officials and chiefs. With a touch of parochialism, the correspondent for the *Daily Telegraph,* observing the festivities from a small plane, comments that "it looked like a huge panorama of the Norfolk Broads." At the center of the colorful flotilla is *Nalikwanda* in which the paramount chief is waiting to receive the Queen Mother, known to the Lozi as "Makoshi." At first the resident commissioner's launch, which has been assigned to ferry her out, refuses to start, causing a moment of panic after so many days of rehearsal, but at last it catches. With a resonant booming of the royal drums, the Queen Mother is welcomed on board *Nalikwanda* by the paramount chief. Together they are paddled to an island in the river where they all take tea. At dusk, they return to the little harbor at Mongu that has been illuminated for the occasion. Here another throng awaits them.

That evening there is a gala party. The inner circle of the high and mighty surrounds Her Majesty, keeping the lower orders at bay. One of the latter is a public works foreman, a diamond in the rough but dressed tonight in his best. As it happens, he is a superb dancer and bets his friends that if he asks the Queen Mother politely, she will dance with him. To the horror of his betters, he approaches her and she happily agrees. What is even more galling, she seems to love being propelled around the dance floor in a graceful whirl. As the dance winds down, she winks at the foreman and, like the true sport she is, whispers "Why don't you take them double or quits? You never know your luck."[42] So he does, and she goes around with him a second time.

The visit is a fantastic success with both Africans and Europeans. Reluctant to see it come to an end, they all fantasize that they might after all prevent her departure by blowing up the airstrip at Mongu—but only after first shipping off the oversized press corps of 85 journalists who have been complaining the whole time about how "scandalous" it is that they have had to stay in a tent camp (fully provided with running water, electricity, and even a restaurant). The Queen Mother proposes that the obvious people (obvious from an English perspective) to do the blowing up are the Irish Fathers in their long gray cassocks and beards: She has met a covey of them at the garden party.

"The visit of Her Majesty the Queen Mother to Mongu," the *Annual Report* intoned, "was the most important event for Barotseland since the signing of the Lewanika Concession in 1900."[43] High noon of Empire on the Upper Zambezi. Or so it seems.

CHAPTER TWO

Libonda: The View from the Kuta

Indirect Rule: Rule by native chiefs, unfettered in their control of their people, yet subordinated to the control of the Protecting Power in certain well-defined directions.

—Lord Lugard, governor of Nigeria (1922)

Indirect Rule came about because in various parts of Africa we'd bitten off more than we could chew. We couldn't possibly administer all these people and these vast territories closely. So our policy was to leave as much as possible to the people themselves and not interfere with their lives unless it was obvious that what they were doing was wrong. If they could settle their own quarrels, so much the better.

—Lord Lugard

The combination of a civilizing mandate with one of ruling through customary authority made colonial rule a Penelope's fabric of doing and undoing.

—Karen Fields, historian (1985)

1959. Libonda. Headquarters of the Native Authority for Kalabo District and home of its chief, the *mulena mbowanjikana*. The incumbent, Makwibi, has just departed to replace the recently deceased female ruler at Nalolo. Makwibi is a large woman who tips the scales at something over 200 pounds while still in her twenties. She is a daughter of the paramount chief, the *litunga,* and blessed with a laugh that ripples down her whole body. The DC has often sat down with her for a good chat. Hazel Japp occasionally sends the Wenela truck to bring her over to Kalabo for a cup of tea on the verandah, and they gossip about children, school, and clothes. During the terrible floods of 1957–58 she did much to raise spirits by touring the worst affected areas. She will be sorely missed in the district. For much of 1959 the ship of native government remains rudderless. Where Kalabo is abuzz with activity (exhaustingly so, in some eyes) thanks to an especially dynamic DC, Libonda is in a state of suspended animation, awaiting a new leader. For months the business of the *kuta* stalls, new appointments are on hold, *indunas* who should be gently retired because of age or infirmity or incompetence linger in office, drainage projects are in limbo. Such are the powers of the Native Authority that colonial officers are powerless to intervene.

Finally, after much delay and much behind the scenes politicking, the paramount chief appoints as Makwibi's successor at Libonda one of his younger half-sisters, Lundambuyu Lewanika, and government can again move forward. In November she is at last installed as *mulena mbowanjikana* with all the pomp the Lozi are famous for and the latest technology they have been quick to appreciate. The government has provided loudspeakers, flags, and transport, and the proceedings have been filmed. The *mulena* arrives in her own barge, paddled by *indunas* from Mongu wearing egret feathers. The DC, resplendent in white ceremonial uniform, waits at the river's edge, flanked by the *boma* messengers, and shakes her hand as she emerges from the white awning and steps ashore. She holds an umbrella in one hand and an eland tail fly-whisk in the other. Together they lead the procession from the river to the *kuta* where the *indunas* await them. Several attendants accompany them wearing printed cloth wrappers, white overshirts, and red caps, carrying rifles over their shoulders. Another attendant carries her chair over his head (see figure 10). There is a festive turnout of men, women, and school children, black and white, officials, clergy, and common folk, who swarm the riverbank and follow the procession. Union jacks bedeck the open area in front of the palace. The dignitaries take their assigned seats and receive the salutes of the messengers who kneel on the ground in front of them and clap. The old Kalabo *indunas* lead a little dance.

The *mulena mbowanjikana* comes third in the hierarchy of Lozi royals, just behind the *mulena mukwae,* who in turn is second only to the *litunga,* the king (or paramount chief in the colonial order of things). The *mulena mukwae* is considered the ruler of the southern half of the floodplain, the *litunga* of the northern half. In earlier times rulers chose their own capitals and might change them at will, but since the late nineteenth-century Nalolo has been the southern and Lealui the northern capital, even though they are actually not very far apart. As for Libonda, it is a bit of off-beat phrasing in the neat symmetry of north and south. Coillard was told that the town was founded by the daughter of the legendary hero-king, Mboo, whose name was Boanjikana, hence the title of her successors and hence her importance in the royal hierarchy.

While the *litunga* is always male, both of these *mulenas* (the word itself can refer to male or female chiefs) have traditionally been female, at least since the years immediately preceding the Kololo invasion of the 1840s. Whether this means the Lozi harbor enlightened views about the capabilities of women is open to question; in a state as prone to civil war and insurrection as this, it may simply make good sense to delegate important posts to women since by definition they cannot be rival claimants to the throne, nor can their children succeed them. Simultaneously considered male and female, the *mulenas* were and are real rulers whose powers and authority parallel that of the king. They have their own courts and retainers, their drums and xylophones; they preside over the *kuta,* discuss state affairs, and judge lawsuits (see figure 11). Like the *litunga,* they are greeted with the salutations reserved for royalty and may use white cloth for the shelters on their barges. Similarly, they are surrounded with many of the same prohibitions. For example, no subject may touch a royal, not even to help him or her out of a barge or vehicle (something that has made life difficult for Makwibi, getting in and out of Wenela trucks). Also, although Makwibi speaks English well, custom demands that she use an interpreter and speak only SiLozi when addressing officials.

A *mulena* may marry, but her husband, the *ishee,* must defer to her and cannot take other wives. On ceremonial occasions, the *ishee* walks a respectful distance behind. Historically, some *mulenas* were known for changing mates with great frequency and unpleasant tales were told about the fate of discarded spouses. Such is not the case with Makwibi. Her husband, *ishee* Mukena, was formerly in government service and has contributed greatly to the efficiency of the Libonda Native Authority.

Since traders and missionaries opened the Valley to foreign commerce and ideas in the 1880s and 1890s, both male and female royals have favored European clothes, furnishings, and houses. They drink tea from china cups and eat cakes from china plates. When the *mulena mukwae* saw the fine rectangular house Lewanika had built for himself at Lealui, first by the Mambari slave traders from the coast, then by apprentices from the Paris Mission, she too insisted on having one at Nalolo. A later DC visiting her palace was somewhat taken aback to find porcelain chamber pots hanging from the walls of one of the rooms along with other European china and utensils. When he asked about this, she replied, "Well, I saw that you had many of our things on the walls of your house, so I sent to Livingstone for English things to hang on mine."[1] Among the gifts brought back by Lewanika when he attended the coronation of Edward VII was a carriage, similar to those that served as cabs on the streets of London. He presented it to the *mulena mukwae* and it is still in use in 1959, drawn by four oxen in lieu of horses.

When European textiles first appeared in Barotseland, *mulenas* used to wear layered *setsibas,* brightly colored wrappers or skirts made from imported cotton prints. Now, alas, they tend to favor more staid British clothes. In the fifties, the designers of these dresses still assumed that ladies, especially ones with ample figures, would wear foundation garments with them. This problem was solved for Makwibi by sending an order by telex to a merchant in Bulawayo.

The present royal residence at Libonda is a large structure, surrounded by a palisade of reeds with pointed ends—only royalty have the prerogative of sharpened stakes around their dwellings. It is constructed of mud brick and has a high, thatched roof held up by wooden pillars. Anyone entering claps gently and offers the greetings appropriate to royalty in a hushed voice, although they no longer have to prostrate themselves on the ground. Around the palace are clusters of more modest houses, a newly opened medical dispensary, and a partially built middle school. When an administrator comes to visit, he stays in the government rest house a little way out of town. It is a square brick house with thatched roof and verandah set on a treeless ridge running north-south. With unbroken plains to the east and west, it offers lovely views of the rising and setting sun.

It is some 20 difficult miles from Kalabo to Libonda at the northern end of the plain. To go between the two on foot takes about five and a half hours. Fortunately, the now much improved Ikatulamwa Canal provides a water route between the Zambezi and Luanginga about 20 miles above their confluence. This means the journey can be made by canoe in three hours, in contrast to the two days needed via the natural waterways with all their twists and bends. Unfortunately the canal is only navigable for half the year: Barges can use it until May, canoes until about July. The older canal to Sishekanu, built in Lewanika's time, is used when the *mulena* moves her court from Libonda to its "omboka" or flood season site in Sishekanu Forest.

The *mulena mbowanjikana* presides over the Libonda *kuta* and also over the 14 subordinate *kutas* of Kalabo District (see Map 3). She in turn is subject to the *litunga* and the government based at Lealui, the Barotse Native Authority. It is a classic case of "indirect rule," owing far less to Lord Lugard and fellow theorists of colonialism than to the rough and ready cobbling of early Europeans on the spot and the skill of Lozi elites. After all, the Lozi had worked out their own system of indirect rule for administering their subject peoples long before Europeans arrived. Thus, the British South Africa Company found a well-developed, highly centralized, and stratified government already in place: They simply imposed one more tier of authority on top. But mostly they left existing institutions in place, gradually whittling down their autonomy.

When the Company yielded to settler agitation and ceded control of Northern Rhodesia to the British Government in 1924, the change was hardly noticed in Barotseland. No doubt, this was in part because there were and are no white "settlers" in the Protectorate. The successive agreements Lewanika concluded with Company representatives guaranteed that there would be no land alienation in the kingdom, and this has continued in effect for the heartland if not for the periphery. Consequently, the few Europeans who reside in Barotseland must lease property from the *litunga* who is, in theory, the owner of all the land in the province.

In simplest terms, indirect rule involves the delegation of power and responsibility to the traditional rulers of a territory. The institution has frequently been likened to the prefectorial system developed by Thomas Arnold in the nineteenth-century British public school that gave both power and prestige to trusted boys in the sixth form, the final grade. Indirect rule, as one DO observed, "was only the prefectorial system writ large, with, *mutatis mutandis,* the District Officers as masters, the Chiefs as prefects, and the tribesmen as the boys. The pattern fitted African tribal society well enough and was easily understood by Chiefs and people."[2] Just as the prefects were supposed to put an end to fagging and bullying, so the chiefs were supposed to end internecine warfare and keep the peace. Not surprisingly, recruiters for the colonial service looked for public school boys ("We couldn't have run the show without them," Furse declared[3]) and former prefects in particular.

By delegating so much responsibility, it was possible to administer the "teeming millions" of the British Empire with what amounted to a handful of men on shoestring budgets. In Northern Rhodesia as a whole, for example, there are some 246 administrative officers governing an area of 290,000 square miles with well over a million and a half inhabitants in 1959. Not quite "two men and a dog,"[4] but almost. What is amazing is how little the system has relied on actual coercion and how rarely even the threat of coercion has been needed. As one historian comments, "The European DC wore the bullet-proof waistcoat of his white skin: it might not stop the bullet, but it nearly always deterred the other party from firing."[5] The inviolability of white skin has been shattered in Kenya with the Mau Mau uprising, but there is as yet no echo of this in Barotseland.

In the early days, indirect rule meant little more than "leave the chiefs alone"[6] (in one memorable instruction), but as the doctrine took concrete shape, it demanded, in Lugard's words, that administrative officers "learn how [local people] govern themselves and assist that process."[7] It assumed that these local people had chiefs and revered them, just as the British revered their Queen, so that nothing should be done to undermine their authority unless they abused the trust placed in them. The role of the district officer remains to advise, not command; administer, not rule. He is to be the "whisper behind the throne."[8] This is why the *boma* is physically separate from the *kuta* and why any tendency to "order" local *indunas* to do something, even something as innocuous as building a latrine, is met with a stern rebuke: "He [the DO] should be instructed that Barotseland is a Protectorate and that he is not empowered to give orders of this nature."[9]

Indirect rule has caused much head-scratching in parts of the territory where chiefs are non-existent or ignored, or where populations are so mixed that local authority is hard to locate. In Barotseland it works much better. Superficially, the Barotse Native Authority still bears a resemblance to Lewanika's government. At the top of what the British like to refer to as a "constitutional monarchy" is the *litunga* or paramount chief who still enjoys great prestige throughout the Protectorate in 1959, as do members of the royal family, although grumbling about their privileges is on the rise. His two chief officers or *indunas* are the *ngambela* (literally "speak for me"), a sort of prime minister, and the *natamoyo* ("master or mother of life"), the minister of justice who traditionally has been able to offer sanctuary to anyone who seeks it and can, in theory, overrule both the *kuta* and the *litunga*. Both of these officials are commoners, appointed by the ruler. The intricate hierarchy of government is translated into the architectural and spatial patterns of the royal capital— the size of the houses and their location in relation to the palace.

Meetings of the national court reflect the same patterns of hierarchy, dividing the assembled notables into three "mats." The ruler sits in the middle. On his right are the officials representing the nation as a whole, including the *ngambela* and *natamoyo;* on his left are two separate "mats," one assigned to the stewards of the royal household, the other to members of the royal family (everyone except the ruler does sit literally on a mat—Lewanika saw to it that the stools that had crept in during the Kololo occupation were disposed of after he felt firmly in power). The stewards are known as "wives" or "boys" of the king but are in fact powerful chiefs in their own right. The terminology simply invokes the fluidity of gender, that what people do defines their gender more than biology does. Behind the mats are the *indunas* or headmen and the common people. In front of the paramount chief sit the royal band and the chief's messengers (see figure 12).

There are several sub-councils: *Sikalo, Saa, Katengo,* and *Situmbu sa Mulonga.* They usually meet separately in between meetings of the full council and include representatives of the three mats; collectively they form a sort of national "parliament." All have their *indunas* or presiding officers, and the most important offices have their own title histories separate from those of the ruling family. These councils are historical overlays reflecting divisions that evolved as the Lozi kingdom expanded and then re-grouped after the Kololo invasion: a map, as it were, of inclusions and exclusions over time and, individually, of who is in favor and who is not, displayed graphically by where one sits in public meetings, not only to the right or left of the ruler but also near or far from the throne. The *kuta* proper is a smaller body, also drawn from all three mats, which handles day-to-day affairs and court cases.

The Katengo Council was the traditional forum for the common people (male) until it fell into oblivion. Now revived as part of the colonial agenda to gradually prepare local populations for self-government, it includes five or six elected representatives from each district. It meets once a year under the chairmanship of the *ngambela* to debate motions and refer matters considered important to the national *kuta.* It seems to be a moot point whether its deliberations are taken very seriously— many people have little idea what the Katengo does and see few tangible results of their experiment in grassroots democracy.

Because it is so inscrutable (at least to outsiders), the system of Lozi government has been notoriously hard to pin down and no two accounts fully agree. Pity the poor officer who takes Lugard at his word and tries to understand how *this* people govern themselves before assisting them. As one recent provincial commissioner exclaimed in despair, the native government is like "a sum in addition badly done. There is little that is neat or precise about it. The outlines are inclined to blur the closer one regards them and the details to re-arrange themselves and to assume new shapes and significance."[10] Half-heartedly the commissioner tried to trim the governmental system down and make it more responsive to modern needs, but in the end the job proved beyond him.

Nevertheless, for all the preservation of titles and royal ceremonial, indirect rule has shorn away many of the prime functions of past Lozi states. No longer can the *litunga* carry out the wars and raids on neighboring peoples that once funneled a rich booty of cattle and slave women and children into the capital at Lealui, whence it was redistributed down the chain of command after the king took the lion's share. No longer can he demand that his subjects hand over elephant tusks or the fat of hippopotami, honey from the forests or all the wild beasts they kill. No longer are citizens obligated to supply an annual tribute of grain or of canoes cut from the forest trees or spears and axes made by Totela and Kwanga smiths. Tribute in goods and services has been transformed into payment in cash. From the *litunga* on down, officials have become tax collectors and salaried employees. It has always been an article of faith that British colonies must pay their own way, and this includes the support not just of the *boma* but also of the *kuta*—and, in this case, of the very numerous royals.

The *mulena mbowanjikana* is the mirror image of the DC in Kalabo. She heads the Native Authority as he heads the colonial administration. At the same time, her government replicates that of the *litunga* in miniature. Like the DC she has her *kapasus* who function much like the *boma* messengers and wear distinctive khaki shorts and tunics trimmed in red. Like the *litunga*, she has her *indunas* who serve as councilors and chiefs of the villages under her sway. (It is a great pity, the DC thinks, that the colonial government has never thought it worthwhile to give the *indunas* proper uniforms such as those worn by their Portuguese counterparts—such a small thing that would mean so much. Nor do the *kapasus* have boots so that they can snap to attention properly like the *boma* messengers.)

On the other hand, the *mulena* oversees a far more extensive bureaucracy than the DC. Each of the subordinate *kutas* has a president and two *indunas*. These *silalo indunas* are responsible for tax collection in the villages within their jurisdiction and also for the administration of justice since the *kuta* also serves as a court of law. They are also charged with recording births and deaths, with keeping their villages tidy and in good order, and with preventing people from moving away without permission—not an easy job given the roving tendencies of some of their subjects. When district officers go on tour, it is these *indunas* on whom they most rely to keep them informed about local affairs. An effective *induna* is worth

his weight in gold, while an incompetent or senile one causes only
gnashing of teeth, since the *boma* may complain but has no authority to
remove him.

Both chiefs and DCs rise and fall according to their success or failure
in keeping track of taxpayers and collecting from them, and on being
able to balance the books at the end of the year. Native courts, too,
are not entirely autonomous. Their jurisdiction covers "native law and
custom," which in practice means mostly matrimonial and inheritance
cases, and lesser criminal cases. In matrimonial cases, courts tend to be
"husband-biased."[11] Nevertheless, women do not always lose when they
ask for divorces on the grounds of neglect, especially when spouses are
long absent on the "line of rail" (in local parlance, the string of mining
and agricultural communities that have sprung up along the railroad).
Adultery is treated as a criminal offence and subject to a stiff fine. Some
cases reflect the unsteady co-existence of old and new, as when an ox
passing by the plaintiff's house got tangled up in the wireless aerial of a
saucepan radio and damaged the set. The *kuta* awarded compensation of
a calf toward the cost of repairing the radio.

District officers are supposed to review the records of native courts
and to correct any glaring miscarriages of justice. But their rulings can
in turn be reversed by the court of the paramount chief, something that
is not true outside of Barotseland. Murder, witchcraft, and other serious
criminal offenses come before the *boma,* not the *kuta,* as do any cases
involving Europeans. The dual legal system does have its quirks. Once an
African man came to then-DO Gervas Clay to complain that his cooking pot was stolen. Clay sent his messenger off to handle the matter.
A year or two later the same man came to complain that his wife had
been stolen by another man. Clay had to tell him that he was powerless
to intervene and that it was entirely a matter for the local chief. "You
mean," the plaintiff said in disbelief, "the pot is more important than my
wife since you will only deal with that?"[12]

In contrast, the beer law is refreshingly down-to-earth. It states that
no one may drink beer but no effort will be made to look for the bev-
erage. However, if anyone quarrels because he has been drinking beer,
he will be severely punished. The sale of hard liquor is strictly forbidden
in Barotseland. Predictably, this means that illegal stills provide abundant
quantities of moonshine liquor. Its base is something known as a "Kaffir
orange," a wild fruit about the size of a cricket ball and much loved by
elephants. When the fruit is not in season, far more disagreeable ingredients are employed: shoe polish, Brasso, or, for the biggest kick of all,
battery acid, siphoned out of Wenela trucks. The effects are hair-raising.

Needless to say, tracking down distillers is a major concern of *boma* and *kuta*.

The powers of the Barotse Native Authority have been increasingly circumscribed over the years, albeit less so in this province than in any other part of Northern Rhodesia. Nevertheless, there are still areas where the *boma* is powerless to intervene. For much of 1959 the work of the Libonda *kuta* has come to a halt because of the interregnum between *mulenas* and the preoccupation with the coming installation of the new office-holder. The power of appointment has been tenaciously guarded by the indigenous government, extending right up to the top and the selection of the *litunga* and his prime minister even over the objections of the resident commissioner of the Protectorate.

Libonda, wrote David Livingstone, "is situated on a mound like the rest of the villages in the Barotse valley, but here the tree-covered sides of the valley begin to approach nearer the river."[13] Beyond lies the thickly forested maze of streams that form the headwaters of the Zambezi, or Lyambai ("river"), as it is known to the Lozi. When Livingstone first visited in 1853, Libonda belonged to two of the chief wives of Sebitwane, the Kololo overlord. The Lozi restoration changed only the dynastic affiliation, not the sex of the ruler. Now the *mulena mbowanjikana* and her *indunas* oversee a vast territory sandwiched between the districts of Balovale to the north, Mongu to the east, Senanga to the south, and the Portuguese colony of Angola to the west, as diverse ethnically as it is topographically.

Some areas are densely populated, others almost deserted. Thus, the endless Liuwa Plain forms part of an "empty quarter" encompassing much of the northwestern reaches of the District. Even had it not been staked out by Lewanika as a royal game preserve, its sandy soils would have deterred human settlement. The same is true of the entire sweep of land along the Angolan border except for the upper Luanginga Valley. The population is most concentrated in the "peri-urban" areas surrounding Kalabo *boma* ("peri-urban" being a relative term), and in the lines of settlements radiating like tendrils from Kalabo along the sandy ridges.

Lozi villages are *sui generis*. There is nothing quite like them elsewhere in Northern Rhodesia. It is often hard to tell where one village ends and another begins. Not only are they very spread out, but sections of one village are mixed up higgledy-piggledy with those of another. A village near Liumba Hill Mission, for example, has five distinct sections, four dispersed along a line east of the mission and intermingled with sections of other, similarly segmented villages. The fifth section lies west of the mission, some two miles from the rest. Some village parts are even farther apart. This pattern is common in Barotseland, sometimes in even more extreme form. Ethnicity plays some role in this: Each ethnic group usually has its own quarter, but sometimes people of the same ethnic group set themselves up in separate parts for purely local reasons. Perhaps their gardens are scattered or their wives have quarreled or perhaps they just like to be alone. Sometimes a man will simply decide to build a large house away from the rest of the village and bring along some of his relations, "rather like the great families made the squares of London."[14]

Whatever the causes of this fracturing, the result is "hopeless confusion."[15] Just figuring out how many villages there are in an area can be a challenge. Even the *silalo indunas,* the local representatives of the Libonda *kuta,* aren't sure. A case in point: The parts of *induna* Chisita's own "village" are 10 or 12 miles apart and it's not clear whether they form one unit or several. All the harder, then, to sort out tax registers, co-ordinate growing crops, or enforce rules about moving in or out of villages. But since the patterns seem to have the "sanction of ancient custom,"[16] neither *kuta* nor *boma* feels quite comfortable about imposing an artificial order on the muddle.

In some areas ethnic differences strike the eye more than in others. The ethnic mix in the district is complicated, but essentially there are the Lozi (and those who have lived among them for so long that they are allied in custom and language even if they are still known by separate names) and the Wiko, the "people of the west," an umbrella label for immigrants from north and west. Differing considerably among themselves, some Wiko have been in Barotseland for a very long time. Thus Mbunda groups in the north harbored refugees from the Lozi royal family during the Kololo domination and have played a prominent role in affairs of state, especially as diviners, thanks to their powerful magic, charms, and ability to foretell the future. Other Wiko are more recent immigrants, streaming across the Angola border in the last 40 years, first to escape local wars, then simply to join relatives or in search of a better life under the more relaxed conditions in Barotseland. There is still a lot of to-ing and fro-ing across the frontier.

Ironically, Wiko are often labeled feckless and untruthful, and yet Wiko villages are universally acknowledged to be better laid out and cleaner than Lozi villages. Houses are solidly constructed of pole and mud with thatched roofs and plastered walls. Grain bins are equally sturdy, and rubbish pits are confined to the outskirts of the village.

There are often trees and flowers and pleasant verandahs. Compare this to Lozi villages with their lack of any discernible order, their flimsy grass huts, often in a state of disrepair, their piles of rubbish strewn about. Houses and grain bins no longer in use are simply left to crumble; even if the owner has long since departed, no one thinks to pull them down. When a Wiko headman dies, the villagers promptly propose a successor to the presiding *induna,* but when a Lozi headman dies, the villagers wait six months or even a year before electing a new one. In fact, the untidiness of villages may be linked to these frequent vacancies, since keeping things tidy is one of the headman's duties. Even when functioning, however, Lozi headmen seem to command far less respect than their Wiko counterparts, which makes them less effective.

The stereotypical Lozi (if there really is such a thing) is portrayed as dignified and somber. The men wear a type of kilt or wrapper and the women well-padded bustles (see figure 13). Wiko file their teeth and wear distinctive hairstyles. Their dress, too, is different, tending toward blues and blacks. They are "gay, irresponsible, bubbling over with song and dance"[17] and seem to have a zest for life not found in the average Lozi. Even Lozi will admit that Wiko women far surpass them in singing and dancing. "Their music has a vigour and panache about it with which the Malozi cannot compete,"[18] although their songs do tend to be a bit racy. They delight in using the call-and-response pattern so typical of indigenous music, improvising to keep their repertoire up to date. And their endurance is spectacular: "I have been accompanied," wrote one DO, "for eight miles by 40 or 50 Mawiko women singing the whole time. It is a moot point who was more exhausted at the end."[19]

By the 1950s the Nyengo of the far western part of Kalabo district are the most famous of all for their singing and dancing. Their *pièce de resistance* is the Kayowe dance that represents a cock looking after his flock of hens and angrily driving would-be rivals from his domain. The "cock" wears a wicker frame swathed in feathers on his head. He squats down on his haunches holding out a short stick. Facing him is a semi-circle of women, also squatting and holding sticks. The man and several of the women have whistles. As soon as the drumming starts, the "cock" struts and postures in front of the woman of his fancy. Then other men arrive and try to compete for her favors, only to be repulsed by the furious cock. The dance lasts about 15–20 minutes, involving "the most incredible contortions of the shoulders and body, a sort of rhythmic shaking of the shoulders in time to the … drums"[20] and ending in the complete exhaustion of the male lead. Seen in the "leaping firelight" it is a memorable sight indeed.

Nyengo songs, like those elsewhere, tend to be topical: cautionary tales for husbands-to-be or paeans to a native doctor across the border who makes a potion guaranteed to "stimulate the most barren of women or impotent of men into fast and furious reproduction."[21] To European ears these songs have no apparent melodic pattern, but the harmony is straightforward and the rhythm easy to grasp. One tune even sounds like the last two lines of "D'ye ken John Peel." A lot of Nyengo dancing is suggestive and the songs Chaucerian in their gusto. But they convey a *joie de vivre,* a gaiety and sense of fun that are unsurpassed even by Wiko standards. The only problem is that the local population seems more interested in teaching their children to dance than in sending them to school. There are few schools in the area and little clamor for more.

The *makishi* is probably the most widely diffused dance in Barotseland (see figure 14). The term *mukishi* (pl. *makishi*) actually refers both to the dancer and to the ancestral spirit he embodies. It appears to have originated in the Lunda-Luvale regions to the north as part of initiation rituals but has long been domesticated in the Lozi heartland where initiation ceremonies for boys and girls are unknown. Livingstone witnessed the dance in 1853:

> Immediately after the service a party of Bakisi [*sic*] came with two drums. Two of the principal actors were dressed as grotesquely as possible. Every part of the body was covered and the face deformed with a kind of snout. One had breasts like a woman, the other something like the male attire, with bells which in his strange contortions made a jingling sound ... some said these are the gods of this river.[22]

Livingstone claimed that his Tswana companions "who had never witnessed heathen orgies like these were horrified" as much as he was.[23] A late nineteenth-century visitor was more taken with what he refers to as the "national saltation." He describes a pair of dancers: one "got up in black and white mask and brown and white jersey and tights with bells, and leopard skins ad lib." The other wore similar attire with the addition of "a really very excellent comical wooden mask, quite a pantomime thing."[24] They were accompanied by a band of two dozen musicians, including three big drums. On this occasion, they danced till one o'clock in the morning when Robert Coryndon, the resident, sent them beer and a gift. Sixty years on, *makishi* still wear elaborate costumes of masks and knitted body suits and they are still called on to perform for important guests, as on the occasion of the Queen Mother's visit to Barotseland.

Constant intermarriage among peoples undermines attempts at "tribal" classification and explains how customs diffuse and change throughout the region. In these patrilineal societies, ethnicity and culture generally follow the father. Thus, Lozi women marrying Luvale husbands, for example, seem to find it natural to adopt the customs of their husbands' families and vice versa. At the same time, however, there can be fierce and impossibly tangled arguments over who is a "true Lozi." On occasion, this may be a matter of importance, the prerequisite, spoken or unspoken, for certain political plums. In most of the *kutas* of the Barotse plain, for example, the *indunas* are all Lozi. Wiko hold positions primarily in the *kutas* near the Angolan border.

One of these is Mwanamungela, president of the Mutala *kuta* on the upper Luanginga. Mwanamungela is an intelligent and well-educated man who was a schoolteacher in Southern Rhodesia before succeeding his father in 1946. Remote as his *silalo* is, he has furthered his education through correspondence courses. His most prized possession is a copy of the *Concise Oxford Dictionary,* which he peruses while hearing court cases. Not surprisingly, his command of English is impressive. Just as interesting is Mwanamungela's genealogy. His great-great uncle, he claims, was the last chief of the Makoma and met his death through Lozi treachery. He was lured into visiting the Lozi capital of Lealui, then sent home in a defective canoe with Lozi paddlers. When the canoe sank, the paddlers swam to safety, but "to save himself from death in this way was inconsistent with his chiefly dignity and he drowned."[25] The Lozi then absorbed his people into their kingdom. There is some debate about whether Mwanamungela's heritage and erudition have made him arrogant and out of touch with his constituents. Certainly he lacks the common touch. On the other hand, perhaps Libonda could find a better use for his talents than this isolated outpost. One thing is certain: He is a first class hunter and fearless lion killer.

A vexing problem is the low birthrate found among many of the Wiko. This is especially true of the Luvale in the northern part of the district. Village after village has only two or three children, and yet others have all the children they could desire. The same variation occurs among individual families. Local *indunas* blame venereal diseases, picked up when men leave home to work on the mines or the line of rail. The problem has been little studied, but the records at the Catholic mission in Sihole show no difference in rates of venereal disease between the

Wiko and non-Wiko treated in their dispensary. There are also rumors, denied by the Wiko themselves, that they employ secret medicines to limit the number of children. An anti-venereal disease campaign has been proposed. It remains to be seen, however, whether it will counter the trend.

Both the Luvale and neighboring Mbunda are renowned for their divination skills and for their medicines. Some medicines are prescribed for disease, others for successful hunting. Most of all they are used to keep demons away. Medicines for hunting and fishing are often quite ornate, in the form of miniature wooden tables with mud figures nearby and a few animal skulls. Anti-demon medicines may be equally elaborate or may simply consist of a cassava planted in a village or a hank of rag tied to a tree. Outside some houses in Lutwi district there are painted "flags" made of a long stick with a bunch of twigs and leaves. The symbols are known as *vimbundi* and intended to cure *mahamba* illnesses: malaria, pneumonia, rheumatism, or headaches. They are made by *mahamba* doctors, specialists, as it were, in these diseases. Other doctors boil up medicines for external application and for inhalation. One touring officer encountered a man who appeared before him "quietly and in his right mind" but who had shortly before been "a naked and uncontrollable lunatic." He had been cured by a potion concocted by a native doctor and forced down his throat by four strong men. An earlier attempt to cure the man by another doctor was not so successful; in fact, the doctor himself went mad and was "still in that unhappy state" at the time of the visit. In his report, the officer commented that "presumably the principle of the Gadarene swine was again in operation,"[26] a reference to the biblical story of Christ driving demons out of a mad man, whereupon the demons took possession of a herd of pigs.

Indigenous doctors pay a substantial fee for their training. Even so, there is a suspicion that teachers probably withhold some of their most precious secrets. The first thing to learn is to distinguish natural ailments from those caused by evil spirits and to treat both types. Doctors often have a considerable knowledge of natural remedies but usually combine them with various charms. Villagers testify to the success of these practitioners and willingly pay for their services. The standard fee is ten shillings, but it is usually payable only on the successful recovery of the patient. Belief in indigenous medicine co-exists with an equal appreciation of European medicine. A short ways south of the *boma,* an African doctor has set himself up with a long white medical coat, a white flag flying above his house, and an "array of enamel ware which would have done credit to a dispensary."[27] He gladly displays his roots to visitors but is reluctant to give away any secrets. "But though the skeptical and sophisticated ... could laugh at these medicines they would not lightly disturb them," wrote an observer, adding, "and nor, I think would I."[28]

The indigenous doctor, the *ng'aka* (often translated as "witchdoctor") is also the first line of defense against witches. In essence he uses the same powers as the witch, fighting fire with fire. The outbreak of witchcraft in late 1956 showed that, whatever the inroads of Christianity, the belief in witchcraft remains deeply rooted. Sometimes accusations extend beyond the village, but mostly they remain within it, directed at kinfolk or co-wives, the circle of face-to-face contacts. Witchcraft (or sorcery—the distinction seems to be fuzzy) is commonly blamed for many misfortunes, but witches, *baloi,* operate in many different ways. Lozi like to blame the most horrendous practices on Luvale migrants from the north and west, but in truth witchcraft is such a tangled web that it is impossible to sort out the origins of the various strands.

Some witches employ familiars who actually do the dirty work. Familiars may be figurines or objects that are animated by the witch, or they may be the spirits of human beings killed for the purpose and then resurrected as slaves. Particularly potent is a form of watersnake a sorcerer may create for himself or a client. The body is that of a snake, but the head is human and closely resembles that of its owner, and the fate of the two is completely intertwined; the death of one results in the death of the other. Familiars have no agency of their own but must do the bidding of their master, although it is a common belief that they may demand opportunities to kill as a reward for their subjection.

In other situations, witches attack directly. While the *kaliloze* guns were the most spectacular weapons used in the 1956–57 outbreak, they were only part of the witches' arsenal. Witches may insert needles under their skin to act as invisible projectiles aimed at a victim, while non-witches may wear the same needles as protection against evildoers. In fact, it is a deadly game. If the attack is parried by the charms of the intended victim, the missile may return to harm the sender. He, too, needs to wear defensive charms of needles or protective beads. Red beads are particularly associated with "killing magic." Most feared of all is a kind of sorcery in which a person sells a kinsman or kinswoman in return for success in life. This is often accompanied by necrophagy: A witch may be required to supply the body of a dead person, preferably a relative, for fellow witches to feast upon as part of the initiation and to eat certain organs of the corpse to increase his or her powers. There is a whole armory of tools and implements ascribed to this practice that enable the necrophager to kill victims, dig up their corpses, and prepare them for eating.

Knowledge of vegetable poisons is also widespread. A self-confessed poisoner eagerly cooperated with authorities during the witchcraft outbreak, showing them "many specimens of roots and herbs which, she alleges, are used in poisoning."[29] Ironically, she was never charged because the post-mortem on the victim was inconclusive. The alkaloid poisons commonly used in Barotseland, it seems, are impossible to detect even when the post-mortem is conducted immediately after death. Nevertheless, her instruction was useful to those eager to analyse the poisonous flora of the region.

It sometimes baffles outsiders that people are not a bundle of nerves, what with all the witches or potential witches around. Quite the contrary. Some of the *kutas* most prone to witchcraft suspicions seem to be the most conspicuous for "gay and carefree laughter and the exchange of banter among the villagers"—a stranger would conclude that they are "among the happiest people on earth." As the Lozi proverb has it: "An ox is not overwhelmed by its horns"[30]; just so the population has learned to live with its *baloi*.

Ethnicity and the kaleidoscope of cultural variations are not the only ingredients that give different *lilalo* in the District their varying flavors. Some are overwhelmingly agricultural; others contain more craftsmen and traders. Immediately around Kalabo there is a "smart residential area,"[31] housing people dependent one way or another on the *boma*. In the eyes of the Lozi landed aristocracy, they are the *nouveaux riches,* not quite acceptable. But they often include people of considerable achievement, such as the first man from Barotseland to matriculate at the new University College in Salisbury. Far more undesirable are the areas of Mankoya and Namulilo, in the far southeast of the District. Long ago this was a no-man's land to which lepers and political undesirables were banished and the stigma haunts it still. To this day it is shunned by members of the royal family, and there are no important ritual sites located here. Instead many royals live in the sparsely populated and largely untroubled *kuta* of Sishekanu, within range of the capital of Libonda.

In 1959, however, all these differences pale before one overriding variable: flooding. Libonda itself spreads out on the banks of the Zambezi, just above the floodline, although the record floods of 1957 came very close. In some years the *mulena* leads the waterborne movement to her *omboka* or flood capital to the northwest; in other years when the flood is more modest, she and her court stay put. For many of her subjects, however, there is no choice. The greater part of 9 of the 15 *kutas* in the District, as well as parts of 3 more, are normally under water from

March till June or July of each year. The result is that most villages in these areas are virtually inaccessible during the flood, with the water in some places too shallow for barges or canoes, in others too deep for wading. Flooding is also at least partly to blame for the casualness in building and maintaining houses in the plain. Why build a good house when it may well be "burned, blown or washed down in a few years?"[32] The strict regulations drawn up by the Native Authority concerning village tidiness refer only to settlements on permanent sites. In the meantime "plain villages will have to rely on the yearly cleansing which they get from the flood."[33]

More serious is the plight of villages outside of the plain that are now waterlogged but have no dry place to move to. In some of the sub-districts immediately southwest of Kalabo, for example, people have no *omboka* homes, no alternative villages. Here the water does not come from rivers overflowing their banks "but instead oozes up from every square yard of ground as if the whole country was a giant sponge."[34] For months of the year, these villages are "squalid in the extreme, water standing all around and in the huts, paths running knee deep in water, rubbish pits and latrines flooded and their contents floating about, villagers not surprisingly sick and dispirited."[35] There is no point in trying to raise standards of living as long as the water continues to rise. Meanwhile, forests that should serve to draw up excess moisture now stand in permanent pools, leaving a depressing scenery of "dead, grey-brown trees ... killed by the rising water table."[36] Ironically, some of these same areas had been deserted only 30 years earlier for lack of water.

The recurrent food shortages and even outright famine that plague Barotseland more and more frequently suggest that something has gone horribly wrong. "If agriculture were the test of civilisation then these are not savages,"[37] Livingstone had declared, and even in the 1930s government experts held the Lozi up as models for their more benighted brethren in other parts of the country. To be sure, Livingstone may have visited the country at optimum moments, when neither drought nor flood disrupted food production, and he had come to the Valley from the parched lands of what is now Botswana. Nevertheless, one cannot entirely discount his picture of a land literally flowing with milk and honey, and grains and vegetables besides, without even the usual "hungry season" before the crops ripen (although the Lozi name for what corresponds to December is "Ng'ulule"—"it is the month of hunger"). Conversely, the 1890s were a time of natural disasters, when for several years the flood failed completely, then came in such torrents that crops were washed away. Locusts ravaged the land and an epidemic of smallpox broke out. Suffering there was, but the country avoided mass starvation. How?

The explanation seems to lie in the sophisticated mosaic of land use that antedated the arrival of the Europeans but was expanded and improved by the system of trunk canals and drainage channels learned from the Paris Mission. The Lozi have fine-tuned their farming methods to the many different soils and water conditions of their environment, allowing them to take advantage of the complementarity of plain and forest and all the gradations in between. Closest to the river, they plant *sitapa* gardens with maize on the rich alluvial soils of the plain when the flood recedes. Equally productive are the *sishanjo* gardens in the zones of sandy peat found along the margins of streams and ponds that dry up between floods—gardens "without parallel anywhere," in the words of two agricultural surveyors.[38] These are made by excavating a lattice-work of deep drainage canals that then link up with the main watercourses and man-made canals. As the soils dry out in the course of the year, the gardens are extended progressively down the riverbanks and planted in maize, sweet potatoes, and some millet. Other types of gardens are adapted to ant-hills or sandy ridges or the cleared forests and thickets of the scarps ringing the plain or its pools. Ideally, a single family farms a number of small, widely dispersed holdings in as many as eight different zones, each producing a different array of crops and requiring work at different seasons. Their variety not only provides a hedge against famine but the possibility of two crops of staples in a single year. Maize, for example, can be planted on the mounds rising from the plain as soon as the rains set in, about November, and is ready for harvesting in January. In lower terrain, a crop can be sown in the damp ground in July, during the dry season, and harvested as the rains are about to begin. Surplus cassava can be sold to the *boma* or to large merchants such as Susman or Wulfsohn. Tobacco also has a local market, mainly in the hands of African traders.

In addition, the sandy loams of the floodplain offer excellent pasturage for cattle. Only Lozi and closely associated peoples traditionally had the right to occupy the mounds dotting the plain, to farm the Bulozi heartland, and to graze cattle on its grassy expanses. The bush beyond was the territory of the Wiko, the Nkoya, the Lunda-Luvale, and other non-Lozi who grow mostly cassava, bulrush millet, and sweet potatoes, supplementing their diet with hunting and gathering. Wiko cultivate little maize and do not share the Lozi passion for cattle, except in the pot.

Until the large influx of Wiko peoples into the District, there has been ample land. What *has* been a problem is the ability to mobilize labor to maintain the system inherited from the past. In Lewanika's day, the Lozi elite could and did draw on both slave and tribute labor for the incessant work of clearing waterways in the floodplain and trees in the bush margins. Slaves were most often acquired through raids or as tribute from subject peoples. A few became slaves in settlement of debts. Like other villagers, they could marry and hold land, but they could not move away and they could not control their own time and labor. The non-slave population could also be summoned by headmen or the king to work on public projects or to participate in the annual hunt. When the British abolished first slavery (in 1906), then tribute labor (in 1925), the intricate 400-mile drainage system created during Lewanika's reign fell into disrepair, leading to the waterlogging that has so concerned the DC and taken so much prime agricultural land out of production in Barotseland.

Even with massive labor migration, there is not an absolute shortage of male labor for communal projects, but it is no longer at the beck and call of the ruling classes nor of the colonial administration. The *makolo,* territorial-cum-kin based units of men that could be called out for war, hunting, or public works, have fallen into oblivion. In some cases, men still volunteer for projects whose utility is obvious, such as road work and digging canals, but the daunting problem of reclaiming, maintaining, and extending the drainage system now requires a long-term commitment of money and supervision, which are in short supply from both Native Authority and colonial administration. The catastrophic loss of gardens in the peat zones of the plain due to waterlogging has put more pressure on bush cultivation on its margins, but bush lands are quickly exhausted and take years to regenerate. The practice of cutting and burning large piles of branches and small trees to provide a fertile layer of ash on the sandy soil also leads to widespread deforestation.

The cattle economy, too, has declined. The grasses of the plain provide lush pasturage and the floodplain proper is free of the tsetse fly so ubiquitous and so mortal elsewhere. However, cattle have to leave the plain for the bush during the months of high water, and grazing in the bush is poor. Many are lost to malnutrition, disease, and even predators. Losses are higher than in the past because herding is left mostly to pre-school boys who lack the skills to provide the best care for the animals in their charge. Older boys and young men who used to do this, voluntarily or otherwise, are now in school or simply consider the job beneath them. While Wiko willingly tend Lozi herds during the flood season, they are poor herdsmen and keep the animals penned up so as to have the manure for their gardens. In the plain itself, two-thirds of the cattle belong to the *litunga* or important *indunas,* but even they cannot command the labor of herders as they once did.

Unlike many other cattle-keeping peoples, the Lozi have never been averse to consuming or selling their animals for meat and hides. Since they escaped the rinderpest that decimated most of southern Africa's herds in the 1890s, they were able to take advantage of the expanding markets of the region, trading large numbers of animals south to Livingstone and north to Katanga. Indeed had it not been for the epidemic of bovine pleuro-pneumonia that hit in 1915, economic development might have taken a different course in Barotseland. Cattle rather than people might have become the country's prime export. The British South Africa Company and the successor colonial state might have invested in infrastructure to move cattle to distant markets. With the export of Lozi cattle embargoed for the 20 years of the epidemic, there was no such incentive. Now, in 1959, there is a modest trade in cattle for slaughter, but the area is too remote to imagine a real expansion in exports, and the waterlogging of so much of the plain has reduced grazing along with garden land.

The net result of this tangled history is that agriculture remains largely stagnant. Experiments in growing wheat and cotton have fallen victim to pest and disease; rice has gained only modest acceptance, much as it has been pushed by extension agents from Namushakende. Even subsistence farming has been drastically simplified. Where once Livingstone remarked not only on the abundance of crops but also on their variety—maize, millet, "caffre corn [sorghum] of great size and beautiful whiteness,"[39] yams, sugar cane, Egyptian arum, sweet potato, two kinds of cassava, pumpkins, melons, beans, groundnuts—the repertoire is now largely limited to maize and cassava. The precolonial array of plants served as a hedge against climatic swings, on the don't-put-all-your-eggs-in-one-meteorological-basket principle. The DC suspects that the greatest sin Europeans have to answer for is the introduction of maize, which has by now largely replaced the variety of sorghums and millets that were so much better suited to local conditions and so much more nutritious. Cassava may be just as insidious an import—it takes little tending but is less nutritious than maize and even more vulnerable to water-soaked soils.

True, when rains and river flooding arrive on schedule and in suitable amounts, the system still works reasonably well. But nature is rarely so dependable. If the flood comes early or is particularly high (or both) it can wash away the early maize and make the ground too soggy for the later planting. Ironically, in 1957, the flood was so late that everyone complained of drought. Then, it swept down with such fury that almost everything washed away. Many people were forced to subsist on water lily bulbs that they gathered at great peril from the crocodile-infested waters and cooked like sweet potatoes.

There is one bright spot. The Zambezi and its tributaries continue to teem with fish: tiger fish, bream, barbel, squeaskers, *mulumesi, nakatenge.* Although technically the river "belongs" to the *litunga,* all the various ethnic groups may fish in it. They use three main methods: trapping, netting, and spearing. The Wiko preserve specially constructed baskets with which to scoop up the fish trapped in ponds left by the flood. As the flood recedes, other groups build fish dams, but these, like the peat gardens, need annual attention to shore them up, and are attached to individual villages. The dams have a downside. They block channels and increase the already too high levels of surface water. In some areas they are banned altogether, but this does not stop the wily fisherfolk from building them anyway. At best, fishing supplies only local needs; there is little incentive for innovation without an expansion of markets.

Both *kuta* and *boma* depend primarily on the local taxes that all adult males have to pay in cash. But where does the money come from? Lewanika once envisioned that his kingdom would be in the forefront of modernization with a railroad running through it and Lozi entrepreneurs leading the way in new crafts and industries, inspired by European example. Unfortunately the railroad that spanned the gorge at Victoria Falls in 1905 runs well to the east of the Barotse Valley through what became the Copperbelt, then north to the Belgian Congo. Rhodes never realized his dream of a Cape-to-Cairo railway, nor did Lewanika realize his of Barotseland as a bustling hub along that line. In 1959, ironically, it is the Portuguese who are taking the initiative and building a railroad eastward from the Angolan port of Moçâmedes, intended to link up with the Rhodesian system. If it bridges the Kwando River at the point that many expect, it will be almost due west of Kalabo *boma.* But will the Rhodesian authorities ever agree on where it should cross the border? Even if they do, is there a ghost of a chance that those who hold the purse strings will match the Portuguese willingness to fund capital projects? Not likely.

Without transport and without mineral resources (except the minor iron deposits once used by indigenous metallurgists), the Protectorate has become not a beacon of modernity but a backwater, valuable only as a reservoir of cheap labor for other more productive areas of southern Africa. Some men find employment in the District as *boma* and *kuta* clerks, messengers and *kapasus,* and house servants of various sorts. With no commercial farming and virtually no industries, however, the road for many leads south to the mines of the Witwatersrand (the "Rand") and the Orange Free State.

On his last trip south in 1888, the trader George Westbeech took along a large contingent of Africans to work in the newly opened gold mines at Klerksdorp in the Transvaal. This is the first record of organized recruitment of Africans from the Zambezi Valley for South African mines. It would not be the last. Wenela, the Witwatersrand Native Labor Association, has been recruiting labor in Kalabo District since 1940, initially in competition with other agencies such as the one, now closed down, that sent men to work on farms and mines in Southern Rhodesia. An annual quota is set for the Protectorate as a whole and for individual districts after consultation with the provincial administration and the paramount chief. In 1959 the Protectorate quota is 5,000 men, of which 1,913 have been recruited in Kalabo by Dick Japp, the local Wenela agent. Wenela also runs a string of camps along the Angolan border, like that at Sikongo managed by Squire Davis, to accommodate recruits from the Portuguese territory and send them along to the main depots. The Barotse Native Government receives a special capitation fee for facilitating the recruit of these aliens from across the frontier, and the Portuguese authorities seem willing enough to bless an enterprise that siphons money into the local economy. The Protectorate quota always fills quickly as men recruit their own brothers and relatives; in fact it fills so quickly that some men pass themselves off as Angolans in order to capture a spot.

Wenela works with extraordinary efficiency, which may account for much of its success. From Kalabo, the men are all taken to Mongu by boat or truck, then flown to Francistown in Bechuanaland and from there to Johannesburg. Wenela has its own fleet of airplanes and crews, mainly DC-3s and DC-4s that have been modified to carry 30 and 99 migrants respectively (in the off-season they may also be used to ferry the Wenela cricket team to distant *bomas*). Recruits sign on for 12 months, with the possibility of a 6-month extension, and are flown back at the end of their contracts. On the way out, they are issued a blanket, a tunic, and a pair of trousers. On the flight back, however, they are loaded down with baggage: gaudy Johannesburg suits and shoes, presents for wives and family, even stocks to trade back home—all the goods that speak eloquently of new-found "wealth" and new-found habits of consumption.

A portion of their pay is deferred until the return, but Wenela also provides for sending remittances home during their term of service. The recruit designates an amount on a slip, then his wife or other family member presents one half of the slip. Dick Japp or another agent has the other half and if the two match, the amount is paid out. This system only applies to Barotse natives, not to Angolans. In fact, there is a real problem if Angolans are injured or killed in the mines: It is very difficult to track down their families, and Wenela is reluctant to pay compensation through the Portuguese colonial government since they can be pretty sure the families will never see a shilling of it. The best they can do is to try secretly to find the families across the border. Most migrants return at the end of their 12 months, but many also sign on again, taking advantage of a provision that if they renew their contracts within 8 months of returning home, they can re-engage at the same rate of pay as when they left, rather than having to start over at the bottom of the heap.

The pattern of migration is more complex than it first appears, however, and does not quite match that found in other parts of Africa where labor migration is also common. For reasons no one can fathom, different villages and different ethnic groups within Barotseland and even within Kalabo District are far more heavily involved than others. While people do move around and intermarry, they still tend to identify with a particular village of residence and to see themselves and others as belonging to specific ethnic groups, still usually referred to as "tribes," and are so listed on the annual census register. The Lozi proper—the "true" Lozi—figure hardly at all in Wenela recruitment. Aside from Wiko immigrants, many of them transient, the most numerous recruits are Nyengo and Imilunga, groups classed as "allied" to the dominant Lozi because of a long history of living together in the Valley (as distinct from the "subject" peoples whose relationship is based on domination). Nyengo and Imilango men are frequently professional mine workers who carry through on six or even more contracts with the minimum interval between them, so that they are able to maintain their pay as specialist workers. Census figures show that in 1959 not only did these two groups provide a disproportionate number of Wenela recruits but also that nearly half came from 3 of the 15 Native Authority *kutas* in the district.

Long before Wenela came to Barotseland, migrants were making their way on foot to the "line of rail" and dreams of a better life, and some continue to do so. Perhaps they haven't paid their taxes (Wenela is legally permitted to garnishee wages for tax payments), perhaps they are under the legal age limit, perhaps they simply prefer to be independent or to try other destinations than the South African mines. The track south to the nearest railhead at Mulobezi used to be known as the "Prostitutes Path" because of the many women lying in wait to relieve the traveler of his money for sex and beer, especially when he was returning with his pockets full of cash. One encampment was nicknamed "Joburg" because often a repatriate from the Rand was so impoverished by the time he reached this point that after one last fling, he had to turn around and head back to the mines without ever going home. The Labour Department has stepped in to improve the miserable conditions faced by the *muselfu,* the migrant traveling on his own. It has built rest camps at intervals marking a day's march and tried to improve security for both the migrants and the villagers along their route. In spite of such measures, there are still plenty of brewers of illicit alcohol, *catchipendi,* and many a man returns home far poorer than he intended. Even the Wenela recruit, once returned to Mongu or Kalabo, has to run the gauntlet of *catchipendi* and *kapenta* ("painted women") before he actually reaches home. An annual report laments that women of the demi-monde have taken to bicycles in a big way to "increase their rate of turnover."[40] But a survey finds somewhat surprisingly that most migrants make it back with a goodly nest egg. If they are single men, this usually goes to find a wife and set up housekeeping. Most of the men, however, are already married and use their savings to build a house, provide for their families, buy cattle, or set up in trade.

Because of their high levels of education compared to other ethnic groups, Lozi who do migrate can be sure of jobs above ground at the mines or as clerks and policemen in the administration not only of Northern Rhodesia but of Southern Rhodesia and Bechuanaland as well. They also command the lion's share of jobs in the Barotse Native Government, which is a major reason fewer Lozi are obliged to seek employment outside the province. Aside from South Africa, some migrants make their arduous way to Lusaka, others to the Livingstone Sawmills in Mulobezi, which supplies high-quality teak used for railroad sleeping cars and timbering in the mines. In the past a small contingent could also be found on the Copperbelt. But the fortunes of copper tend to a boom-and-bust cycle, making employment there uncertain. Besides, the Copperbelt is considered Bemba territory (even though the Bemba are outsiders, from the northeastern part of the colony), and the Bemba and Lozi do not get on very well. Southern Rhodesia has a far worse reputation for working conditions than the Rand, so that it is a destination of last resort.

Men go to the mines first and foremost to earn money. They also go out of a sense of adventure, a chance to see the outside world. A survey of Wenela contract workers found that the higher the education level of the recruit, the more he mentioned a wish for adventure as a motive for signing on—this regardless of his age or marital status. To be sure, men with more education may be better able to analyse and articulate their reasons, but studies elsewhere have found the same correlation. The survey also revealed that men with mine experience were very apt to recommend to young men looking for a career that they accept a Wenela contract. Most interesting of all, respondents were unanimous in asserting that women in their home villages preferred the company of mine workers to the stay-at-homes. A self-serving response? Since the women themselves were not asked, we will never know. But there is no doubt that working with Wenela confers a relative well-being that sets them apart from their non-migrant neighbors and often wins them positions of prestige as village headmen when they retire.

By 1959 migrancy has become a way of life in Kalabo. It seems perfectly normal for men to sign a contract with Wenela or to head off on their own to Livingstone or Lusaka or points farther afield. Depending on the individual *kuta,* anywhere from 10 percent to 79 percent of its taxpayers are away from home. The average is around 40 percent. What is the impact on the District of having such a high rate of absent males?

First of all, the immediate economic benefit to Kalabo/Libonda from Wenela recruitment is striking. If one adds up payments to the Barotse Native Government in fees and rents, remittances and deferred pay to Kalabo repatriates, and payments made locally for labor, foods, and materials at Wenela posts and stations in the District, the total for 1959 comes to some £50,000. Since all of this enters the local economy at the village level, it is unquestionably the largest single contribution to the prosperity of the District, seven times the amount of taxes collected for the year and 50 percent greater than the total budget for the Libonda Native Authority. This does not include the even more numerous Angolan repatriates who are paid out at the station in the Caprivi Strip but sometimes travel north through the District on their way home. Without Wenela, the economy would be even more precarious than it is.

But what is the cost, the price paid for this infusion of money? It is not necessarily where one would most expect to find it—in the realm of family and village stability. According to a carefully done survey, divorce rates among these "professional" Wenela migrants do not seem to be any higher than among the non-migrant population. Put differently, there is an enormous range in the divorce rate among the different *kutas* of the

District and it seems to be quite unrelated to the pattern of migrant labor. Nor is there any correlation between birth rates and migration. The eight-month grace period between sign-ups is usually sufficient for wives to become pregnant before their men take off again. This is presumed to serve as a guarantee of marital fidelity over the next 12 months. Women are happy with the presents their husbands bring back and claim to be confident the men will return punctually from their contracts. In a sense these women experience migration vicariously and, like any other topic, it becomes grist for the songs they sing during their daily chores. Are they jealous that their men come back with their own songs about "Egoli" (Johannesburg) and the things they have seen in the city of gold? Do they wonder about "town wives" their menfolk may have in that other world?

Kuta court records indicate that migrants are no more or less law-abiding than their fellows. At the time of the outbreak of witchcraft killings, some suspected that the particularly brutal forms it took may have been influenced by experiences abroad, especially in South Africa. Forty-four of the 50 convicted gunmen had worked outside the Protectorate, more than half of them on the Rand. Some were initiated into the gunmen's society while living in the mine compounds and either took charms with them or had them made there. What is more, the activities of the "Kaliloze gunmen" first came to light in an area of the District most heavily involved in Wenela recruitment.

In spite of all this circumstantial evidence, however, it seems more likely that while mine service may have reinforced some ideas and influenced some practices, the outbreak in Barotseland was at bottom an indigenous affair; it was too consistent with the beliefs of Lozi and their neighbors to be explained simply as a foreign import or a symptom of social breakdown caused by migration. Thirty years earlier there were reports that Balovale sorcerers killed their victims with "night-guns" made from a thigh or leg bone or of carved wood and metal. Guns were loaded with bullets carved from human bones and only the victim knew that he had been fired on. He was doomed to die and it was left to the diviner to discover who had bewitched him. Then it might be up to the witchdoctor himself to take revenge on the witch. In one form or another, these beliefs about witches and their repertoire of power objects have been common currency in Barotseland for a long time.

The verdict that the outbreak of witchcraft was essentially local in origin is reinforced by the evident conservatism of the population and their resistance to change in their daily habits, no matter how much time they have spent abroad. They may eat mine food day in and day out in

South Africa, for example, but when they get home they can hardly wait to return to the old staple of sour cassava with fish relish. Even when they can afford grinding mills that would give women much more time for other things, Lozi men reject them, saying they don't like machine-ground flour and anyway the women might just use the extra time for extra-marital dalliance. Still, the Lozi were quick to adopt the three-legged iron pots that became plentiful in the 1920s and replaced the clay pot perched precariously on the burning logs of the cooking fire (there were no stones in the plain), an innovation that freed women to do other tasks while dinner was cooking since children could safely be left in charge. Ploughs were even more radical. Although they clearly saved a great deal of labor, they were resisted for a long time because of the well-founded belief that they destroyed the soil's ability to retain moisture. Nevertheless they became increasingly common from the 1930s on.

Social custom, then, serves as a sieve, determining what is borrowed from other cultures and what is not, and all in all the experience of migration over a generation or more has introduced fewer changes than one might imagine.

Even in the realm of agriculture, the effects of labor migration are not obvious. This is because of the unusual pattern of family structure and production in this land of subsistence farming. Each family is responsible for all stages of production. There is no communal clearing of new fields and gardens. If the taxpayer is absent when this needs to be done, women do it, or, more commonly, they hire someone else to do it with the wages of the family head since even with relatively high levels of migrancy in many areas, there is still a surplus of labor. The more individualistic agricultural system in Barotseland seems to have the effect of tying the migrant more firmly to his village than is the case elsewhere. More generally, the smaller family unit involved means that the migrant is not obligated to spread his wealth among a bevy of extended kin but concentrates it within what is essentially a nuclear family. If anything, migrancy intensifies the individualism and narrower sense of family obligation already a feature of local peoples—if it continues, there may be a clamor for individual ownership of land that could spell trouble for the Native Authority.

The most serious effect of labor migration, then, may be less what has happened than what has not. The men from the District who have spent most of their prime years as labor recruits outside the Protectorate are among the best educated and most energetic. What would have been their impact if these men had spent the same years in their home villages? Would they have been able to push both the Native Authority and the colonial administration toward projects that would expand local opportunities, to change the prevailing image of Barotseland as the most backward of the provinces of Northern Rhodesia?

Early on, Lewanika saw the immense potential of Western education but grew impatient with the missionary baggage that came with it. He wanted literacy and also training in all the industrial crafts that Europe could offer and that seemed to account for Europeans' evident material superiority. Local artists could work beautifully in wood and clay, metals and grasses. Lozi basketry was a particular marvel, "excelling anything produced by basket-factories of civilized countries," wrote a visitor in 1891, "for scarcely would our workers in basketry undertake to weave an impervious vessel from reedy grass, to carry five or six gallons of water."[41] This was not enough for Lewanika; he wanted to train his people as carpenters and masons and eventually as engineers and surveyors. After his trip to England in 1902 and all the wonders it entailed, he became even more passionate in his pleas for training in the practical arts.

Disappointed as he may have been, Lewanika did succeed in pushing the Paris Missionary Society to upgrade the level of its schools by skill-fully whipping up competition from other sources. One of the most important of these was the Barotse National School, set up in 1906 and in 1959 still the only school in Northern Rhodesia that is not church-affiliated. What most galled the *litunga* was that the British South Africa Company contributed not a penny to the school—it was paid for out of a percentage of the hut tax—and yet it insisted on tightly controlling both the budget and the day-to-day management of the school. Located in the malarial Kambule Valley, near Mongu, the school got off to a wobbly start but eventually did offer an education that combined technical train-ing and basic education up to Standard V, later upgraded to Standard VI. Its pupils were almost exclusively sons of the royal family and senior *indunas* who paid no fees and were provided with room, board, and uniforms at no cost. Since there was no age limit for entry, many of the students were married men with families in the early days. In contrast to the mission schools, there was no compulsory church attendance or religious instruction.

At first the staff was entirely European, but gradually Africans were added and finally an African became headmaster in 1951, four years after the school was purchased from the Barotse Native Government, at last becoming a government school under the eye of the provincial educa-tion officer in Mongu. By 1959 it admits both boys and girls and covers the whole span from elementary through secondary education, with a trades school built largely by the students. Lewanika may finally be at peace.

Most students, however, do not attend the BNS; it remains the bastion of the elite. For the past year school attendance has, in principle, been obligatory for children "of apparent age of eight" residing in the Protectorate, but the law must be qualified to apply to those who live within a reasonable distance of a school where a vacancy exists. There are some 60 schools in the District, most of them at the elementary level and many of them overcrowded. Parents must pay school fees for all children and provide food for boarding students in secondary schools. For poorer families, then, schooling is out of the question for some or all of their children. In certain of the more remote corners of the District such as Lupui *kuta,* the population is just too scattered to justify any schools at all. Who knows what "mute inglorious Miltons"[42] will remain forever undiscovered?

Even the mission schools (Paris Missionary Society, Catholics, and Seventh Day Adventists) receive at least 90 percent of their funding from the colonial government. This is altogether in keeping with the Ministry of African Education's declaration that "Christianity is the declared basis of education in Northern Rhodesia and the practice of Christian principles, except in the case of *bona fide* Moslems, is included in the code of professional conduct which a teacher undertakes to do his best to adhere to when he joins the Unified African Teaching Service."[43] Indeed, virtually all indigenous teachers have been trained in mission schools, and religious instruction is prescribed for all grades. Missions are represented as a matter of course on government education boards and committees.

Locally, however, the battle over the curriculum still rages. The missionaries tend to emphasize academic subjects, while the Barotse Native Government favors practical training and points to its model gardens to prove the point. The Catholics feel that life in the bush is always improved by a knowledge of Latin. No new mission schools can be opened without the permission of the BNG. So great is the eagerness for education that once permission is granted, everyone turns out to clear the land and build the school under the watchful eye of the missionaries within three or four days. While the government pays teachers' salaries, villagers themselves are responsible for building and maintaining the schools in their districts, whether missionary- or state-run. In areas where schools have to *omboka* every year along with the rest of the population, this means maintaining two schools.

Although extension of the Libonda Middle School buildings is still lagging in 1959, the Libonda Education Authority schools have made great progress, not only in repairing schools damaged by the floods but also in drawing up a comprehensive education plan for the District. There are local school councils and teachers' conferences. Nevertheless many schools must crowd several classes into a single room with only the most minimal furniture. Added to this, teachers have the daunting task of teaching much of the material in a foreign language, English. English is taught to children of all levels; arithmetic is taught in a mixture of English and Lozi.

But when the DO and the inspector from the Native Authority come on tour, the students and teachers are eager to display their accomplishments. Sometimes it is a thriving garden filled with carrots, lettuce, tomatoes, onions, and pineapples; sometimes a display of marching to a young drummer; sometimes a mural painted by a talented master. One inspired teacher has laid out a map of Barotseland in the sand near his school with sticks hammered into the ground, its scale 1" to the mile. "To allow pupils to walk on the map is an excellent way of putting over the rudiments of map-making and use of maps,"[44] reported a DO (himself an accomplished mapmaker). A rare school actually possesses a football "in a state of inflation."[45] Would that the powers that be realize how good an investment it would be to provide more footballs—surely attendance would skyrocket!

The highpoint of the school year is the annual field day that marks the end of exams with games and competitions. It is a direct descendant of the festivities Lewanika attended on New Year's Day, 1890, in Sefula during which he observed the exams, then watched with probably even more fascination (if not bewilderment) as William Waddell, the gifted mission carpenter, taught the school boys to play cricket. The day ended with a feast and magic lantern show. In 1959, the school sports day in Kalabo tops even that: It takes place the same day as the Liyoyelo regatta with all its pageantry and the paramount chief in attendance. Victorious schools proudly display their trophies. Or in the case of the Libonda school, its two live oxen won in the football match and the barge race.

The juxtaposition of school field day and regatta symbolizes the Lozi penchant for absorbing the new while clinging tenaciously to the old, a trait that often surprises outsiders. The Lozi consider their royal family to be descended from Mbuywamwambwa, daughter of the supreme god, Nyambe. According to some traditions, Mbuywamwambwa gave birth to her children by parthenogenesis; according to others she sometimes took the form of a white cow. When faced by a revolt on the part of some of her sons who felt that women should not exercise political authority, she abdicated in favor of her son Mboo, retaining for herself the role of *éminence grise,* the power behind the throne. This has remained the acknowledged role of royal women. Similarly, all claimants to the throne must be descended from Nyambe and Mbuywamwambwa.

But ancestry alone is not enough to confer divinity: The prince chosen by the national assembly to become *litunga* must go through a sequence of purification rites that remain largely secret but that demonstrate his power over nature. He must spend a night naked save for his cloth wrapper at the grave of Mboo, the first *litunga* of the Barotse, at Ikatulamwa. Here he is presented to his distant ancestor by the guardian of the shrine, but what else happens at the grave has remained a secret. One tradition says that he sits alone beside a small lake wherein dwells a fabulous cow called Liombé-Kalala. It is a good omen if this creature comes out of the lake and licks the king; in any case, he sits waiting for it. At dawn the ordeal is over. He puts on his clothes and emerges from seclusion to the beating of the great *maoma* drums awaiting him on the river bank. Then, in a public ritual, the new king sits on one of the drums during the enthronement ceremony and is invested by Kashambatwa, the chief steward of Mboo's grave, with the power "of the night" and "of the day." Men perform a dance as the royal drummer plays another type of drum, while women collect wood to rekindle their cooking fires that were extinguished at the death of the previous king. Finally the new king goes on a ritual hunt where he has only to cast a spear at an animal to fulfill the requirements. At the end of these rites of passage, the initiate emerges as a different category of being. He is no longer the "owner of his body." Henceforth he must not be brought into contact with death. He cannot attend funerals, even of his own wife or child, nor should any bereaved person enter the capital. Blood, too, is taboo: The ruler must not go to a queen who has recently borne a child nor to the first menstruation ceremony of his daughter.

While Lozi kings have not been as secluded as some in other parts of Africa, their public appearances are limited and they can communicate only through intermediaries. The *litunga* also speaks through his musicians. Wherever he goes he is accompanied by his bandsmen and they are always present when the *kuta* meets, sitting directly in front of the royal dais. The band consists of drums and a xylophone. Every night of the king's life, one of the drums, the *mutango,* is beaten at intervals as a sort of surrogate heartbeat. It falls silent only when he dies. Far from the capital people will inquire of any emissary, "Are the drums still beating?," meaning "Is the king still alive?" Lesser chiefs also have their bands as well. Their musicians and instruments are a mirror of the different ethnic groups that have been incorporated over time into the Barotse nation. Except for the *mulena mukwae,* however, none of the other chiefs is entitled to *maoma,* the great cylindrical war drums covered with hides of bulls and spotted with red. Possession of these drums symbolizes kingship, although oral traditions differ about just when and where they were acquired.

In death a king becomes even more powerful. A century of missionary contact has not weakened the veneration accorded the royal graves. "One can recognize them a long way off," Coillard noted, "by the magnificent clumps of trees which shade them."[46] The tombs must always be constructed within Bulozi proper and on mounds where the earth remains dry even during the flood. Some of the oldest and most sacred are in Kalabo District, including those of Mbuywamwambwa and Mboo. Each king has a separate burial site and a grave keeper whose position is hereditary and who must know the history of the king whose grave he guards. Access to the graves and to their custodians is tightly controlled, not only because of reverence for the dead but also because dead kings are actively consulted by their successors about current affairs. They must approve the choice of a new king, for example, and he in turn must make a tour of all the royal gravesites in the country, offering sacrifices and seeking ancestral blessings.

Europeans are forbidden to visit the royal tombs. It is said that a man named Whiley of the colonial Veterinary Department violated this prohibition and entered one of them in 1917. He died soon after and is buried near Makono. Forty years later the story is still well known and visitors are shown the grave, a simple patch of sand surrounded by a fence of reeds, tended by a villager. There is no marker of any sort. The story serves as a warning to other inquisitive Europeans, but the effect is diminished by a variant tradition that Whiley in fact died of the DTs.

A ruler often instructs the custodians of the graves to pray for the well-being of the nation and of individuals—Lewanika, newly restored to his throne, repeatedly implored the departed kings to pray for Westbeech's recovery when the trader fell ill. "In every way," Coillard observed, "the king, dead for generations past, is treated with as much deference as if still living and reigning. They present him with libations of milk and honey and offerings of beads and white calico. They bid farewell to him before starting on a journey, and on their return they come to salute him, and to tell him the news."[47] To the missionary, this suggested a welcome hook to preach the message of resurrection of the dead and eternal life; to the Lozi, it confirms that royal ancestors can intervene actively in the present and that rulers had better secure their loyalty and that of their priests. One wonders, too, if Lewanika was speaking more than metaphorically when he drew aside the curtains and exposed the portrait of Queen Victoria in his dining room saying, "I have heard white men speak of her since I was a little boy. She was queen then, and she is still alive. I do not believe she will ever die."[48]

During his long reign Lewanika also had to contend with other centers of spiritual power, particularly those in the hands of rival ethnic groups such as the Mbunda diviners. In some of his contests, he had the support of Coillard and his fellow missionaries. They were pleased when he declared that there was no such thing as witchcraft and put an end to the witchcraft ordeals that had so shocked Livingstone and Arnot. But Lewanika was also engaged in a power struggle with the missionaries. This was why he demanded that they leave offerings of white calico when passing by royal graves in the floodplain. He enjoyed theological discussions with the missionaries, frequently attended Christian church services, and sent many of his children to mission schools, even as far away as Lovedale in South Africa. However, there was never a real question of conversion. How could there be when political power depended on polygamous alliances with influential families and spiritual power depended on alliances with royal ancestors?

Nevertheless, there are unresolved strains within the body politic. When education was largely limited to royals, it could reinforce their monopoly of power, but now a generation of "new men," educated commoners, is chafing at the bit, demanding a greater role in government and more access to its rewards. Why should they be excluded in favor of members of the ruling family and their cronies whom they often view as barely literate incompetents? Education and Christianity are, as Lewanika recognized, a double-edged sword. This disaffection of the educated elite is matched by an equal disaffection among branches of the royal family who also feel left out. Both are looking to make the most of new institutions beginning to take shape: the Katengo Council with its expanded role for commoners and the territorial constitution, which, for the first time, provides for an elected representative from Barotseland.

The paradox is that these groups are as attached to the rituals of royalty, if not necessarily to their present rulers, as anyone else, for these rituals symbolize what it is to be Lozi. Lewanika was a master of royal pageantry and his successors are not far behind. On a national level, the climax of the ritual calendar comes with the annual move to higher ground during the floods, the *kuomboka* ceremony. *Kuomboka* means literally "to get out of the water," and this is what everyone living on the floodplain does unless it is a year of unusually low water. But no one can make a move until the paramount chief sets the date because he is the one who has power over natural forces. Libonda is the lone exception: Lying upriver from Lealui, the river rises sooner here, and the *mulena* can signal her intention to move before the rest of the country. In the meantime, the rains fall, the waters encroach, and space on the diminishing mounds has to be shared with snakes and vermin and insects, all trying to keep dry in the damp houses. It is a very unpleasant time until at last the new moon appears. As in many parts of central Africa, this is the auspicious moment for new undertakings.

Two days before departure, the *maoma* drums are beaten, resonating across the waters all the way to Mongu. They are calling everyone to the capital at Lealui: the keepers of the royal graves, the paddlers of the royal barges, and all the commoners who will join the armada. Just before sunrise on the appointed day, the tall royal drum *mwenduko* sounds, indicating that the *litunga* will not spend the next night in Lealui. There is a flurry of last minute packing. Long lines of men and women file out of the palace carrying the ruler's goods to the waiting boats to the accompaniment of the royal bands of drummers and xylophone players. When everything is ready, the three *maoma* drums are lifted onto *Nalikwanda:* first the big drum, the male, then the slightly smaller one, the female, and finally the child. This is the signal for the royal procession to make its way from the palisaded enclosure of the royal palace. In front come the carriers bringing the royal spears and rifles, then the musicians, and finally the paramount chief dressed in the splendid gray top hat and Edwardian morning-coat of his father, Lewanika. He walks with stately gait to the boat landing to the accompaniment of shrill ululations from the crowds of women. An elderly praise-singer joins the chorus.

The state canoe, *Natamikwa,* leads the fleet out into the channel and serves as a sort of scout during the voyage. It is followed by the two state barges, *Nalikwanda* and *Notila,* then the assorted barges of the royal family, government ministers, *indunas,* stewards, and commoners, once more mirroring the hierarchical order of Lozi society. The royal barges are enormous affairs; they are recognizable by the black and white stripes on their sides and by the basketwork shelter in the middle, covered with white calico. *Nalikwanda* is usually built new each year, following the lead of Lewanika who had a passion for boat design (see figure 15). It is rebuilt from many smaller canoes and symbolizes the nation as a whole, even the power of the people to dispose of their king. When a king dies, *Nalikwanda* is scuttled.

Betty Clay has stitched a pennant for the barge: a red flag with a white elephant embroidered on it since the elephant is the royal symbol. The boat is manned by 70 paddlers wearing only antelope skin loin-cloths and red caps with swatches of lion's mane attached. No one turns down the honor of paddling, but many of those chosen are well past their first youth and it is hard work in the heat of the mid-day sun. If a paddler slackens or fails to keep in time with the rest, he is flipped overboard by the *induna* in charge. *Natamwika* comes to the rescue, but tradition has it that in earlier times—when of course standards were higher—the unfortunates were left to the crocodiles.

The *litunga* himself begins and ends his voyage on board *Nalikwanda,* but it is large and cumbersome, so that if he wants to hunt hippos along the way, he shifts to the smaller, more maneuverable *Notila,* his second boat. Princes and other royal males are also allowed to travel under *Notila's* white canopy, propelled by members of the royal household, bare-chested and wearing colorful pieces of cloth around their waists, with black plumes over scarlet caps on their heads. (*Notila* is also the boat the *litunga* takes on all other occasions such as visits to the royal graves.) Women are never allowed on board.

The great drums are beaten, the *litunga's* band plays, and the huge flotilla makes its way slowly across the water. Swarms of birds rise from the water. Snakes slither out of the semi-submerged bush as the boats pass. At lunchtime, the resident commissioner's barge pulls up. Dressed in full uniform, he joins the *litunga* for a lunch that has been cooked over an open fire in *Nalikwanda.* The food is excellent, a match even for Lewanika's *haute cuisine.* It turns out that the chef was trained at the Victoria Falls Hotel, the great colonial pile across the Zambezi in Southern Rhodesia.

Although the winter capital of Limulunga is only about 11 miles from Lealui, it takes three or four hours for the fleet of boats to get there. During a sort of intermission in the strenuous paddling, women on the various vessels shriek "Aciii, ac, acicicici." This is the signal for the pad-dlers on *Nalikwanda* to shake their lion mane caps, swing to and fro, and propel the huge craft first one way, then the other, as if out of control. All the while the *maoma* drums beat wildly. Then, just as suddenly, the boat reverts to its more sober course at the head of the fleet. Finally they reach the narrow Mwayowamo canal, a dangerous stretch for smaller boats as they all jockey to be among the first to reach the harbor and frequently capsize instead (see figure 16).

Limulunga has served as the royal residence for the three or four months of the flood season only since the 1930s and has its own

European-built palace up the hill from the water's edge. Swarms of people are waiting to greet the chief and his entourage. They sing,

> Hail our King
> Greetings, Oh King.
> To travel, travel
> To travel with the King

At last the great drums roll, the curtains are pulled aside on the royal barge, the crowd goes down on its knees, and Mwanawima III, *litunga* of Barotseland, emerges to the roar of the multitudes, resplendent now in his gold-braided uniform. The musicians strike up a processional, and the ruler makes his way slowly up the hill, looking neither to right nor left. As he passes, the crowds rise to their feet, row after row, "like a field of wheat in the wind," as one observer puts it.[49] Then they fall in behind and dance in the wake of the royal parade.

For the next three days there is dancing and celebration. *Indunas,* village headmen, and office holders come to do homage in the traditional manner. Missionaries and administrators also come to pay their respects and exchange pleasantries, but avoid the Lozi salutations that are altogether too obsequious for their taste. Nowadays the *kuomboka* is broadcast over the airwaves by the Central African Broadcasting Station. The mass migration to higher land is too much fun, too much a symbol of Lozi identity to abandon, although truth to tell, more and more people are living year round on high ground. Nor is *Notila* the only means the paramount chief has for touring his domains. He now has a white Land Rover for which Betty Clay has also made an elephant pennant. During the dry season he can make the rounds of many of the *kutas* by car, albeit tortuously given the condition of the roads, accompanied by the omnipresent musicians and the rest of his entourage in a fleet of vehicles. The white speck of his Land Rover on the horizon brings the same feelings of excitement and anticipation to the village people as the speck of the Queen Mother's red airplane to the British colony in Mongu. The villagers build three-sided straw shelters specially for his visit so he may sit in the shade with his *indunas* and hear the concerns of the people, who will greet him not with curtsies and tears but with clapping and kneeling, with ululations and the ancient cry of "yo sho, yo sho, yo sho." High noon of the Barotse Native Authority. Or so it seems.

CHAPTER THREE

Salisbury: The View from the Federation

The drama of Africa's political evolution is not of the type which can be handed ready-made by the playwrights to the actors. Its action will be largely developed by the actors themselves.
> —Lord Hailey, proconsul (1951)

Joining with the white man in a federation is like trying to share a small stool with someone with a big backside.
> —Kenneth Kaunda, African nationalist leader

They tell us to come to terms with the black Nationalists. Pah! We might as well come to terms with a black mamba.
> —John Gaunt, former DC, leader of Northern Rhodesia's
> white settlers

A man who gathers honey expects to be stung by the bees.
> —African proverb, quoted by Kenneth Kaunda

Salisbury 1959. The city honors the nineteenth-century British prime minister, Robert Cecil, Lord Salisbury. (It barely escaped the more ethereal "Cecilia" to immortalize both the Lord and Cecil Rhodes.) Little is left of the town created by Rhodes's Pioneer Column in 1890 with its tin-roofed, one-story houses, some with slender cast-iron pillars, others with bulky stone ones supporting gingerbread balconies overhanging the sidewalks. Meikle's Hotel is one of the few reminders of earlier times. Its white building sprawls comfortably, even elegantly, as if there is all the room in the world for its meandering verandahs and gardens. A little tower is flanked by two relaxed lions. Inside, the vast lounge and dining room display high ceilings of plaster-work imported from South Africa—which are not really plaster at all but white-washed pressed tin. Nowadays cattle are rarely herded through its public rooms as they were in the old days of "hard drinking, hard swearing and hard living,"[1] so much a source of nostalgic pride to present residents of the city. Whatever the changes, Meikle's remains a white bastion. Salisbury may be the capital of the Federation of Rhodesia and Nyasaland whose by-word is "partnership," but "partnership" most emphatically does not mean "opening Meikles's to the Munts overnight."[2] The "Munts" are the Africans, and the word (usually prefixed by "bloody") has the same connotation as "Nigger" in the United States. Ironically, it is derived from "muntu," the perfectly neutral word for human being in many Bantu languages.

There is a monument to Rhodes's Pioneers in the garden laid out on top of what is known to Europeans simply as the Kopje, the Afrikaans word for hill, rising steeply in the middle of the city (its African name is Harari, after an outcast who took refuge there). Legend has it that Fort Salisbury was supposed to have been built on Mount Hampden, ten miles away, but the Pioneers settled for the lesser hilltop because they came to it first and nobody wanted to push on any farther. Perhaps it was just as well, since Mount Hampden had been named by the big-game hunter and explorer Frederick Selous after the seventeenth-century champion of English liberalism in the struggle against Charles I—not necessarily the patron saint the Pioneers and their descendants would have chosen.

As in other white towns in Africa, the villas of Salisbury's European inhabitants, set in their big gardens, encircle the downtown. Segregation is marked not along class lines as in England, but along those of color since the working class is by definition black. The original African quarter, Old Bricks, is close to town but set apart from European neighborhoods. It is a disheveled slum. The newer African townships, like those of South Africa are far from the city center, and workers spend long hours and much of their pay getting to and from their jobs.

Salisbury has little culture to boast of. Through private efforts, it has acquired an impressively modern art museum, but still lacks anything to put in it. When the newly arrived director made a plaintive request for residents to lend works to mount on its walls, the most promising reply came from a settler who offered him a "Rubens." Unfortunately, it turned out to be an embroidered chair cover. Still, before the museum came to Salisbury, the only claim to culture was a subscription library established in memory of Queen Victoria and housed in a building as dowdy as the old queen herself. As for public monuments in the city center, the statues on the main thoroughfare commemorate not the heroes of the Pioneer Column but the giants of imperial capitalism: Cecil Rhodes at one end of the avenue, his financier Alfred Beit at the other. David Livingstone's statue is sequestered in a courtyard of the federal office building. In Salisbury's central park, however, is a working model of Livingstone's most famous discovery, The Victoria Falls.

Salisbury wears two hats. Since 1923 it has been the capital of the self-governing colony of Southern Rhodesia; since 1953 it has also been the capital of the Federation that embraces the two Rhodesias and Nyasaland (see map 1). The overlap leads to a somewhat ludicrous duplication: two parliaments, two civil services, two governors-general. No wonder the Federation has been called "the world's most over-governed country."[3] On the other hand, it has brought a new prosperity to Salisbury. The swampy Makabuzi River has been tarred over to make way for Kingsway, one of the city's smartest thoroughfares (see figure 17). Skyscrapers are "rising like a great cliff,"[4] symbolizing, some say, the bright economic future of a united Central Africa. British Prime Minister Harold Macmillan rhapsodizes about the city that "soars from the veldt," its architecture responding "to the challenge of the air as clear as a diamond." Invoking the civilizing mission of its European—nay, British—inhabitants, he declares, "It has brought the Central African plains, which not much more than a generation ago were the home of nothing but nomadic herdsmen, into the full swing of the modern age."[5] But even the injection of federal monies and the spectacular building boom have not been enough to dust off Salisbury's image as a dull town without any identifiable character of its own, unlike Bulawayo, its less prosperous but livelier rival to the west. As one observer put it, "Bulawayo seems to have the vitality and sophistication of a city which has grown up from its own roots, whereas Salisbury is like a large plastic flower grafted upon an African tree."[6]

In 1959 the Federation is presided over by Sir Roy Welensky. Welensky's ideological pedigree might read: by Rhodes out of Huggins. Where Rhodes was the master builder of British southern Africa, Godfrey Huggins served as midwife and first prime minister of the Federation, its last imperial bastion in Africa. Welensky is the spiritual heir of both in the fervor of his devotion to Britain and Empire—ironic for one who has not a drop of British blood in his veins (he would later describe himself as "50 per cent Jewish, 50 per cent Polish and 100 per cent British").[7]

His father was a Lithuanian Jew from Vilna who had wandered over much of the Western world before washing up in Salisbury: Sweden, Germany, the United States, South Africa. His mother was a ninth-generation Afrikaner from the Cape Province of South Africa; he was her thirteenth child, born in 1907. When Roy was eleven, his mother died. She was attended in her last illness by the Salisbury doctor, Godfrey Huggins, who later became her son's close friend and political mentor.

Roy had a rough-and-tumble childhood on the streets of the still rough-and-tumble town over which the Union Jack had first been raised only 17 years before his birth. His family lived on Pioneer Street, at the base of the wooded *kopje* around which the settlement sprawled and across the Makabuzi River from the administrative center. Into Pioneer Street straggled prospectors returning from the bush after their usually fruitless searches for the gold, for the "second Rand" with which Rhodes had lured them into this wilderness. They came to Michael Welensky's saloon to drown their misfortunes and to his hotel to sleep it off. But Welensky's father never prospered, too inclined as he was to join his clients at the bar. Often he had to earn what money he could as a *wocher,* a watcher for the dead for the Salisbury Hebrew Congregation. Roy left school at 14 to earn his own living. A burly boy with a quick temper, he had early learned to take care of himself: By 19 he was the professional heavyweight boxing champion of Southern Rhodesia. After a series of dead-end jobs, he became a fireman on Rhodesia Railways, eventually graduating to engineer. An appropriate job, perhaps, for a boy who had grown up on the wrong side of the tracks—or, rather, the wrong side of the muddy Makabuzi—and one that eventually allowed him to realize his talents as an organizer and leader of men.

While the pay was not high, especially during the Depression years of the 1930s, railway men were the elite of the working class. It was railroads, after all, that were the key to opening up the wildernesses of southern Africa, just as they had been for the American West. Hadn't Rhodes's ambition been to unite Africa with his Cape-to-Cairo railroad? For the landlocked Rhodesias, railroads were the lifeline to the outside world, the key to development. Lewanika had understood this perfectly when he lobbied hard but unsuccessfully to have the line of rail run through Barotseland. But it was copper-rich Katanga in the Belgian Congo that lured the railroad builders, and the line passed far to the east.

Welensky's work as a railroader shaped him in many ways. He and his two brothers quickly became active union organizers. In retaliation, the company banished him in 1933 to Broken Hill, a particularly depressed lead mining town in Northern Rhodesia. Broken Hill would be his base for the next 20 years as he built his unlikely career in trade unionism and politics. In the thirties, Broken Hill was home to a small but truculent group of Fascists, an offshoot of Oswald Mosley's British Union of Fascists. Viciously anti-Semitic, they attacked Welensky as "that fat Jew boy" and as a Mason, to boot. Until then, Welensky had had little sense of his Jewishness. Now he fought back, first with his fists, then with union organizing. In Broken Hill the "race question" was still a matter between Jews and Gentiles, not blacks and whites. The railway employed only a minority of Africans, and it became a cornerstone of union politics to maintain the "colour bar" at all costs, that is, to reserve the skilled positions for Europeans. While Welensky eventually came around to supporting some unions for Africans in other industries, he and his Rhodesia Railway Workers Union never gave an inch on the question of African advancement in their domain. He also resisted any efforts to open up membership in Rhodesian unions to all races.

Since the union operated, as did the trains, on both sides of the Zambezi, it is hardly surprising that Welensky was a fervent advocate of amalgamation of the two Rhodesias. Various permutations had been in the air for decades: Southern Rhodesia and South Africa, Northern and Southern Rhodesia. Supporters argued that amalgamation made economic sense and would encourage investment. Opponents pointed out that Southern Rhodesia, which had been self-governing since 1923, was firmly dominated by a small group of white settlers who were determined in any future reconfiguration to maintain their privileged position. This was part of the appeal of union with South Africa, given its similar racial ideology. But if the two Rhodesias were amalgamated, what would happen to the African population of the Protectorate of Northern Rhodesia whose rights the British government was charged with safeguarding?

The whole, thorny question was tabled during the Second World War. Meanwhile, union organizing had proved to be the stepping-stone to politics for Welensky. In 1938, he was elected to the Northern Rhodesian Legislative Council (Legco) for the first time. Asked what his policy was, he replied belligerently, "I've no need for a policy—I'm just pro-settler."[8] This would be his credo for the next quarter century. Three years later he formed the Northern Rhodesian Labour Party and gained control of *The Northern News,* which he used effectively to publicize his views. During World War II he held the crucial post of director of manpower. After the war ended, he became the leader of the "unofficials" in Legco, those members who did not hold their position by virtue of colonial office and who were often at odds with official policies.

In this role, he scored an early triumph in 1949 when he took on the target his countrymen most loved to hate: the British South Africa Company. Although the company had given up its direct rule of Northern Rhodesia in 1924, it still held onto its hugely valuable mineral rights and continued to draw considerable royalties from mining companies operating on the Copperbelt, all the while paying no taxes. Welensky argued that the original agreements between the company and Lewanika were invalid because Lewanika had no right to dispose of subjects' lands without consulting them and that, in any case, what became the Copperbelt was not really within his domains to begin with. "The sovereignty of the King of the Barotses never extended to the Copperbelt," he maintained. "Some tribes never recognised Lewanika as their king and he had no right to part with their heritage at all." He condemned the British government for approving what was obviously an illegal deal: "Could the [Northern Rhodesia] House have a worse example of the selling of the birthright of the people of this country and by a Government that was responsible for them?"[9] Welensky was almost certainly correct in his claim that Lewanika's sway had never extended to the Copperbelt and that the company conveniently and knowingly fudged the matter when it came to staking its claim, although he was hardly the first to point this out.

In any event, the issue gave him a chance to pose as the champion of all people, black and white, in asserting their right to the fruits of the land against a company that still evoked much hostility. Furthermore, with the boom in copper demand and rise in prices following World War II, the company's annual royalties had skyrocketed to some two million pounds. Welensky's motion demanding a 50 percent tax on these royalties was seconded by an African member of the Legislative Council, a rare occurrence indeed, then or later. But the irony, of course, is that Welensky associated whites as well as blacks in his argument when logically only the original inhabitants of the Copperbelt would have had a legal claim to share in the profits realized by the company. Welensky's campaign succeeded in revising the company's status. It would be allowed to enjoy its mineral rights until 1986 when they would be transferred to the Northern Rhodesia government without charge, but meanwhile it was obligated to pay the government 20 percent of its net revenue from the mines in lieu of taxes. What was not known at the time was that Welensky had met secretly with company officials and reached an agreement with which they were altogether content, even relieved. After all, 20 percent was a lot less than the 50 percent originally demanded.

At best, however, this was a side issue. For Northern Rhodesia's white settlers, whose interests Welensky wholeheartedly represented, the more important concern was still how to gain control over their own affairs. It was a source of constant annoyance to be outvoted by the "officials," the representatives of the Crown, in the government of the colony. Even when they gained parity in the legislature in 1948, they were far from satisfied. Most of the settlers saw their best hope in self-government, along the lines of Southern Rhodesia, which had exchanged the stricter supervision of the Colonial Office for the tolerant sway of the Commonwealth Relations Office. On this, however, the British government refused to budge because of its commitment to African interests—to keeping the Zambezi as the northern limit of settler rule—and the British government still had the final say in Northern Rhodesia. While it was not ready to allow more than token membership in Legco or the Executive Council to the Protectorate's more than two and a half million Africans, it was not about to hand the government over to the seventy thousand whites either. Ironically, in this very British territory, the majority of these settlers were not British—they were and are a polyglot mixture of Afrikaners from South Africa, Italians, Greeks, and others, many of them transients, in the territory only long enough to make their fortunes on the Copperbelt.

Welensky was shrewd enough to see that amalgamation, his old dream, might offer a way around this impasse. Even as he led the settler campaign for "responsible government" in his adopted territory, he worked ever more closely with Godfrey Huggins who had been prime minister of Southern Rhodesia since 1933. Separated by both age and class, the two formed an oddly effective partnership: Welensky the hulking, blunt, pugnacious railroader; Huggins the urbane, impish, little doctor. They shared, however, a profound loyalty to Africa—a quintessentially white and British Africa. To them Rhodes was not an anachronism; his ideals were still their ideals. Determined to bring about the amalgamation of the two Rhodesias as a bulwark against the rising tide of anti-imperialism in the postwar world, they might have succeeded if the Labour Party had not come to power in Britain. In the end they were forced to settle for something far more problematic: the Federation of Rhodesia (that is, the two Rhodesias) and Nyasaland. Nevertheless, with skillful handling, the Federation may yet be the backdoor through which can be smuggled Huggins's and Welensky's dream of indefinite white hegemony in Central Africa.

Nyasaland was the poor relation, the price of Rhodesian federation. It had not figured in some earlier schemes of union, and certainly holds little appeal to the Southern Rhodesians. When pressed about why it was included at all, a Conservative Party spokesman replied gamely that "the

Civil Service mentality felt that it was a tidy thing to do."[10] It is a desperately poor colony, endowed mainly with beautiful scenery. It was founded by missionaries rather than capitalists, albeit missionaries who saw commerce and Christianity as natural allies. There are only 7,000–8,000 whites in the whole country that runs like a sliver along the western shore of the deep, narrow lake from which it takes its name. With its mountains and lake, it is almost a tropical Scotland until one encounters the oppressive heat of the Shire Valley leading down to the Zambezi. Scottish, too, were many of the missionaries who, following in Livingstone's footsteps, aimed to make this land a beacon of enlightenment in Central Africa, substituting wholesome agriculture and trade for the horrors of slave raiding. Although many of their early enterprises failed, they have left a legacy of solid Scots education and evangelism that will come to haunt the Federation in their nationalist reincarnation. The Church of Scotland, now known as the Church of Central Africa Presbyterian, still retains a fiercely proprietary interest in Nyasaland and in the rights of its citizens. It is also one of the few institutions that both preaches and practices racial equality and does not hesitate to speak out on political issues.

Welensky and Huggins sold the Federation to their white constituents and to the British government above all by concentrating on the economic boom it was expected to bring, thereby deflecting attention from the political ramifications. They won the enthusiastic endorsement of big business (including the British South Africa Company that has come to think very highly of Welensky) and the main Rhodesian newspapers (which belonged to a South African conglomerate). At first the boom seemed real enough. Copper prices were still soaring and alone sufficed to buoy the economy of the whole Federation. Some Northerners grumbled that the South was reaping all the benefits, getting rich on Northern Rhodesian copper. Lusaka, the Northern Rhodesian capital, watched helplessly as one after another the copper companies moved their headquarters to Salisbury to be near the seat of power. The luxurious Ridgeway Hotel, built in Lusaka at a cost of £200,000 in 1951, stood virtually empty. Investment poured in, but it was particularly federal enterprises that benefited. All told, the Federation hemorrhaged £77 million from Northern Rhodesia, mostly southward although some of it went to Nyasaland.[11] White immigrants as well as capital answered the call with gusto: some 100,000 came in the first five years of federation, primarily to Northern and Southern Rhodesia.

But it was the Kariba Dam on the Zambezi that would come to symbolize the hubris of federation, the megalomania of its leaders. In 1955, two years after union, the federal government unilaterally decided to build the dam at a cost of £90,000,000 [$316,000,000], overriding the agreement made only 18 months earlier that a more modest dam would be built on the Kafue River in Northern Rhodesia and ignoring the fact that £500,000 had already been spent on preliminary work at the Kafue site. Huggins, now Lord Malvern, made no bones about the fact that Kariba was first and foremost a prestige project: "Its size and all that sort of thing makes such a popular appeal and it will be an excellent advertisement for the whole Federal area."[12]

He was quite right. The 420-foot high Kariba Dam would create the largest man-made lake in the world, swallowing up some 2,000 square miles of hill, bush, and riverbank upstream from Kariba Gorge. The gorge lay at the head of the Gwembe Valley, one of the most inhospitable and inaccessible corners of Central Africa, so inaccessible that its inhabitants had been shielded from conquest for generations. There were no roads to the site and no nearby towns. Tracks would have to be bulldozed down the steep escarpment, housing built overnight, and everything necessary brought in from far away. Those working on the dam could expect sweltering heat, plagues of insects, and endemic disease. Their schedule would be dictated by the ineluctable rise and fall of the great river—more indeed than they ever anticipated.

Like its better-known contemporary, the Aswan Dam in Egypt, the project epitomized post-war international capitalism on a grandiose scale. The World Bank and other international banking houses would put up most of the money; an Italian firm would build the dam following plans drawn up by French engineers with labor imported mainly from Italy and southern Africa; finally, it would primarily benefit mines controlled by financial interests based in the United States, Britain, and South Africa.

Kariba had many critics, especially in the North, and they included some of the very industrialists who had supported federation. The Kafue dam, they argued, would be more than sufficient to supply the industrial requirements of the Federation, which in any case were mainly on the Northern Rhodesian Copperbelt, and would also provide water for irrigation on a large scale. Kariba was absurdly ambitious. It would provide more power than Central Africa had any need for, would monopolize the government's credits for years to come, and would not provide any irrigation. What's more, it would require moving roughly 40,000 people living on either side of the Zambezi, 29,000 in Northern and 11,000 in Southern Rhodesia, something that seems to have been ignored by planners. (By the time the dam was completed in 1959, the number of people moved far exceeded the original estimates and totaled some 70,000.)

Colonial officials in the North who had been neutral on the issue of federation now became increasingly suspicious of the federal government. Others were even more outspoken, condemning the decision as an outright betrayal. It was, they said bitterly, Lord Malvern's private monument, a "monument big enough to retire on—like Rhodes and Rhodesia."[13] Welensky had been an ardent exponent of the Kafue dam, but now he found himself forced to defend the Kariba project at stormy meetings of Europeans all over Northern Rhodesia. By loyally doing so, he guaranteed his succession as prime minister of the Federation the following year. But at what cost?

The dam's most immediate victims, the Gwembe Tonga who faced removal, had no political voice at all. Prophetically, they warned when the dam was begun that the spirits of deceased ritual leaders would be angry and cause problems if their old homes were abandoned. When the terrible Zambezi floods arrived, first in the 1957 season, then even more destructively the following year (the same floods that wreaked such havoc in Barotseland), few were surprised. Nor were they surprised when the torrents washed over the coffer dam and swept away a footbridge and tower, and when millions of crickets rose above the valley floor, filling the air with their chirruping, and armies of scorpions, mice, and shrews clung to any vegetation they could find. Worst of all, 14 Africans and 3 Italians, working on top of one of the vertical water intake shafts in 1959, fell 230 feet when their scaffolding gave way and they were buried in 80 tons of wet concrete.

Soon, rumors sprang up that the unprecedented floods and other disasters were the work of the angry river god Nyamenyame, a huge serpent living in the Zambezi who could with the flick of his tail destroy the works of man. Nyamenyame seems to have been a figment of the European imagination, suitably hyped by the Southern Rhodesia press and exploited by an enterprising carver of statues for the tourist trade. Before the dam, there was no Tonga belief in any form of river deity, but in due time the story made its way back across the river and did indeed become entrenched in local lore.

Some Gwembe Tonga, however, did not leave things to their spirit allies. Chief Chipepo's people refused to move from their riverbank villages to a new site 100 miles to the northeast on the Lusitu River, claiming they had never been consulted about matters that so profoundly affected their future. They had been told so many conflicting stories, they were not even sure their alluvial gardens by the river really would be permanently flooded. The protectorate government had no power to force them to move and counted desperately on persuasion. By now, however, the district officers—very much the "men in the middle" since they also had not been consulted about the dam—had lost the credibility they once enjoyed because plans changed so often. Were they after all, the Gwembe wondered, any different from the European settlers? Wasn't the dam simply a "cover for a European land-grab"?[14] Even a visit from Governor Benson, arrayed in full gubernatorial white uniform with plumed hat and sword and accompanied by a military band, failed to sway the villagers who felt the government had consistently deceived them.

The government of Northern Rhodesia was on the spot. It was acknowledged colonial policy that Britain should protect the rights of native peoples, indeed that the sanctity of their rights should take precedence even over those of European settlers—the territory was, after all, a protectorate (unlike the self-governing Southern Rhodesia). Nevertheless, special powers were decreed and police units brought in to force the issue. The Gwembe resisted with spears, the police responded with gunfire. Eight Africans were killed and 34 more wounded. Soon after, trucks came in and hastily moved the people to their distant home at the hottest season of the year. Many of their possessions were lost, broken, or stolen in transit. On the Southern Rhodesian side, there was no resistance because people were quite aware that the government, being free of colonial restrictions about indigenous rights, had the legal right from the beginning to force inhabitants to move. In the end, of course, it amounted to the same thing on both banks of the river.

At the time the switch to Kariba as the site of the dam was first announced in 1955, it was protested by the nascent nationalist movement in Northern Rhodesia. The head of the African National Congress (ANC) sent a petition directly to the Queen of England pointing out that the entire area to be flooded was either Native Reserve (on the Northern Rhodesian side of the Zambezi) or Native Trust Land (on the Southern Rhodesian side). It had been set aside "for the sole use and benefit, direct and indirect, of the natives"[15] of the two territories. The petition was ignored; the ANC had no legal status and no recognized niche in the political structure. Agents of the ANC also encouraged the unsuccessful resistance in Chief Chipepo's villages and shared the blame when it failed.

The Gwembe dispossessed in Northern Rhodesia received fairly generous compensation; those in Southern Rhodesia (outside the purview of the Colonial Office) were forgiven taxes for two years but received not a farthing in cash. In Great Britain, the whole affair received little attention. There was more outcry about the fate of the rhinos and elephants and antelope that were imperiled by flooding, such an outcry, in fact, that federal authorities had to mount an expensive scheme, known as "Operation Noah," to haul stranded animals out of the rising waters.

Although federation supporters paid much lip-service to the notion of racial "partnership," they made it quite clear that "partnership" was not a synonym for equality. Huggins dismissed any thought of transplanting democracy onto African soil. "It is irresponsible," he declared, "to place such a dangerous weapon as the vote in the hands of people who still seek the solution to their problems by studying the entrails of a goat"[16] — a remark that showed his ignorance of native peoples in Central Africa who do not practice this form of divination. He had confused them with the rulers of classical Rome.

Addressing a white audience at an agricultural show, Prime Minister Huggins declared that the partnership of whites and blacks should be like that between rider and horse, an analogy that caused him much grief later in spite of his attempts to explain that he was thinking of his old polo-playing days and the ideal of horse and rider forming a perfect unit, their success depending totally on their rapport with one another. He and Welensky subscribed to Rhodes's slogan, "Equal rights for all civilized men," assuming that Africans would become "civilized" in due time, and that as they did so they could become part of the political process. "Due time" they reckoned to be 50 to 100 years; in the meantime, Welensky declared, "the African has an important part to play here, but he has to play that part as a junior partner, and I am prepared to accept him as such."[17] They declared candidly that only Europeans could manage "this vast territory which the indigenous inhabitants were quite unable to develop." If he played his assigned part, the African would "get his rewards the same as everybody else."[18] For the present, neither blacks nor whites want racial integration, Welensky argued; in any event race relations cannot be legislated, just as "all the differences between Africans and Europeans cannot be wiped out at the stroke of a pen,"[19] but improvements will come naturally through the economic development of the country. Against charges of racism, Welensky retorted that he knew Africans far better than any of his critics—as a child hadn't he swum "bare-arsed in the Makabuzi River ... with [the] piccaninnies"?[20] He had, indeed, but since then the personal contacts had grown rare.

Even the official position of gradual—very gradual—inclusion was more liberal than many whites could stomach. For all their protestations that they had no intention of giving Africans more than a token political voice for the foreseeable future, Huggins and Welensky were often attacked from the right as "Kaffir-Boeties," African-lovers. One group pointed out that it was absurd to expect Africans to achieve in 50 or 100 years the level of advancement that it took the people of Britain 1,000 years to reach; any talk of a shorter timespan was useless or dangerous. (Huggins even had his doubts about the people of Britain after a millennium of evolution. In an outburst of annoyance with Colonial Office control, he grumbled, "Why should the destiny of millions in Central Africa be left in the hands of persons elected to look after the drains in Shoreditch?"[21])

Much as it was touted as a great experiment in multi-racialism, federation had in the end been voted in by only 25,570 citizens out of the nearly eight million in the three territories, almost none of them black. As a disgusted white liberal commented, "in this Christian country" neither Welensky nor his sympathizers "would have thought Jesus and the Twelve Apostles fit to vote."[22] Paradoxically, Africans in Northern Rhodesia and Nyasaland were defined not as British subjects but as "British Protected Persons" and therefore ineligible to vote. True, they could become British subjects by paying £5 and declaring their loyalty to the British Crown, then meeting other property and literacy (in English) qualifications. As of 1953, only three Africans had thought the purchase of citizenship in their own country worth the investment. In Southern Rhodesia, although they were British subjects, property qualifications excluded most Africans from electoral rolls.

The new federal constitution closely reflected the views of Huggins and Welensky. It provided for a total of 35 representatives from the three member territories. Although six of them were to be "elected Africans," the catch was that in each of the territories they would be chosen by voters from either the "common roll" (Northern and Southern Rhodesia) or the Convention of Associations in Nyasaland. The common roll in Northern Rhodesia consisted of 11 Africans in 1953, while in Southern Rhodesia it was 99 percent white. The Nyasaland Convention was entirely white. There was a separate category, "nominated Europeans for African interests," in Nyasaland and Northern Rhodesia, a lame recognition that the colonial government had an obligation to look out for African interests—far from acknowledging that Africans might be entrusted to do this for themselves. The result, as anticipated, was that white settlers controlled the Federal Assembly and could dictate the token Africans with whom they served.

White dominance was further reinforced by revisions made in 1957 that increased the total number of members of the Federal Assembly without increasing African participation. Of a total of 59 members, only 15 were Africans or "Europeans representing African interests." The two-tier system of general roll and special roll, based on higher and lower property qualifications (except where it privileged African chiefs and ministers), meant essentially that while Europeans had a large voice in electing African representatives, even the small number of African voters had no part in electing Europeans. African MPs thus owed their seats to Welensky and his backers. At the same time, any future enlargement of the African franchise would depend on the will of the European majority, and as they showed in 1957, they were more inclined to go the other way. Majority rule or even parity was out of the question.

Theoretically, the British government had the power to block any changes. At a public meeting, Welensky had been asked what would happen if the British government disallowed any measure passed by the federal government. Sir Roy (he had been knighted in 1953) replied: "There is such a thing as sedition and I don't want to be charged with incitement to disaffection but you may recall a certain historical tea-party"[23]—a response that had the audience whooping with delight. As his biographer comments, "Even the slightest hint of pitching the constitutional tea-chest into the Zambesia gave the Colonial Office a delicate fit of the jitters."[24] Besides, the colonial secretary was eager to show his gratitude for the prime minister's wholehearted support of Britain during the 1956 Suez crisis and overruled the objections of the African Affairs Board, the chief watchdog for African interests under the federal constitution. The Nyasaland member for African interests resigned from the board in protest. With the elections in 1958, the board has become simply an appendage of the ruling United Federal Party.

The federal constitution stipulates that there should be a full-scale review seven to ten years after it first went into effect, that is, between 1960 and 1963. There is increasing pressure to have it sooner rather than later. For Welensky and his supporters the stakes are high: They are aiming for nothing less than dominion status for the Federation, a possibility anticipated in the preamble to the federal constitution. This would remove the northern territories, Northern Rhodesia and Nyasaland, once and for all from Colonial Office and parliamentary surveillance, giving the settlers a free hand to run the entire show just as they had been running Southern Rhodesia for the past 35 years, with only the most distant and benign nods from the Commonwealth Relations Office. Welensky will need all his skills to bring along the four parliaments (Federal, Northern and Southern Rhodesia, Nyasaland) on the one hand and the British government on the other. The African partners, he continues to insist, are still too junior to need consulting.

For all his bluster, Welensky has considerable personal charm, as even those who do not share his personal views grudgingly admit. "Off the war-path, [he] had a warm, friendly, paternal manner," one journalist reminisced. "He held out his big bear-like paws with genuine affection. He liked people (white) and they in turn liked him."[25] Even more incongruous than his friendship with Huggins is his friendship with Sir Stewart Gore-Browne. Gore-Browne is a slightly eccentric English patrician who fell in love with an out-of-the-way corner of Bembaland during a survey mission in Northern Rhodesia just before World War I. He returned after the war to create his own private Shangri-la at Shiwa Ngandu ("Lake of the Royal Crocodile Clan"), a 22,000-acre estate in the middle of the African bush. Here he has built a great stone mansion in the Italianate style (inspired perhaps by John Buchan's *A Lodge in the Wilderness* of 1907), where he presides over several hundred African dependents with the fatherly solicitude of a feudal lord. He runs his own *boma,* as it were.

In 1935 Gore-Browne decided to stand for election to the legislative council from the huge constituency that encompassed most of north-eastern Northern Rhodesia. Its only real center of (white) population, however, was Broken Hill and Welensky was "the uncrowned king of Broken Hill."[26] The engine-driver and union boss had already announced his support for Gore-Browne's opponent, but when the two met they immediately took to each other and remained friends for the rest of their lives. Gore-Browne wrote, "I really and truly like and respect [Welensky] for he has a slow, winning smile, and a shy confidence which is very attractive."[27] Welensky was equally attracted to him, even though he found him "every bit as much an aristocrat as the Governor, probably more."[28] "I owe him a great debt," Welensky wrote in *4,000 Days,* "primarily because he taught me to think for myself."[29]

Thinking for himself was precisely what Gore-Browne did and what set him apart from most other white settlers. It enabled him to move beyond the benign paternalism of his relations with Africans of his early years in Africa to an ever deeper belief that Africans could and must manage their own affairs. For more than a decade he was leader of the "unofficials" and also represented African interests on the Legislative Council (Africans were not permitted to represent their own interests), encouraging fledgling African organizations on the Copperbelt and insisting that educated Africans, not just chiefs, have more of a role within the colonial state. He resigned his position as leader of the "unofficials" in 1946 when he found that he could not wear both hats and maintain his credibility with Africans, especially as Europeans continued to ignore African opposition to amalgamation and demands to be included in the franchise.

On the other hand, he was sympathetic to settlers' frustrations with Colonial Office rule. "I cannot believe it is impossible to find some means to enable white people to stay on in this country and prosper, and at the same time to deny the black man no advance of which he is himself capable," he declared at the end of a long debate in the Legislative Council.[30] His 1948 proposal for greater self-government in Northern Rhodesia, however, was more than a little quixotic: He envisioned changes whereby a motley group of Africans (including one nominated by the paramount chief of Barotseland) and Europeans representing Africans could ally with "officials" to block any legislation by white settlers. Although it included an overall increase in African representation, it immediately provoked a storm of protest from Africans who denounced it as a cover for white domination and a prelude to amalgamation. Many Africans felt that Gore-Browne had flung them "like felons into the gallows of self-government," as he put it.[31] African protest may have had some effect in making amalgamation unthinkable thereafter, but for Gore-Browne it was a painful reminder of the limits of paternalism. Federation came anyway, and with none of the safeguards Gore-Browne had fought for. He became more and more disillusioned with its false promises of partnership, but, remarkably, his relations with Welensky never soured. Even after Gore-Browne had dismissed federation as a scam and its vaunted "racial partnership" as "humbug,"[32] Welensky wrote to him, "We do not see eye to eye, but there is no reason why we should not work together for the common good."[33]

The greatest irony of federation and all its works is that it has called into being what it most fears: the Frankenstein monster of African nationalism. African nationalism was virtually non-existent in Northern Rhodesia in the years before federation. It was clear to any who cared to notice, however, that Africans opposed amalgamation all along and that they opposed federation as amalgamation in disguise. Their greatest concern was that they would lose their land, as Africans had lost their land in Southern Rhodesia and South Africa: "Europeans were vultures hovering over the land to pounce on their African victims."[34] Game parks and forest reserves, it was hinted, would be opened to a rush of white immigration. It didn't help that Welensky warned Africans to come into the federation with the Europeans or else "they will face the fate of the Red Indians in North America."[35] Many uneducated Africans could not believe that the Queen would have imposed federation on them and imagined that she would surely right things if they could only communicate directly with her.

Rumors spread like bushfires, especially rumors about vampires. Vampire beliefs had been widespread in eastern and central Africa in the 1920s and 1930s. Initially they revolved around the idea that Europeans needed African blood and organs to make medicines for their diseases. The long drawn-out illness of King George V in 1929, for example, inspired a wave of panic, for surely the king would require a great deal of blood if he were to survive. As federation approached, vampire beliefs re-surfaced with a vengeance as the projection of African fears and took myriad forms. Suddenly vampire-men, *banyama,* were everywhere, especially in Lusaka and on the Copperbelt. Supposedly victims lost their will-power and supported federation in a somnambulist trance, manipulated by agents of the Capricorn African Society (one of the few organizations that promoted interracial dialogue, albeit among a small elite)—how else to explain why any African would accept federation? *Bacapricorn* soon became a synonym for *banyama.* Other rumors hinted darkly that Europeans were determined to poison the African population through sugar or tinned meats (Hadn't a low-grade product recently come on the market, labelled "For African consumption"?). When a soap company on the Copperbelt gave away free samples to Africans, something that had never happened before, the Africans threw them away unused, believing that they were intended to sap their free will and make them accept federation. In Nyasaland people claimed that vampires used a gray Land Rover with a shiny metal back that looked a little like an oversized bully-beef tin to spirit away their human cargoes—a Central African variant on UFOs and alien abductions, it would seem.

Then, abruptly, the flock of vampire rumors came to roost squarely on the Central African Broadcasting headquarters in Lusaka. "How could the announcers broadcast 'bad news,' news which displeased Africans, unless they had lost all their will-power? How else could they be made to read pro-Federation propaganda on the air?"[36] Clearly the station was under the thumb of the Capricornist vampire-men. Its African employees lived in fear of their lives. To make matters worse, they often worked late into the night and were driven home to the compounds in an ominous green van. By the end of 1952, a few months before federation became a *fait accompli,* the vampire scare had reached such proportions that the African National Congress condemned the government for "failing to deal with the Vampire men threatening the peace and order ... of the country."[37]

These rumors took on a new life at the time the Kariba Dam was being built a few years later. Laborers who went there to work for the white man, it was hinted, would never return because they were being fed to the vampires. The metaphor of consumption is a common one for unspeakable acts. In short, as a young broadcaster discovered, many Africans believed that Welensky was determined to kill all the natives one way or another and be done with it.

African views had in fact been ignored in the talks that led up to federation. No African had even been invited to the crucial conference at the Victoria Falls Hotel in 1949 (an omission later justified by Welensky on the grounds that Africans wouldn't have understood what was going on anyway), and none were included in discussions of changes to the federal constitution. Partisans of federation confidently insisted that Africans would quickly rally round once they saw the economic benefits federation would bring and that they would be fully reassured by guarantees of existing land rights. Political rights, Welensky declared, meant very little to a man with an empty belly and could come later. Across the continent in Ghana, however, the nationalist leader Kwame Nkrumah was electrifying fellow Africans with the exhortation: "Seek ye first the political kingdom." Europeans in Central Africa would have done well to listen.

Just as Sir Roy Welensky has come to personify federation and the battle to preserve white domination north and south of the Zambezi, so Kenneth Kaunda has come to symbolize African opposition to white domination and demands for political power in Northern Rhodesia. Kaunda was born in 1924, the second son and eighth child of a Church of Scotland evangelist from Nyasaland, long settled at the Lubwa Mission station in a remote rural area of northeastern Northern Rhodesia. His African name was Buchizya, "unexpected one." His father died when he was eight, and he, his mother, and his other siblings had to maintain the farm that had all along been their main source of income even though his father was a minister and his mother the matron of the girls' boarding school at the mission. His happiest memories of his father were the times he gathered the family around him before setting out on his tours and they all sang hymns in Bemba. Indeed, two abiding loves from his childhood were music and farming.

Kaunda began school at age seven. As a promising student, he acquired the best education then available for Africans in Northern Rhodesia: He went through Standard VI at Lubwa Mission school, then on to a teacher training course, also at Lubwa, and finally two years at Munali, the secondary school for boys that had just opened in Lusaka. In his memoirs he vividly describes his country bumpkin's arduous journey by truck and

train to the "new and wonderful world" of the capital.[38] In true British
fashion, the school emphasized both games and liberal arts. Although history had been his strong suit, he did not do well, perhaps, he notes lacon-
ically, because it was all South African history. When he became captain
of his house, he attempted to prevent the bullying that made life miserable for the younger boys. Already as a prefect, he insisted on discipline
and order, as he would when he was a teacher himself—and as he
attempted to do later as a political leader under much more difficult cir-
cumstances. At school, too, he joined the debating society, but of course
politics was out of bounds and the topics assigned were so bland as to be
meaningless. The guitar became his real passion, and during one school
holiday he and one of his masters formed a dance band and went touring on the Copperbelt. It was not the success they had hoped for.
Someone stole most of their earnings and Kaunda's travel document, then
the DC to whom Kaunda went for help, chose rather to humiliate him
by ostentatiously ignoring the fact that he spoke English well.

After two years, Kaunda was recalled from Munali to teach at Lubwa.
He stayed for four years. He continued his earlier involvement with the
Boy Scouts (called the Pathfinders because the original Scouts were as
yet unwilling to accept Africans) and discovered the Chinsali Welfare
Association, one of the many such organizations springing up throughout Africa that brought educated Africans together for "improvement"
and for social activities. Now at last he had enough money to indulge
his love of clothes. For the time being, he settled for having them specially styled by a Chinsali tailor; in the later 1950s he would affect togas
in the manner of Ghanaian nationalist leaders. His mother found him a
wife, Betty, a young woman with more education than most of her peers
and, fortunately for him, the patience to put up with a life that would
be lived more and more away from home. Together they would have six
sons and, at last, a daughter—"the joy of our hearts."[39]

But the obedient son of the mission was growing restless, eager to break
out on his own, eager to see more of the world. After four years at Lubwa,
he tried several ventures, none of them very successful. For a brief period
he was employed as a welfare officer, then as a teacher on the Copperbelt.
Here he had his first experience of the "colour bar" and a rude shock it
was. Up until now, the most serious discrimination he had encountered
was the fact that the missionaries in Lubwa had padded seats in church
while his father, who had served longer than most of them, had to sit on
a wooden bench with the rest of the African congregation. On the
Copperbelt, discrimination was pervasive: in jobs, housing, public accom-
modation, hospitals, cafes, and restaurants. Average wages for whites in the

mining industry were ten times those of Africans even though Africans in practice often performed many of the same jobs as Europeans. At post offices, there were separate windows for Europeans and Africans. In shops, Africans had to go around back or be served through hatches (likened by one observer to "lepers' holes in medieval churches").[40] At butchers, they often had no choice but to accept rotten meat (Kaunda's disgust over this turned him into a life-long vegetarian). Africans were referred to disdainfully as "Kaffirs" or "Munts." The Copperbelt politicized Kaunda, and when the African National Congress was founded in 1948 by a small group of urban intellectuals he was one of the first to join.

When Kaunda decided to end his brief period of wandering and head back home to Lubwa, he had a three-fold agenda: to trade in second-hand clothes from the Belgian Congo, to farm, and to engage in political organizing. He had discovered that there was a good market for clothes from the Congo and that even with the long, dusty bicycle ride there and back, he could make just enough profit to support his family. He also cycled all around the Northern Province organizing branches of the ANC, a feat as daunting as his trips to the Congo, given the terrible state of roads and bush tracks and the danger of lions. To pass the time— and perhaps to shore up their courage—he and his fellow organizers sang the Bemba hymns that had been so much a part of their mission youth. Kaunda even turned his hand at writing songs for the young nationalist movement:

> Others cry out for smart berets;
> We cry for our country.
> Others cry out for suits;
> We cry for the iron in our soil.
> Our wealth has been taken from us,
> Alas, our iron.
> Mothers, cease your weeping;
> Fathers, do not cry.
> I ask, "What are you going to do about it?"[41]

Their most effective ploy at meetings was to appeal to the many men who had fought in World War II to defend the British Empire and who now found themselves second-class citizens in their own country, unable to eat at the same table with those they had fought beside or to vote for their country's leaders.

In 1953 Kaunda was elected secretary-general of the ANC and moved his family to a small, grass-roofed house in an African township of

Lusaka. In its cramped quarters politics competed for space with domestic life. After the ineffectual leadership of its first president, Godwin Mbikusita, a member of a junior branch of the Lozi royal family, the organization was in poor shape organizationally and financially. It had also been badly shaken by well-founded reports that Mbikusita had denounced Simon Zukas, one of the few Europeans to support the nationalist cause, as a Communist, leading to his deportation from the country. Kaunda was determined to restore faith in the leadership, expand membership, and bring greater accountability to its shaky finances, but he was relatively inexperienced. In May 1957 he and ANC President Harry Nkumbula went to England at the invitation of the Labour Party to attend a conference of commonwealth and other leaders, all of a socialist persuasion. The conference was held at the Beatrice Webb House near Dorking and was Kaunda's first visit to England, in fact his first time out of Central Africa. It marked a watershed in his political maturation. Not only did he meet more radical Labour MPs such as Barbara Castle and Jim Callaghan, but he also met delegates from Australia, West Africa, and the Caribbean.

In many ways he and Nkumbula were a study in contrasts: Nkumbula was long familiar with London and its pleasures, ready to lavish money on new shirts and ornate cufflinks; Kaunda, the shy son of the soil who could never forget who was financing their trip. At their first official lunch in Dorking, he was too reticent to mention that he was a vegetarian, but when the good-natured housekeeper saw that he had eaten only the carrots and potatoes, she henceforth prepared special meals for him. Though not by nature a pub-crawler, he was surprised at the ease with which whites and blacks could mingle at the local pub of an evening. He formed an improbable friendship with the Ghanaian representative, a cheerful rogue who freely admitted the corrupt election practices that had brought the Convention People's Party to power in his country a couple of months earlier.

The conference took a strong stand against imperialism, specifically condemning the Central African Federation and its minority government. It called for the speedy introduction of "a common roll ... which should be based on the principle of universal adult franchise."[42] Kaunda stayed on in England for another six months to study British political institutions and, specifically, the organization of the Labour Party. While he learned much about the political process, he also did his best to publicize the problems of Central Africa on speaking tours throughout the country. He was pleased by the sympathetic reception he received but amazed at the innocence of his audiences and sponsors. "Like my

European liberal friends in Rhodesia, they were political babes in the wood. They would never really believe what I said about the oppression of my people in the rural areas."[43] Just as troubling in its implications for the future was Nkumbula's conduct. Kaunda's discomfort with his chief's lifestyle paled before his irresponsibility. With much difficulty, a meeting had been arranged for Nkumbula and Kaunda with the Conservative colonial secretary, Lennox-Boyd. When the time came for the meeting, however, Nkumbula had already flown back to Northern Rhodesia. Kaunda was left to offer what lame excuses he could for Nkumbula's absence and fobbed off with Lord Perth rather than the colonial secretary himself. The meeting was a dead loss. In a patronizing tone, Perth counseled patience.

The next year, 1958, Kaunda made his first trip to India, following in the footsteps of several of his lieutenants who were eager to learn firsthand the secrets of the movement that had led India to independence without bloodshed. The teacher-farmer-trader-of-used-clothes was becoming a cosmopolitan figure in the intensifying anti-imperialist movement. He was beginning to see his own country's struggle in the wider context of world history. And India was a sobering reminder that independence alone does not usher in a Golden Age, that independence may be won without bloodshed but violence may be waiting in the wings.

At home, however, the ANC continues to face problems. After the unsuccessful campaign against federation, the organization had been somewhat adrift; it was several years before it found both a structure and a message that would give it mass appeal. Like the welfare associations, the early membership of the ANC had consisted primarily of more "advanced" and educated men like Kaunda and his friends. Initially, it had little strength in rural areas, and on the Copperbelt relations with the African labor unions were tenuous, marked as much by personal rivalries as by common interest. Gradually, however, the ANC has built up a network of branches, instituted boycotts and the picketing of merchants who humiliated Africans, and kept up pressure on the government through public meetings and petitions. There have been some successes, such as the outlawing of the hatch system and the modification of the colour bar on the Copperbelt (achieved primarily by miners' unions), but there have also been actions that flopped and meetings that turned violent in spite of the ANC's avowed policy of non-violence. Organizers in turn constantly complain of police harassment and frequent arrests and imprisonment.

What has finally galvanized the movement and made it a force to be reckoned with is the continued failure of the powers that be, whether in Lusaka or Salisbury or London, to acknowledge African political demands. In Northern Rhodesia, the last straw for the ANC has been the so-called Benson Constitution. When the White Paper outlining proposed electoral reforms was made public in early 1958, it had the dubious distinction of infuriating both ends of the political spectrum—perhaps the only sense in which it achieved its avowed purpose of "multiracialism." Welensky commented that it was so complicated that constitutional lawyers "have been known to burst into tears at the sight of [it]."[44] Even in their revised form published later in the year, Welensky found the proposals totally unacceptable because they "offered no advance whatever towards self-government,"[45] that is, control of the territorial government by its European population. Africans, on the other hand, were dismayed by the glacial pace of change: They would still only hold a minority of seats in the Legislative Council. Not only was the African franchise extremely limited by property and education requirements, dividing the electorate into "ordinary," "special," and "ungraded" (voteless), it was further diluted by weighted voting in favor of Europeans. The final straw was a new provision that any candidate contesting a rural seat had to get two-thirds of the chiefs in his constituency to approve of his candidacy in the presence of a representative of the Crown duly appointed by the governor. Most constituencies were rural, with villages scattered far apart, and this imposed an almost ludicrous burden on candidates forced to beat the bush for chiefs and representatives of the Crown.

Kaunda and Nkumbula had met with Governor Benson to present their proposals. They were still willing to accept parity of African and European representation, but even that was dismissed by the governor: "'Mr. Kaunda,' he asked, 'don't you think Europeans would paralyse Government if we accepted your proposals?' In reply I said, 'Are you implying, Your Excellency, that for our demands to be met we have got to be in a position to paralyse the Government?' My question was never answered."[46] Nkumbula's response was to publicly burn a copy of the White Paper when it was issued. Shortly before, Governor Benson had sent a letter of concern to Kaunda when the latter was struck by lightning, but now personal relationships take a back seat to struggles for power.

Another struggle for power is building within the ANC itself. Like many nationalist movements, it is facing a crisis in leadership. Just as Mbikusita had been replaced by a more militant cadre of leaders in 1951, so the current president, Harry Nkumbula, now faces a revolt by those who see him as no longer effectual, even compromised. Nkumbula had long been revered by young nationalists, including Kaunda, who saw him as the "Man of Destiny." He had studied on a scholarship at the London School of Economics, his education largely underwritten by

Gore-Browne. He took over the reins of the ANC during the critical struggle against federation and led the effort to turn it into a mass movement. But Nkumbula has always had a taste for extravagance, something the perennially impoverished ANC can ill afford, and has now embarrassed the organization by missing a second crucial meeting with the colonial secretary in London. Within the organization, he brooks no dissent. At the same time, he seems to have lost his fire and his taste for dusty journeys to the far ends of the territory. After one brief stint in jail, he has little stomach for more, and yet jail appears more and more inevitable in the coming months.

Worst of all, he has begun flirting with liberal white parties and associations that are springing up in Northern Rhodesia; he seems quite willing to accept their gradualist agendas simply because they are less racist and less gradualist than that of the dominant United Federal Party. Harry Franklin, one-time district officer, later Northern Rhodesian director of information and father of the "saucepan special" (a battery-operated radio at a price many Africans could afford), seems to have become his *éminence grise*. There are even rumors that Nkumbula has made a pact with the authorities who now view him as the devil they can deal with, the lesser of nationalist evils. What seems to give credence to these rumors is that he has done an about-face on the Benson Constitution and decided to stand for election—this after his dramatic burning of the White Paper only a few months earlier. Can the "two Harrys" be trusted as events become more and more tumultuous and the stakes rise higher and higher?

In late October 1958 the split comes. The dissidents break off and form the Zambia African National Congress, often referred to simply as "Zambia." It is the first time the name, a contraction of Zambezia, passes into common currency (it was apparently first coined by Arthur Wina in a poem written while he was a student at Makerere College in Uganda). Kaunda is elected president of the new organization. In contrast to the "playboy" Nkumbula, he is an ascetic disciplinarian, a vegetarian who doesn't smoke or drink, a deeply religious man whose model is Mahatma Gandhi, the Indian prophet of non-violent nationalism. A commanding figure in his signature toga (often mimicked, rarely with success, by his admirers), wearing his hair brushed straight up, Kaunda has conquered a childhood stammer to become an effective speaker. But the decision to break with Nkumbula has been difficult, both personally and politically. Furthermore, the new organization has no money and no headquarters, other than Kaunda's little house in Chilenje. On the day the party is founded, Kaunda and his old friend and fellow leader,

Simon Kapwepwe, have just two shillings between them. He has to borrow 2 shillings 6 pence from his wife, the only money she has in the house.

By 1959 the lines are drawn. The tempo of political agitation is intensifying on all fronts, even among schoolchildren. On both sides, the cry is for "independence now"—but independence for whom? For Welensky, it is independence for the Federation as an independent dominion within the British Commonwealth. The white electorate is far from monolithic, divided between those who oppose any more concessions to Africans (there have been too many already in their view) and others who are willing to acknowledge the legitimacy of African demands but are not yet ready to accept African majority rule. Neither has been able seriously to challenge the prime minister's party at either the federal or territorial level. A very few whites such as Sir Stewart Gore-Browne throw in their lot with the Africans, realizing that federation has been a scam and that anything less than majority rule is neither just nor realistic.

For the Zambia African National Congress, the battlecry is "Africa for Africans": independence for Northern Rhodesia as Zambia, based on a system of one man, one vote. Parity between Africans and Europeans is no longer acceptable, nor is federation (which Kaunda once characterized as the "partnership of the slave and the free.")[47] Even as it escalates pressure on the Northern Rhodesian government, ZANC is not sure how much the breakdown of unity has damaged the movement, how many of the ANC rank-and-file will fall in behind its banner. Confrontations between ZANC and ANC followers often turn nasty. But the attention to rural voters that characterized Kaunda's early organizing is paying off: Rural branches, especially in the Northern and Luapula Provinces, are gravitating toward ZANC. ANC's main strength is in Nkumbula's home Southern Province. When the two now opposed leaders attend the All African Peoples' Conference in Accra, Ghana, in December 1958, it is clear that the other African leaders see Kaunda as the man of the future, not Nkumbula.

Kaunda is committed to non-violent action and a non-racial society. ZANC has publicly affirmed the same objective. It is very difficult, however, for the organization to control all of its far-flung members, not all of whom share this commitment. "In any nationalist organization," Kaunda acknowledges in his autobiography, "there are bound to be 'roughs and toughs' who want to force the pace and a way must be found of dealing with them."[48] It is all too easy as well for hooligans to use the movement as a cover for acts of pure lawlessness, especially in a society where many young people feel disaffected not only from the government but also from their own elders. ZANC's most immediate objective is to discourage Africans from taking part in the territorial election scheduled for March 20, the first to be held under the Benson Constitution. Persuasion is the avowed policy, intimidation impossible to avoid. There are sporadic outbreaks of violence in both Northern Rhodesia and Nyasaland where, after 40 years abroad, Dr. Hastings Banda has returned to lead the Nyasaland Congress. A ZANC official in Broken Hill exhorts Africans to "hate anything white on two legs."[49] Just as many Africans believed Welensky was out to kill them all at the time federation was imposed, so now Europeans believe, just as irrationally, that the more extreme nationalists, represented by ZANC in Northern Rhodesia and ANC in Nyasaland, are determined to murder all of them.

Until the present moment, the government has played the game of "white man's bluff"[50] and played it well; brute force has rarely been needed. In the early months of 1959 nationalists in both Rhodesia and Nyasaland are calling the bluff, and the government overreacts. As a contemporary observer puts it, "When the bluff is first called, the ghost of a vanishing prestige becomes immensely important; we must not yield they say, because it would be seen as weakness."[51] A state of emergency is proclaimed in Southern Rhodesia (where very little is happening) and in Nyasaland where federal troops are sent to quell disturbances.

No state of emergency is declared in Northern Rhodesia because to do so would mean postponing territorial elections, and Benson is determined that these proceed on schedule, come hell or high water, especially because he is soon to retire. Even without a formal state of emergency, he uses his powers to ban ZANC. He orders more than 50 leaders of ZANC rounded up and "restricted" to distant areas of the country, especially to Northwestern Province and Barotseland. ZANC has infuriated Sir Arthur by calling him "cruel, imperialistic, inhuman, Satanic and brutal."[52] He replies in kind, claiming that the party is planning nothing less than a violent revolution in concert with the nationalists in Nyasaland and has instituted a virtual reign of nighttime terror in villages and towns, "invoking witchcraft and unmentionable cursings."[53] He compares the organization to "Murder Incorporated," the notorious Chicago racketeers who "established protection rackets, corrupted the local governments, ruled by the gun, the sap [blackjack], the knuckle-duster, the bicycle chain;"[54] they are, he declares, ready to use any means, however violent, to prevent the African electorate from voting under the new constitution. In fact, an official enquiry turns up not a single instance of violence that can be attributed to the party before the banning and arrests.

An outbreak of lawlessness does occur, however, as an immediate reaction to the government's actions. Shops windows are smashed in Lusaka, cars damaged, fires lit. Remarkably, the only occasion in which anyone is hurt is during a riot in Northern Province: Four Africans are shot dead after the DC and his assistant are wounded with spears. Ninety people are jailed. However, the election does take place in late March, albeit with a majority of eligible Africans abstaining. With the top leadership of ZANC in detention, political activity comes to a near halt for the rest of the year. Ironically, by the time Benson retires, he has lost all faith in federation.

Kaunda cannot resist a Parthian shot at Benson. He claims that when he and his fellow detainees arrive in Kabompo in the northwestern corner of the country, the inhabitants shrink from them in fright: "Mothers dashed to their houses with babies in their arms." On investigation "we found out that those in authority had spread a very wicked story about us. Villagers had been told that these Zambia men were cannibals. They especially liked children since these provided tender meat."[55] Anyone who would go to such extremes needs treatment, he comments, but such are the workings of imperialism. But are the local people really so unsophisticated, so oblivious of national events as to swallow such tall tales? It makes an effective yarn, if not an entirely credible one. Kaunda finds the few months spent in Kabompo a bittersweet experience. He marvels at the beauty of a landscape he had never seen before and comes to love nature in a way new to him:

> I would walk for about a mile and then come to rest at a very high place overlooking one of the most beautiful scenes in the country .... Here the silent waters of the Kabompo River gather in one great sheet of water. On both sides of the river are huge trees, deep green in the rainy season. They seem to be jealous of one another and appear to be pointing fingers of strange accusation at each other as the wind blows them backwards and forwards. Just as this one great sheet of water makes a sharp bend at the grassy feet of this princely high ground of Kabompo Boma, the silent waters burst into noisy protest as they clash with the enduring rocks ... As the quiet breeze blew from the Kabompo River the trees and the grass around seemed to dance to a strange tune which made me feel that I was in the midst of music which would never come the way of my ears ....[56]

He longs to photograph the trees from various angles that please him, but has no camera. He imagines that trees and all growing things have a

language of their own, a secret to all but God. Someday this secret will
be revealed to man as other secrets have been revealed. One day he is
visited by a black mamba about five feet long. Remembering that the settler leader John Gaunt had called him a black mamba, he wonders dryly
why "this particular member of 'my family' did not stop to greet me."[57]

He manages to keep up a correspondence with many of his fellow
leaders and with sympathizers abroad who jokingly refer to Kabompo as
provisional HQ of ZANC. They adopt nicknames and remind each
other that they have nothing to lose but their chains. But exile is lonely
business—Kabompo is, he writes, "a St Helena on the mainland."[58]
Sikota Wina, a fiery Lozi journalist, is detained in far off Bembaland. In
a letter to his cousin he quotes from a poem by the Russian poet Boris
Pasternak, himself no stranger to internal exile:

> I am lost like a beast in an enclosure;
> Somewhere are people, freedom and light;
> Behind me is the voice of pursuit
> And there is no way out ....[59]

Kaunda suffers from a lack of fresh food and accuses the government
of deliberately trying to starve him. At one point he falls very seriously
ill with dysentery, aggravated by malaria and, perhaps, by malnutrition.
He is also much troubled by the drunkenness he observes around him.
He admits he has tended to romanticize rural life, believing that "moral
decay" is rampant only in urban areas. In fact the problem is much more
widespread: "The Western way of life has been so powerful that our own
social, cultural and political set-up has been raped by the powerful and
greedy Western civilization." People have lost their bearings and think
only of aping the West. How can he and his fellows hope to make a
nation out of an utterly demoralized people? he asks in a letter to a fellow
nationalist. "Who do we hope to lead to our cherished land of Canaan?
A nation half-drunk, half-thinking, half-corrupted, possessing only many
other halves of what makes LIFE what it should be?"[60]

In June he is re-arrested and imprisoned first in Lusaka, in the cell he
had occupied several years earlier when he and Harry Nkumbula had
been jailed for possession of banned literature, then in Salisbury. Like so
many political detainees the world over, he uses the enforced leisure to
read and to take a correspondence course in economics. As his lawyer
notes, he has now joined the "growing number of men in the history of
the Commonwealth ... who have graduated ... from the University of
the Territorial Prisons."[61] Indeed, "a spell inside"[62] has become *de rigueur*

for any nationalist worth his salt (in Ghana, they proudly wear "PG"—Prison Graduate—on their caps), and Her Majesty's Government is willing to oblige.

What echoes of this time of troubles and uncertainty reverberate in Barotseland? Very few. Kaunda has never set foot in the province and neither ANC nor ZANC have a presence there, in spite of the fact that several prominent nationalist leaders are Lozi of origin, including Sikota and Arthur Wina, the two sons of the former *ngambela*. The split between the two organizations has gone virtually unnoticed. The brand of nationalism most in vogue here is a nostalgia for past greatness, a defiant isolation from the rest of the country. As one official puts it, "The Barotse leaders evidently wish to drive as lonely a furrow as possible."[63] When Gervas Clay returned as resident commissioner in 1958 after 19 years elsewhere in the territory, he could only remark, "*plus ça change plus c'est la même chose* ... The Barotse way of life has, to an extraordinary extent, remained the same."[64]

No wonder it seems natural to rusticate troublesome nationalist leaders to Barotseland and neighboring North Western Province where, it is thought, they can do little harm. Several are sent to Mongu and Sesheke and three to Kalabo, referred to in the *Annual Report* for 1958 as "perhaps the least politically conscious district in Northern Rhodesia."[65] Indeed, there are no visible signs of political discontent in Kalabo at all.

Nevertheless the DC is not happy to have them. He complains in his report for 1959 that, unavoidable as this strategy may be, it is "most unsatisfactory" as far as the districts involved are concerned. For the most part the "Zambia men" are polite but distinctly resentful. In a confrontation strikingly similar to one described by Kaunda during his time in Kabompo, the detainees barge into the DC's office on one occasion without first making an appointment through the clerk in the outer office. The DC refuses to see them, they refuse to leave; there is a standoff. Furious, the DC orders the messengers to haul them off to the local jail, becoming even angrier when the messengers don't do this energetically enough to suit him. Then he turns to his cadet and scolds him for not having intervened when he saw that his superior had acted intemperately, something that of course no cadet would ever consider doing. Hierarchy is hierarchy.

This is not the end of the affair. The Zambia men (who know the law and probably intended their action to be provocative) claim that they were imprisoned without cause. What makes it especially dubious is that the case will be heard in the first instance by the DC himself—a reminder of the potential for conflict in his multiple roles of executive, police chief, and magistrate, the one who must ultimately keep the peace in his domain. The cadet writes home that it was a mistake to have charged the men in the first place. But the Devonshire Courses have never included instruction on how to get on with "that new phenomenon on the African administrator's horizon of the 1950s, the political party." If politics tends to be a dirty word for the average DC, " 'politician' [is] not far removed from 'trouble-maker.' "[66]

Perhaps all politics *is* local. There may not be much interest in political stirrings on the larger stage, but local intrigue is, in the words of one British administrator, "practically an occupational disease" among the Lozi:[67] intrigue between cliques of *indunas* jockeying for power in the *kuta* and between branches of the royal family angling for lucrative offices. It takes a sensational twist on the night of August 29, 1959—the night of the DC's grand regatta at Liyoyelo—with the murder of Akashambatwa Imwiko, son of the late *litunga* Imwiko and nephew of the present ruler, Mwanawina III. Word of the death spreads slowly; it is several months before it becomes generally known. Then, public opinion jumps to the conclusion that Akashambatwa was killed on the paramount chief's orders, first to exorcise the evil spirits that have been abroad and unappeased since the death of the old *mulena mukwae,* then to get rid of a potential rival who might challenge Mwanawina's own son when the paramount dies (he is already over 60). The idea is not as outlandish as it might appear since it was and still is widely believed that Mwanawina poisoned Imwiko in order to clear the way for his own accession a decade earlier. The official report at the time was that Imwiko had died of a sudden stroke but this did little to allay suspicions. Now the investigation is being carried out by the DC Mongu, he who was DC Kalabo during the witchcraft epidemic of 1956–57, and by the CID. So byzantine are Lozi politics that it is next to impossible to determine whether the crime was plotted by Mwanawina or by his enemies in order to discredit him.

Although he may have his detractors, the paramount chief has skillfully navigated the treacherous seas of federation. Since the idea of amalgamation was first bruited in the 1930s, Lozi of all stations have voiced their

Table 3.1 Lozi rulers

	Lewanika (1878–1884; 1886–1916)	
	|	
Yeta III (1916–1946)	Imwiko (1946–1948)	Mwanawina III (1948–1968)

Figure 1 Lewanika in England, 1902 (Caplan, *Elites*, between pp. 94–95)

Figure 2 Kalabo *boma* from the air (Murray Armor)

Figure 3 DC's house, Kalabo (John Herniman)

Figure 4 Touring camp (John Herniman)

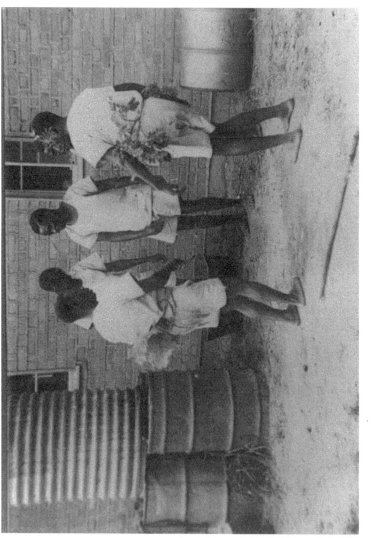

Figure 5 Prisoners dancing as Christmas trees (John Herniman)

Figure 6 Grace Hart at Hart's store, Kalabo (John Herniman)

Figure 7 DC: Ndoka Canal (John Herniman)

Figure 8 The DC leaves Kalabo, May 1960 (Murray Armor)

Figure 9 H.R.H. The Queen Mother, *litunga* Mwanawina III, and Gervas Clay, Resident Commissioner, 1960 (Murray Armor)

Figure 10 The installation of the *mulena mbowanjikana* (Murray Armor)

Figure 11 Queen Mokwae—Slaves bringing her food (Coillard, *Threshold*, facing p. 213)

Figure 12 Lewanika holding court (Johnston, *Reality versus Romance*, p. 94)

Figure 13 Lozi women wearing bustles, 1959 (John Herniman)

Figure 14 *Makishi* dancers (Murray Armor)

Figure 15 "Nalikwanda"—A royal progress (Coillard, *Threshold*, facing p. 408)

Figure 16 *Kuomboka* arriving at Limulunga (Murray Armor)

Figure 17 The Makabuzi River in 1959—the *vlei* runs under Kingsway, a handsome thoroughfare in the heart of Salisbury (Garry Allighan, *The Welensky Story*, p. 81)

Figure 18 Mwanawina III receives his knighthood at Limulunga (Public Record Office: CO 799/39)

Figure 19 Margery Perham in Darfur, Sudan, 1937 (Heussler, *Yesterday's Rulers*, p. 20)

Figure 20 Government House, Lusaka (John Herniman)

Figure 21 President and Mrs. Kaunda and *litunga* Mwanawina on the royal barge during the 1965 *kuomboka* (Caplan, *Elites*, between pp. 194–95)

opposition because of their distaste for the system of white domination in Southern Rhodesia and the ill-treatment of their migrant laborers. Touring the province in 1947, Gore-Browne found "a great deal of talk ... about amalgamation." He concluded, "There is no doubt that people in rural areas are exercised on this matter just as much as those in towns."[68] Royals and *indunas* have an added reason for hostility, given the undermining of chiefly power that has accompanied "responsible government" in their neighbor across the Zambezi. The National Council threatened that if amalgamation were to occur, they would take Barotseland out of Northern Rhodesia and seek recognition from the Crown as a full protectorate similar to the High Commission Territories of Bechuanaland, Basutoland, and Swaziland. Mwanawina reiterated this position as soon as he became paramount chief, which brought hasty visits from the governor and the colonial secretary.

So eager has the government been to placate Mwanawina and to win him over to the idea of federation—to be able to display him as a trophy of African support for federation—that he has been able to bargain for some of the powers whittled away by the colonial government in past reigns. The jurisdiction of the courts of the paramount chief and the *mulena mukwae* has been extended, and the former has been given the sole right of appointing and dismissing *indunas*. In return he and the Lealui *kuta* declared that they would not object to federation if the rights specified under the original Lewanika Concession were guaranteed, and if Barotseland were henceforth styled as the "Barotseland Protectorate" and the provincial commissioner renamed "resident commissioner." In gratitude and in the hope that his example would inspire other chiefs still hesitating about federation, the British government flew Mwanawina, his *ngambela,* and others of his entourage off to London in 1953 to attend the coronation of Elizabeth II, just as his father Lewanika had attended the coronation of Edward VII and his half-brother Yeta III the coronation of George VI.

What would have happened if Mwanawina had stubbornly refused to accept federation? Would he have been deported like his contemporary, the *kabaka* of Buganda, who held out against the colonial administration in Uganda? Deportation at least had the benefit of increasing the *kabaka's* popularity at home, something that Mwanawina could well have used. While he has gained support from the elites in his fight for the rights and privileges of the entire, rather numerous ruling class, he has managed to antagonize important constituencies.

First of all, his election as paramount chief—the third successive son of Lewanika to rule—means that other branches of the royal family have been shut out, with little chance at the throne in the future. This has particularly frustrated the hopes of the children of both Yeta III and Imwiko, but there are also plenty of children sired by Lewanika's many other sons eager to play the game of royal intrigue rather than sit idly by and watch the throne pass to Mwanawina's own son whom he seems to be grooming for the job and who is commonly regarded as an idiot. Senior *indunas* attach themselves to the various princes and mastermind the scheming, which in turn provokes purges and counterpurges, accusations of disloyalty, and even acts of arson.

The other constituency clamoring for a place in the sun is the self-styled "African intelligentsia": clerks, teachers, medical orderlies, and the like, who have often been to school in Basutoland or South Africa. They have several grievances. For one thing, their pay and living conditions are far inferior to those of whites with comparable education doing the same jobs. In Kalabo, for example, the local school superintendent possesses a school certificate and spent 18 months in a teachers' training college in England. His salary has finally been raised to £500 per annum, but he must still live in a small hut in the African area with the messengers because there is no provision for better African housing nor the possibility of living with Europeans. Furthermore, the intelligentsia resent their exclusion from a political system dominated by chiefs and *indunas*. In Mongu this group has formed a welfare association to further the ends of its members. Mwanawina has been smart enough to invite senior members of the association to fill clerical posts in the Barotse Native Government. Understandably this co-optation provokes its own resentments. "The whole of Mwanawina's court, they are backward fools," one *boma* clerk opines in an unguarded moment. "A few of them used to be okay, but then they had their mouths closed with big jobs and now they are just like the uneducated ones."[69]

Since the BNG, *boma,* and other local enterprises can only absorb a limited number of educated men, many must leave Barotseland for jobs on the line of rail or even farther afield in East and Central Africa, where Lozi educational accomplishments are much in demand. Here they have often been attracted to nationalist politics, especially when they realize that they are still disenfranchised while Europeans of less education run the country (Welensky himself jokes that if Standard VIII were a voting requirement, most of the African nationalist leaders would qualify but he would not). Their brothers at home, however, focus their resentment primarily on their exclusion from local power and all the perks it entails.

And perks there are. The court at Lealui continues to live on a lavish scale; indeed, Mwanawina lives more grandly even than his predecessors, thanks to the fees paid into the native treasury by the Zambesi Sawmills Company for logging the teak forests in Sesheke District and by Wenela for the ever-increasing army of men recruited to work on the mines in South Africa. On the eve of federation, the treasury showed a balance of £102,000, most of which went for salaries for the Native Authority and for maintaining the royal establishment at Lealui. Compared to other native rulers, the *litunga* is very wealthy indeed, but the bulk of this wealth is monopolized by the inner elite at Lealui. They also control much of the best land in the floodplain.

The colonial administration is understandably dismayed by the extravagance of the court and its conservatism, indeed its preoccupation with feathering its own nest at the expense of the population at large—all the more so since Barotseland is one of the poorest, most underdeveloped areas of Northern Rhodesia, surviving mainly by the export of its men as migrant labor. Even during the dark years of the 1930s when depression, floods, droughts, and cattle diseases brought so much misery, the Native Authority, supported mainly by government subsidies, showed little inclination to support projects to develop the country. The *kuta* even balked at leasing land for the establishment of the Development Centre at Namushakende which, however imperfectly, would seem to have embodied Lewanika's dreams of modernization.

Over the years, there have been attempts to trim the native government and force it to become both more responsible and more inclusive. The administration has abolished what it considers superfluous titles and offices and redefined others to suit the changing times. Thus certain *indunas* have been charged with agriculture, health, and education. Soon after World War II, the anthropologist Max Gluckman, the acknowledged authority on Lozi society, offered a plan of reform but it was so complicated no one could understand it (a bit like the Benson Constitution) and in the end too conservative as well. All that came out of it was the revival of the Katengo Council in 1947, a quasi-traditional assembly of commoners elected to represent all five Barotse districts.

Matters came to a head with the Konoso Affair. Sekeli Konoso was secretary of the Barotse National Association, a group of Lozi working on the line of rail who organized to demand reform of the Barotse Native Government. Early in 1957 he was arrested for insulting the paramount chief and plotting the overthrow of the BNG: He had demanded that Mwanawina resign after he had appointed his favorite as *ngambela* in a particularly devious manner. The Lealui *kuta* convicted Konoso and sentenced him to three years in solitary confinement, later reduced by the Federal High Court to six months at hard labor. So many of his supporters attended the trial and demonstrated outside the Mongu prison where he was interned that the administration was obliged to appoint a commission to look into the constitution of the BNG and the procedures of native courts, and to make recommendations for reform. The commission was headed by C. G. C. Rawlins, a DO with considerable experience in Barotseland. Except for Rawlins and a European missionary, the commission consisted entirely of Lozi, but they were virtually all relatives and friends of the ruler. It heard a large number of witnesses, many of them highly critical of the paramount chief, and collected vast amounts of evidence. Predictably, it called for only modest change. Yes, many office holders were doddering incompetents, and should be replaced by younger, better educated Lozi. And yes, the national council should become more representative by including the five members of the Katengo as full members. All in all, however, the paramount chief was a wise statesman, as his appointment of the commission so amply confirmed, and the BNG "essentially sound and adaptable to changing conditions."[70] Once again the administration proved that it could not afford to alienate so valuable an ally.

The scene is set for the federal elections in late 1958 and the territorial elections in March 1959. Just to make sure, Welensky had paid a formal visit to Mongu in May 1958 and met with the paramount chief and *kuta* in full session. He repeated that the federal government had no intention of meddling in Barotse affairs. Many Lozi resented the visit and their ruler's willingness to deal with Welensky, but Mwanawina can afford to ignore their objections. He has read the signs well: The Queen's 1959 New Years Honours List includes the name of Sir Mwanawina Lewanika III, KBE, the first—and last—chief in Central Africa to receive a knighthood. In May, Sir Evelyn Hone, newly appointed governor of Northern Rhodesia, comes to Limulunga to present Mwanawina with the insignia of office: Mwanawina in the British admiral's uniform, Hone looking as if he is still not quite used to all the plumage on his cocked hat (see figure 18). The investiture takes place "amid scenes of enthusiasm"[71] according to the official report. The paramount chief, however, is really holding out for a full-blown investiture at the hands of the Queen.

Initially Mwanawina opposed participation in the territorial elections, seeing them as a threat to his own power. Now, however, armed with his knighthood and Her Majesty's assurances (yet again) of the sanctity of Barotse treaties, he comes around. Taking advantage of the provision that chiefs can reject candidates, he rejects three—two because he dislikes them and the third because he allegedly supported the hostile Barotse

National Society and is, to boot, a member of another branch of the royal family. Finally he finds a candidate to his liking, both educated and loyal. Since all his *indunas* and headmen are eligible to vote, he can be pretty confident his man will be elected.

In Kalabo, as elsewhere, district officers belatedly make the rounds, signing up voters. The *mulena* and her husband, *ishee* Mutena, top the cadet's list in Libonda, and he joins them for a spot of tea after the day's work. In truth, very few of those eligible register to vote. This is partly because of the delay in making known the paramount chief's acceptance of the constitution, partly because of conservatism. As the DC Kalabo notes in his annual report for 1958: "There is probably no district in the territory where less interest is evinced in political development or non-parochial matters. The Federal elections went unnoted, the territorial constitutional proposals attracted little interest and the Rawlins report proposals are generally ignored."[72] Overshadowing all these events is the drama going on in Libonda itself during the course of 1959: the elevation of the *mulena mbowanjikana,* the eventual choice of her successor, the elaborate rituals of installation. Preoccupation with these matters brings the native administration of the district to a virtual standstill for much of the year—and confirms those who see the Lozi as living in a curious timewarp all their own.

Kwalombota Mulonda, the anointed candidate, wins easily. A few months later *litunga* Mwanawina makes a royal progress, accompanied by the *ngambela* and senior *indunas.* They visit Lusaka, the Kariba Dam, Livingstone, Bulawayo, and Salisbury. The inclusion of Salisbury on his agenda despite the warnings of Mulonda and many members of the national council shows a certain amount of bravado, even cockiness. What does it matter that the crowds who turn out to greet him along the way are conspicuously thin? He is indisputably the best known chief in Central Africa, honored by the Queen, pampered by government officials, wooed by the prime minister of the Federation.

Welensky seems equally secure in 1959. He has forced Whitehall to accept the 1957 changes in the federal constitution, to declare an emergency in Nyasaland, and to acquiesce in sending leading nationalists in both Nyasaland and Northern Rhodesia to prison or internal exile. "Politically, Welensky is winning, if something is not done and done urgently," writes the nationalist journalist Sikota Wina bitterly. "He is winning not because he is getting African support but because there is *no* African National movement here, literally."[73] Federation Day dawns on October 29 with nary a demonstration, nary a protest banner to be seen anywhere in the three territories and with more than 500 leaders still in detention. Small wonder that Welensky expects the Federal

Review Conference to smile on his plans to transform the Federation into a dominion.

True, the British government has insisted that it must be preceded by a fact-finding commission, led by Lord Monckton, which will propose possible changes to the constitution. The commission includes a broad spectrum of members from the United Kingdom, Australia, and Canada, as well as both African and European representatives from the Federation and from its individual territories. Elspeth Huxley, who grew up in Kenya and then turned her hand to writing autobiography (*The Flame Trees of Thika*), mysteries (*Murder at Government House*), and political tracts (*White Man's Country*), is the only woman on the commission, appointed presumably because of her knowledge of Africa and her familiarity with the problems of settler colonies. Welensky has made sure—or thinks he has—that certain topics are off limits for the commission, specifically majority rule and secession of any of the three members of the Federation. The Queen has just made Sir Roy one of her privy councillors, and he can count on his friends in the Whitehall, he confidently believes, to protect his interests.

On January 9, 1960, Kaunda is released from prison. He goes directly to the little house in Chilenje to join Betty and their children. Neighbors gather, and soon a crowd of supporters ring the verandah singing Christian hymns and nationalist songs. He demands independence but also urges Zambians to be calm and patient. Several weeks later he is elected president of the United National Independence Party (UNIP), the phoenix that has risen from the ashes of the banned ZANC. Almost immediately he once again hits the dusty roads with his message of one man, one vote. As befits a vegetarian, his slogan is not the proverbial "chicken in every pot" but the clunkier "an egg a day for every Zambian."[74] This time he tours the country not by bicycle but in "Mother UNIP," the Land Rover given to the party by Reverend Merfyn Temple, a Methodist minister. In February, Temple oversees the publication of the pamphlet, *Black Government,* a dialogue between Kaunda and the radical cleric, Colin Morris, with a foreword by Stewart Gore-Browne, about their sometimes divergent visions of the future. It is a hurried book, Temple acknowledges, "for events march swiftly in Central Africa today."[75]

That same month the Monckton Commission arrives in Livingstone and holds its first meeting at the venerable Victoria Falls Hotel. Twelve days earlier, British Prime Minister Harold Macmillan delivers his "wind of change" speech in Cape Town.

CHAPTER FOUR

London: The View from Whitehall

Our opponents in Britain wanted, at six thousand miles' distance, to create a Parliamentary democracy like their own: we fought to maintain the civilisation we had made.

—Sir Roy Welensky, prime minister, Federation of Rhodesia and Nyasaland

Africans think that they should be given independence now. Europeans think that they are not ready for independence. The tragedy of this situation is that both are right.

—Hywel Griffiths, provincial community development officer

The broad expanse of Whitehall curves ever so slightly as it makes its way from Trafalgar Square to Parliament Street and Parliament Square. On either side it is lined with public buildings and government offices, including the Home Office, Commonwealth Relations Office, Foreign Office, and Treasury. Its main claim to architectural fame is the magnificent Banqueting House designed by Inigo Jones. One of the finest buildings in London, it was intended once upon a time to be the anchor of a vast royal palace that would dwarf Spain's Escorial in size and splendor. In contrast to the classical lines of the building's exterior, its interior ceilings are flamboyantly baroque. Peter Paul Rubens painted the allegorical scenes of the Apotheosis of James I while he was in London in 1634 to collect his knighthood. In 1649, James's successor Charles I stepped out through one of the Banqueting House windows onto the scaffold where he was beheaded by the rebellious Puritans. Ironically, one of Rubens's panels depicts Minerva driving Rebellion to Hell. In 1959 the hall is no longer used for banquets or beheadings but houses the "absurd and unfrequented Imperial Services Museum, full of howitzers, faded flags and dusty models."[1] Near the southern end of the avenue stands the wreath-bedecked Cenotaph, the memorial to Britain's dead in two world wars. At right angles to Whitehall is Downing Street, the location of the prime minister's official residence.

Whitehall has become a metonym, the part standing for the whole. The street conjures up the "opaque and impenetrable regions of the bureaucracies,"[2] the civil servants who remain largely anonymous behind its high classical facades and looming cupolas. Governments may rise and fall, politicians come and go, but the minions of Whitehall remain. When a government changes in Great Britain, only seventy officials leave their desks in Whitehall; when a government changes in the United States hundreds flock out and hundreds flock in.

In 1959 the professional civil service is barely a century old, dating only from the middle decades of Queen Victoria's reign. Its members take a perverse delight in the familiar caricatures—the gloomy offices, the doddering attendants, the "contrived squalor" of the halls and ante-rooms, the clacking of knitting needles in the typing pool, even a trade union magazine titled *Red Tape*.[3] Its powers have escalated far beyond anything dreamed of before the Second World War, as have its numbers. Theoretically, the permanent civil service does not make policy but only carries it out. The line between the two functions is a thin one which few could explicate and fewer still would want to. Certainly many of the most important decisions affecting the lives of Britons at home and sub-ject peoples in the far corners of the Empire are taken inside the palaces of Whitehall, not in Parliament. Deluged with a flood of files, memos, and urgent telegrams, often on subjects in which they are quite out of their depth, cabinet ministers are of necessity reliant on the guidance of the faceless figures within Whitehall's labyrinthine corridors. This is especially true of colonial secretaries, for whom the post is often seen simply as a "stepping stone to higher things."[4] To some, Whitehall collectively is still Charles Dickens's "Circumlocution Office" writ large: "Whatever was required to be done, the Circumlocution Office was beforehand with all the public departments in the art of perceiving How Not To Do It."[5] To others, however, it is the indispensable and incorruptible backbone of British public life, the repository of collective experience and wisdom, unsullied by hustings or marketplace.

But Whitehall is hardly monolithic. Intense rivalry characterizes inter-departmental relations. "They spend so much time fighting each other," commented one civil servant, "that it is difficult to remember they're all supposed to be serving the same government."[6] The Foreign Office, housed in its gaudily decorated Palladian pile half way between Whitehall and St. James's Park, looks down its collective nose at the upstart Commonwealth Relations Office installed in an adjoining corner of courtyard. In some areas, the two have duplicate experts and bureaucracies and make a point of not letting each other know what they are doing. The Colonial Office has its own quarrels with both Commonwealth Relations and the Foreign Office, but most of all with the Treasury, "a department without bowels of compassion or the throb of imperial feeling."[7] The CO is not actually lodged in Whitehall proper but in Church House, Great Smith Street, between Scotland Yard and Westminster Abbey. At the end of World War II the government drew up ambitious plans for a magnificent new home for the Colonial Office on Parliament Square, to be built at a cost of more than £3 million. Work was begun in 1952 but halted two years later, first for reasons of economy, finally because by the mid-1950s a grandiose monument to imperialism no longer seemed like such a good idea. Or even very necessary: Winston Churchill himself acknowledged that before long, all that would be needed would be "a fine dining room and kitchen and a big office."[8]

The Colonial Service (since 1954 technically known as Her Majesty's Overseas Civil Service) operates in all the areas over which the Colonial Office holds sway: East, West, and Central Africa; the Caribbean; South East Asia; the islands of the western Pacific; and miscellaneous bits of real estate such as Gibraltar, Bermuda, and St. Helena. Its officers are recruited by the heirs of the redoubtable Sir Ralph Furse, lodged within the Colonial Office but not of it. The Furse system of selection, depending as it does on close contacts within the major universities (especially Oxford and Cambridge) and the interviewing skills of his team, has been called "one of the secrets of the Empire."[9] For some four decades, from 1910 to his retirement in 1948, the Eton and Balliol-educated Furse demonstrated his belief that what were needed were men of character and that character could be instantly recognized in the applicants who appeared before him and his aides: "Their eyes were steady, their mouths firm. It was abundantly clear that without exceptions these paragons possessed in the fullest possible manner the qualities essential to a successful colonial administrator: fortitude, fair dealing, integrity and supreme self-confidence."[10] Or as Jan Morris has put it, "Whatever their motives, they had no doubts ... brisk young cadets, so fresh, so pink, so assured."[11] Alas, for the poor aspirant with "flabby lip or averted eyes" or any sign of "nervous disorder."[12] Off to the counting house with him. His eyes steady, his lip firm, the successful applicant actually receives his appointment from the governor of the colony in which he will serve. He draws his pay from the colony's exchequer and must abide by its laws and regulations. Since colonies vary in their ability to generate money from taxes and customs duties and vary equally in their legal systems, officers find themselves serving under very different conditions according to what corner of the Empire they land in. Lacking the Gallic passion for tidiness, the British cheerfully accept the bewildering particularism of their many colonial outposts.

One thing one must never do is to confuse the Colonial Office and the Colonial Service. They themselves are never guilty of such folly; indeed, the two barely speak to each other. Those in the Service thank God they have escaped the dreary routine of Whitehall, while those in the Office remind any and all that, unlike those boy scouts warding off snakes in the bush, they have gained their jobs through competitive examination. There was, commented one officer, "a deep-rooted prejudice against the Colonial Office and all its works in the minds of the majority of officers serving overseas ... too much paper and not enough realism, and too many instances of officers home on leave being patronized by men many years younger than themselves, who had never been near the countries with whose affairs they dealt."[13] Or as another put it more succinctly: "They weren't one of us."[14]

In the 1860s, the Colonial Office was described as "a sleepy and humorous office ... where there seemed no enthusiasm, no *esprit de corps,* and no encouragement for individual exertions"[15]—an intriguing comment when one considers that the Scramble for Africa erupted only a decade or so later, bringing much of the continent under its sway (albeit in somewhat haphazard fashion, given the tug-of-war with the Foreign Office). It was revitalized by Joseph Chamberlain when he became secretary of state for the colonies in 1895. In the noontide of empire, as George Orwell, the ex-colonial policeman in Burma, observed, "nearly every inch of the modern colonial empire was in the grip of Whitehall. Well-meaning, over-civilized men in dark suits and black felt hats, with neatly rolled umbrellas crooked over their left forearm, were imposing their constipated view of life on Malaya and Nigeria, Mombasa, and Mandalay. The one-time empire builders were reduced to the status of clerks, buried deeper and deeper under mounds of paper and red tape."[16] Furse claimed that he was one of the few in the CO who had ever actually seen a colony.

By the 1950s, however, the Colonial Office is far from sleepy and no doubt much less humorous. Over-civilized they may still be, but the best and brightest Oxbridge graduates compete for appointment to its ranks. By now, too, the "derision gap"[17] between the Colonial Office and the Colonial Service has narrowed somewhat, although to officers in the field Whitehall still seems the remote Olympus of "god-like creatures."[18] Rare is the officer who has actually crossed the invisible barrier between the two: the "beachcomber" of the Colonial Office getting a taste of life in the territories or the "retread" of the Colonial Service signing on for post-retirement employment in Whitehall. One of the former is Sir Andrew Cohen, a reform-minded and influential under-secretary of state for Africa, who was given a chance to put theory into practice as governor of Uganda from 1952–57. It has been rumored that more than a few members of the Service were privately gleeful when Cohen ran into trouble as a result of his deportation of the *kabaka* of Buganda in 1953. Among the "retreads," Rowland Hudson has been brought in to head the African Branch at the CO after a distinguished career in the Service in Northern Rhodesia that began right after World War I. Nevertheless, much as the two groups share class and educational backgrounds and often belong to the same clubs in Pall Mall (to say nothing of serving the same Empire), the "us" versus "them" mentality persists.

The Colonial Service has found its stoutest champion in the unlikely person of a female Oxford don. For 30 odd years Margery Perham has traveled the length and breadth of Africa (and many other parts of the Empire as well), equally at home in Government House and in the *boma,* confidante of governor and district officer alike. She can hold her own at a formal dinner party or out on tour, riding for days on horseback with officers on their rounds (see figure 19). While some find her obsession with the minutiae of colonial administration wearing, most appreciate her unique knowledge of the field—her ability to combine the researches of the scholar with the realities of life as it is lived by those in the Service. Even more, officials appreciate her powerful connections in England and the role she has played in bringing colonial questions and colonial administration before the public.

Margery Perham is one of the remarkable cohort of women who came to prominence in Great Britain during the interwar years, making reputations in anthropology, archaeology, history, literature, and public affairs. On colonial matters, they had the field almost to themselves, their only rivals being Lord Hailey and Sir Reginald Coupland. Perhaps they would have achieved eminence no matter what; perhaps they filled the vacuum left by the slaughter of a generation of young men in the First World War. Perham herself lost a much-loved brother in the First and would lose an equally treasured nephew in the Second. Her studies at St. Hugh's College, Oxford, coincided almost exactly with World War I. She then accepted a lectureship in history at Sheffield University but in 1920 suffered a nervous breakdown. Her doctors advised a change of scenery. Instead of a walking tour of the Lake District or the Swiss Alps, Perham—in the best tradition of her Victorian foremothers—chose British Somaliland, a desolate waste on the northeastern extremity of Africa, where her sister's husband served as district commissioner. In this Gehenna she found her vocation.

By all accounts a tall, attractive, and intensely feminine young woman, an excellent swimmer and horsewoman (and a ruthlessly competitive croquet player), Perham contended with conflicting pulls in her life. Just below the surface of the scholar, an artist was struggling to get out—her first published works were two novels. The better known, *Major Dane's Garden* (1925), based on her experiences in Somaliland, vividly recreates the tumultuous worlds of colonial and indigenous politics in a barely tamed land: scheming officials, native insurrections, battles and massacres, impossible love. Not quite Kipling, but a good read nonetheless. In the end, however, the don won out. Nevertheless, in an interview years later with the writer Elspeth Huxley, Perham wondered whether she had made the right choice. "Anyone can write ... these sort of dull, conscientious books," she mused, "but to do imaginative work would have been wonderful."[19] In fact, she gave the lie to this dichotomy by infusing her writing with her own love of words, people, and things.

A second dilemma followed on the heels of the first: the classic choice between ambition and marriage. As she almost single-handedly created the new academic field of colonial administration, Perham concluded that in the Britain of her time, it would be impossible to be an influential public figure and at the same time have a conventional private life, and she very much wanted to play a public role. In *Major Dane's Garden* her heroine protests, "I don't see that it's a woman's business to worry about the problems and administration, and principles of native government."[20] Just as Rhona changes her mind in the course of the novel, so Perham found herself very much worried about these very problems; they took the place of "the lost home and depending family."[21] She became, in a manner of speaking, den mother to that most masculine of institutions, the Colonial Service. And to the African Colonial Service, in particular, for Africa was her lifelong passion. Although she never held a position in government, she not only influenced a generation of officers but also

came in time to symbolize "the enlightened conscience of British colo-
nial rule."[22] Was it an adequate substitute for a life of command? "Ah,
Dame Margery Perham!" exclaimed a senior officer later in her career,
"Now there's a woman who should have been a colonial governor."[23]
Perhaps she thought so, too.

Perham spent much of the 1930s traveling, thanks to funding from the
newly endowed Rhodes Trust and from the Rockefeller Foundation. On
her first trip, she encircled the globe, visiting British outposts in the
Pacific as well as in East and Southern Africa. In subsequent years, she
visited Africa almost every year. In these years she also took to journalism,
partly to support herself and partly to reach a larger public than her more
specialized work. Letters to the *Times* soon made her a name to conjure
with as far as colonial issues were concerned, for the *Times* columns were
an incomparable bully-pulpit (one observer refers to her "almost posses-
sive use of the *Times.*")[24] To print journalism, she added broadcasting and
became a familiar voice on the BBC and in the pages of its weekly
Listener magazine.

Oxford provided Perham with a base at her old college, St. Hugh's,
but it served largely as a springboard for her tours of Africa with local
DOs. Later she reminisced happily about her travels in the 1930s: "[T]he
fascination of Africa with the sheer fun and interest of travel and
the enhancement of my own position which my experience gave me.
The self-importance [?and] pseudo-romance of this woman traveller
were a comforting change—with all the male company thrown in—from
the chill corridors of a woman's college" (i.e., St. Hugh's).[25] She translated
these experiences, this "long romance with District Officers and other
colonial officials,"[26] into her courses and writings on colonial administration and imperial studies. On the eve of World War II, she helped to
run two very successful summer schools at Oxford that offered refresher
courses for colonial officers from the field and a chance to socialize with
the Olympians: Lord Lugard, Lord Hailey, a smattering of governors, and
a contingent from Whitehall. On those occasions, she warned of the
dangers inherent in the lack of accountability of colonial administrators
vis-à-vis the peoples they administered and in Britain's tendency to take
its empire for granted. She also lamented a lack of spiritual and aesthetic
sensibility in British rule—something to be learned from the French, a
view shared by Ralph Furse who thought that "in respect of the spiritual and aesthetic aspects of the life of coloured peoples," British officials
"have too often had both eyes shut."[27]

Margery Perham's name is linked above all to that of Frederick
Lugard, architect of indirect rule. Perham first met him in 1929 when

she was only 33. His introductions opened many doors for her during her travels and she revered him as the model proconsul. She became an outspoken champion of the doctrine of indirect rule and, in her best known work, *Native Administration in Nigeria,* demonstrated how the system worked on the ground and how it might meet its own goal of "the political education of the people."[28] She agreed with Lugard that indigenous chiefs should be "supported in every way and their authority upheld" and that indirect rule provided "a system by which the tutelary power recognises existing African societies and assists them to adapt themselves to the functions of local government." She acknowledged that the system also appealed to a thoroughly British conservatism "with its sense of historical continuity and its aristocratic tradition."[29]Although Northern Nigeria had been the incubator for Lugard's theories, Barotseland would have done just as well.

With her wide experience of Africa and colonial administration, to say nothing of her literary skills, Perham was the obvious choice to write Lugard's biography. She at last tackled the work in 1945, the year of his death, little dreaming what a formidable task it would turn out to be nor how long it would take. Not the least of her problems was that by 1945 she realized that the world, and Africa with it, was changing. The cracks in the doctrine of indirect rule were becoming all too visible, tending to preserve Africa as "a sort of Whipsnade [Zoo]," as one critic put it, something quaintly exotic.[30] Even Lord Hailey with whom Perham had worked on his monumental *African Survey* (1938) warned that "we must not act as if the system had come to us graven on tablets of brass."[31] Lugard was not quite Moses.

Her own African graduate students at Nuffield College, where she was the first Founding Fellow, came to be prime exhibits of what was wrong with indirect rule: It left little room for Western-educated "new men" such as they. More and more, these students became the teachers, jolting Perham into a realization that new forces were at play and new nationalisms aborning that she would have to come to terms with. It was no longer so clear that "backward people" wanted to be brought into the modern world through the efforts of a hardworking and incorruptible colonial service—administration was receding into the background, political bargaining taking center stage.

The evolution of Perham's thinking mirrored that of the more forward-looking in the government. While the Second World War (1939–45) is generally seen as the watershed, in fact the seeds of change were sown in the late 1930s, above all by Malcolm MacDonald during his tenure as colonial secretary from May 1938–May 1940. Until then, the Colonial Office "did not appear to possess anything," as Sir Ralph Furse put it, "which you could call a general policy."[32] It was administered rather than governed. Decisions were left to the men on the ground, the colonial governors who were responsible directly to the King or, in 1959, to the Queen. They lived in drafty palaces and mouldy castles (always known as "Government House") (see figure 20). On ceremonial occasions they donned their tall, cocked hats bedecked with swan plumes (£20, Moss Bros., London) (see figure 18) and toured their domains to the accompaniment of smart brass bands. Governors were "monarchs, prime ministers, judges rolled into one."[33] As long as they stayed within budget and kept the peace, all was well.

In 1939 the Empire was at its zenith, embracing nearly one-fourth of the world's population. But there were warning signals. Disturbances broke out on the Northern Rhodesia Copperbelt in 1935 and again in 1940; in 1937 a massive holdup of cocoa deliveries threatened the Gold Coast economy; two years of rioting brought chaos to the West Indies, Britain's oldest tropical dependency; finally, there were reports of serious malnutrition in Kenya. The Moyne Commission, appointed by Parliament to look into social and economic conditions in the Caribbean, painted a grim picture. Its findings seemed to vindicate the few critics of Empire such as W. M. Macmillan and Leonard Woolf. The former prime minister, Lloyd George, was "perfectly appalled at the conditions" in the West Indies and ashamed that this "slummy empire" had been tolerated.[34]

MacDonald determined to wake the Colonial Office out of its complacency, to reform a system of governance damned by one peer as "lethargy tempered by riots."[35] First, he opened the ranks of the Colonial Service to women, although there is no record that a woman served as a district officer (they did serve in the secretariats as well as in various specialized branches). Then, even more radically, he pushed the CO to take an active role "as the head and ruler of its empire, where policy would be formulated and imposed."[36] He called into question the assumptions of minimal intervention, implicit in the Lugardian model of indirect rule and territorial autonomy. To the extent that Britain had any policy, it had been summed up in the notion of "trusteeship," but this had always been left deliberately vague—"a quasi-theological doctrine," which, "as with the Trinity, it was tantamount to heresy to reduce ... to comprehensible dimensions."[37] MacDonald called the bluff, insisting that trusteeship was meaningless without an active policy of social and economic development, financed not by native treasuries but by the imperial government. Hitherto, neither the British Treasury nor private capital had shown any interest in investing in most of the colonies, so that public works had to be financed through private borrowing, to be repaid from meager colonial revenues. As a result most colonies were still the "undeveloped estates"[38] they had been during Joseph Chamberlain's tenure at the Colonial Office almost half a century earlier. MacDonald's greatest achievement was the passage late in 1940 of the Colonial Development and Welfare Act. For the first time, Britain accepted responsibility for the economic and social conditions in her colonies. The Act provided £5 million per year, initially for ten years. A historian of the Colonial Service refers to the measure as "a fine act of faith in days darkened by Dunkirk, when the blitzkrieg was on us and our very existence hung in the balance."[39]

It may have been an act of inspired expediency as well. Great Britain was fighting for her life and hugely dependent on her colonies for men, materials, and credits. In the 1930s, a disgruntled voice in the Commons had asked, "What is it for?," referring to the colonial empire.[40] Now he had his answer. Of necessity, the war put colonial development on hold, but it did force other equally important issues to the fore. Britain's American allies did not like the idea that they were fighting Nazi imperialism only to maintain another empire, conveniently forgetting that they had an imperial history of their own. When Roosevelt and Churchill signed the Atlantic Charter in August 1941, declaring that their countries respected "the right of all people to choose the form of government under which they will live," it caught the Colonial Office off guard. Surely, Churchill had not been thinking of *his* empire but only of nations under Nazi domination—Did the colonial millions really have a right to choose their own form of government? Only the year before, Churchill had articulated his dream that the British Empire would last a thousand years (a dream that sounded uncomfortably like that of Hitler's thousand-year *Reich*). Roosevelt's hatred of imperialism was heightened by a visit to the Gambia that he recalled as "the most horrible thing I've seen in my life.... Disease is rampant.... For every dollar the British, who have been there for two hundred years, have put into Gambia, they have taken out ten."[41]

In fact, except in the case of the Indian sub-continent (which did not fall within the purview of the Colonial Office), no one in the British government had given much thought to the endpoint of colonialism, when the White Man might lay down his Burden and under what conditions. There seemed to be a general sense that imperial rule would go on for an "indefinite time ahead," if not forever. Malcolm MacDonald had spoken vaguely in terms of "generations, perhaps even centuries."[42] Even Margery Perham, who *had* given it some thought and had proposed ways to make native government more responsible, assumed that there was plenty of time and that independence, while it must surely come some day, was "very distant."[43] After much wrangling among the Allies—the Soviets also weighed in against imperialism—the British government committed itself to eventual self-government (avoiding the word "independence") for its colonies, persuading itself that this had been its intent all along. Left for later were the definition of "self-government" and a timetable for its achievement. This and the new policy of development were enough to satisfy the Americans, especially as the war went on and they began to cast their own covetous eyes on some of the Japanese islands in the Pacific. Privately, Churchill instructed his foreign secretary: "Hands off the British Empire is our maxim and it must not be weakened or smirched to please the sob-stuff merchants at home or foreigners of any hue."[44]

Churchill's bravado notwithstanding, the loss of much of her Empire in southeast Asia to the Japanese, culminating in the fall of Singapore in 1942, had a devastating effect in Great Britain. It burst the bubble of imperial invulnerability. In the end, she regained her lost territories but never her sense of imperial mission. As one historian has commented, World War II brought about "what may be described as a complete change of heart on the part of the ruling race. The cult of 'Imperialism' was almost wholly extinguished; what had once been a high-minded political doctrine passed into a term of vulgar reproach. Britain, to all appearances had lost all sense of pride in her Imperial position.... The task of empire had come to be regarded as an incubus rather than an obligation."[45]

Margery Perham expressed a similar view. Shaken by Britain's near defeat in the war, she acknowledged in 1948 that "the age of confidence and power has passed and it has been very brief as the history of Empire goes."[46] In *Major Dane's Garden* she had put an irreverent theory of empire into the mouth of one of her favorite characters, the Irishman Rankin. "It's not enterprise or genius for organization that holds your Empire together," he exclaims,

> it's dressing for dinner in the Solomon Islands, and playing football in Southern Nigeria, and talking scandal in the club at Baluchistan, that's what's done the trick; and you'll be all right so long as you don't stop for a moment to think what you are doing. You can go on glutting yourself upon a quarter of the world. See how patiently Africa bears with you, like a huge elephant at the prick of the goad. There's no law here either of reward or retribution.[47]

But people were stopping to think what they were doing and the elephant was showing signs of impatience.

The task of defining and re-orienting postwar colonial policy in Africa fell largely to two men, one a career civil servant, the other a politician. On the surface, Andrew Cohen and Arthur Creech Jones were an odd couple. Cohen, the burly giant, brilliant, charming, wildly energetic, descended on his father's side from a prominent Jewish business background, on his mother's from a radical Unitarianism. He graduated from Cambridge with a double first in classics, more than a little snobbery, and a healthy dose of romanticism. As a younger son, he could not inherit from his father but he preferred anyway to aim higher, to carve out a career in government as a "Platonic philosopher-king,"[48] no less.

Creech Jones was the son of a journeyman printer in Bristol with no particular advantages of birth or endowment. A scholarship boy at his preparatory school, most of his further education came during his two-and-a-half year imprisonment for opposition to military conscription during World War I. Like so many "political prisoners" before and after (including Kenneth Kaunda), he used the time for self-reflection and for reading voraciously in history, politics, and economics. After the war, he gradually made his way into politics through the trade union movement, specializing more and more in colonial questions. As a boy he had been horrified by the atrocities committed by the Belgians in the Congo and deeply impressed by the determination of E.D. Morel and Roger Casement to expose them. As a trade unionist, he responded to the struggles of African workers in South Africa. So frequently did he raise questions on imperial topics in Parliament that he was dubbed the "unofficial member of the Kikuyu at Westminster."[49] Somewhat shy and self-effacing, he lacked Cohen's overwhelming presence and sense of heroic mission but shared his passion for colonial improvement, his energy and persistence, and above all his "colour-blindness" in matters of race.

In 1943 Creech Jones became chair of the Labour Party's advisory committee on imperial questions. Three years earlier he and Dr. Rita Hinden had founded the Fabian Colonial Bureau, dedicated to working on behalf of colonial peoples and providing information for government policy (surprisingly little was available). When Labour came to power in 1945 at the end of the war, Prime Minister Clement Atlee grudgingly appointed Creech Jones as undersecretary, then secretary of state for the colonies. The fact that Atlee could not even spell his name correctly says something about the antipathy between the two men. At bottom, Atlee had little interest in colonial affairs and couldn't fathom his colleague's enthusiasms—understandable, perhaps, in a postwar Britain facing terrible shortages of food and fuel and desperate balance of payment problems, a "financial Dunkirk."[50] When Creech Jones lost his seat in the general election of 1950, it would have been easy to find him a safe seat in the next by-election, but this was not done, nor was he given the peerage customary in such cases. Nevertheless, in his brief tenure Creech Jones joined forces with Cohen to engineer a revolution that provided nothing less than a blueprint for the end of empire in Africa. How did this happen?

After a dreary year at the Board of Inland Revenue, Cohen was rescued in 1933 by an influential family friend and transferred to the more congenial Colonial Office with its large contingent of fellow-classicists; his absorption with African affairs was largely serendipitous—"Africa had become his life by chance."[51] On his first visit to Africa in 1937, he was dismayed by the reality of "trusteeship." In Northern Rhodesia, for example, colonial rule and the wealth of the copper industry seemed to have done little for the African population. This was to be his yardstick: that colonial rule could only be justified by the degree to which it advanced native interests. Cohen was also appalled by the unofficial color bar he encountered in Rhodesia and Kenya, and took time out to visit the United States in hopes of finding a solution to the problem of race. Unfortunately, the United States had little to teach him.

Cohen's visit to the United States was cut short by the outbreak of World War II. He was soon sent to the colony of Malta in the Mediterranean to organize civilian supplies during the long siege of the island. "It was," as his biographer notes, "his first taste of power (for which he was voracious), in an embattled Government organizing a society to meet an emergency."[52] The experience left him with "a towering impatience to cut red tape" and the Fabian socialist's conviction that it was the "duty of the state to improve the social order."[53] For all his driving ambition, Cohen had an appealingly distracted side. During his tenure in Malta, dockyard workers became so disgruntled with the bad food they were expected to eat that they sent their leader to meet personally with Cohen (then acting as lieutenant governor). Beforehand Cohen was sent a piece of mouldy bread that had been served at the workers' canteen as Exhibit A. When the angry leader arrived, the primary evidence had disappeared. Cohen had absent-mindedly eaten it.

By the time Creech Jones took office, Cohen was back in the CO and had risen to be the key man in the African division. His official title was assistant under-secretary in charge of the African Division, but he was generally known by the less formal title "King of Africa."[54] Both men believed that the Lugardian doctrine of indirect rule was a "relic of reactionary imperialism,"[55] fossilizing the status quo and enshrining tribalism. As Lord Hailey had pointed out with his customary understatement, "The principles of indirect rule, if not incompatible with the ideal of self-government by representative institutions, are at all events so far alien to it as to suggest that native institutions must be materially modified if they are to fit into any scheme involving an elected parliament."[56] With the war finally over, it was indeed time for Whitehall to take command and to chart an entirely new course for Africa as a whole, rather than leaving decisions to individual governors. While his boss was beset with a host of problems in Palestine, Cohen, the philosopher-king, mapped out a comprehensive plan to develop colonial Africa socially, economically, and politically. Its endpoint would be nothing less than self-government, the transfer of power from Great Britain to her colonies.

The Local Government Despatch of February 1947 informed the colonial governors that the old system based on supposedly traditional African structures was incapable of adapting to the needs of the nation-state, above all its modernizing agenda. "The modern conception of colonial administration," the Despatch insisted, required a "democratic system of local government."[57] Where was the model to be found? Why, in the English system with its complex pyramid of power from local to national, from town clerk to prime minister. Change would come about in four stages, allowing for different conditions in the various African territories and the need to give people time to learn the arts of government; the sequence would be the same for each, but the timetable would vary. Local authorities would be directly elected and these in turn would elect the legislative councils. Gradually, Africans would gain a majority of seats on the legislative councils and be brought into ministerial positions. In the final stages, a presumably sophisticated electorate would elect the national assembly by universal franchise, leading to a full-fledged parliamentary system on the Westminster model. In some cases, this might happen within a generation, in others it would take longer. Ironically, this developmental scheme was derived from settler colonies such as Kenya and Northern Rhodesia where Europeans were only part way up the ladder to self-government by 1947 and Africans had barely begun the climb at all.

Crucial to the plan were the new educated African elites who had been frozen out of the system of indirect rule because of its reliance on traditional elites. For Creech Jones and Cohen, educated Africans (that is, Western educated Africans), not chiefs, were to be the cornerstone of local government. Furthermore, even under the pressures of domestic austerity in the immediate postwar years, the Labour Government was committed to expanding the Colonial Development and Welfare Act, and development most assuredly required local initiative and local know-how: "Development from above can only ever make limited progress. It must come in addition from below."[58] Creech Jones and Cohen had little faith that the existing Native Authorities were capable of the planning and execution required. Education on all levels, technical, administrative, political, was therefore a top priority so that Africans could gradually replace not only the chiefs but also in due time the cadres of European officials and specialists who were themselves multiplying with the postwar emphasis on welfare and development.

The 1947 Local Government Despatch and the follow-up Report were not a response to nationalism, at least not African nationalism—at this moment it was barely visible, even in West African colonies such as the Gold Coast and Nigeria that boasted much larger communities of well-educated and articulate Africans than East and Central Africa. With an eye to newly independent India, however, Cohen and Creech Jones realized that nationalism *would* come to Africa and that it would be fostered by the very expansion of education they envisioned. Indeed, nationalism was preferable to the tribalism inherent in indirect rule since the goal, after all, was nationhood. The problem was to stay in front of the pitch: to guide the Empire toward a peaceful demise and ensure that the successor states would continue to be friendly and loyal trading partners. The virtue of the local government plan was that it would force future nationalist leaders to court rural populations because under the system of indirect election, they could not gain power on the basis of urban support alone. The scheme therefore accelerated political development at the same time that it put the brakes on nationalism. Creech Jones and Cohen knew they were in a race against time, but surely they had at least a generation to guide their charges through their crash-course in democracy, English-style.

Africans, of course, were not consulted about the far-reaching changes of which they were to be the chief beneficiaries. Nor were colonial governors, although several conferences were arranged to brief officials at various levels and to solicit their comments on what was presented as no more than a draft report. But much as Cohen and Creech Jones might protest—too much?—that the 1947 proposals really did not mark a revolutionary break with the past but were the logical and historical next step toward indirect rule, many of the older generation of governors did not buy it. Some argued that the plan was woefully out of step with African realities, that Africans were not ready to move to self-government in the foreseeable future. Others argued that it was wrong to impose an alien system of government on Africa, however well it might serve

England; still others maintained that the pace of change was simply too fast. One governor worried that "democracy is not a patent medicine. Democratic institutions improperly understood and badly handled may become perverted."[59] Nevertheless he supported the policy because it could serve to check any headlong rush to independence. The governor of Nigeria, however, objected that Africanization would corrupt administration at every level. Cohen retorted that "self-government is better than good colonial government,"[60] a sentiment shared by critics who were impatient with the slow pace of change hitherto. As one left-wing MP insisted, "The colonial peoples do not desire Britain to be good to them. They desire freedom to decide their own good."[61]

So great was the governors' resistance that details of the plan were never made public. At the 1948 Africa Conference, Creech Jones felt obliged to limit himself to discussing generalities about creating "conditions of free nationhood and societies that are responsible and democratic." Lamely, he reassured the Conference that "there is … a plan. We know what we are doing. We are not fumbling, we are organising things at this end to help. We are making great demands on you, but do believe that we have some conception of the overall picture, the kind of thing we want to reach."[62]

In the end, however, officers in the field had the last word; they could make or break a policy. "Theory in Whitehall and practice in Northern Rhodesia were as opposite poles," Harry Franklin observed, "which yet attract each other and so maintain an invisible current which runs uselessly round and round for ever unless directed to a practical task by interested electricians."[63] The district officers were the electricians. Indirect rule may well have been abandoned by Whitehall in 1947. It was not necessarily abandoned on the peripheries of empire.

Indirect rule had been tailor-made for Barotseland. As hierarchical and confident as the Fulani emirates of Northern Nigeria that inspired Lugard's blueprint, Lozi chiefs slipped easily and mostly comfortably into their imperial role. When Governor Arthur Benson toured Barotseland in August 1957, it was an altogether happy experience. The fishing was superb, and he felt at home not only with his old friend from Oxford days, Resident Commissioner Glyn Jones, but with the indigenous system of government. Benson was a conservative, regarded as "old fashioned in his respect for the chiefly system and its longer term significance."[64] He heartily approved of a paramount chief who received distinguished British guests in top hat and tail-coat of Victorian vintage. As his private secretary commented, the visit provided "justification of all his pet theories about indirect rule and the vital importance of the chiefs

in British colonial rule." He approved equally of Glyn Jones as "the epit-
ome of a relaxed colonial paladin, in complete and comfortable control
to his province and on excellent terms with the traditional chiefs."[65]
From the commissioner's magnificent new residence high on a bluff in
Mongu, Benson had a splendid view out over the Zambezi floodplain.
And he saw everything that the British had made, and, behold, it was very
good. This was the way things should be and the proof of its rightness was
the absence of political agitation in the province.

Two years later, in 1959, the governor still seems bewildered that his
countrymen with their own loyalty to the Queen "are so slow to understand that the indigenous people of tropical and sub-tropical Africa
found their focus and continue to find their focus in the persons of their
Chiefs, and in their chiefly institutions which we have today in
Northern Rhodesia.... It is the Chief," he insists, "who, in African religion, holds in his person the entire spiritual welfare of the tribe, and
therefore its material welfare."[66] No wonder he has little sympathy
for African nationalists (or democratic enthusiasts in Whitehall). What
spiritual sanction could Kenneth Kaunda claim?

In fact, there was no noticeable impact of the 1947 Local Government
Despatch in Barotseland. That same year the provincial commissioner had
on his own initiative pushed *litunga* Imwiko to revive the long-dormant
Katengo Council as a more popular counterweight to the National
Council (*kuta*). It consisted of five representatives from each of the five
districts in Barotseland. The first members were appointed by the local
kutas in consultation with the DCs. Thereafter one of the five would retire
each year and be replaced by a member elected by universal male (and in
Senanga District, female) suffrage, with secret ballot. Normally it met
once a year, debated motions, and raised questions, to be passed on to the
National Council for consideration. Five of the Katengo councillors were
allowed to take part in that body's deliberations. In practice, the Katengo
was toothless; it had only advisory power and was to all intents and pur-
poses dominated by the *ngambela* who could veto any of its actions. Even
so, it was resented by the *indunas,* the hereditary elites, as elections increasingly favored ambitious teachers and clerks. In Kalabo District the DC
was unimpressed with the calibre of men elected and the domination of
the larger *kutas*. People tended to vote for the local candidate, whoever he
was. Nevertheless, the DC hoped, without much conviction, that the
experience would prove "a useful introduction to the electoral system."[67]

Ignored by the national *kuta,* forbidden by the provincial commissioner
to discuss political matters of any significance or to express hostility to
Europeans, the Katengo in the end satisfied no one. Far from proving a

training ground in grassroots democracy, it heightened conflict between the local intelligentsia and the traditional elite, and turned both against the colonial administration.

The pyramid of representative bodies created by the Northern Rhodesian government fared little better. At its base were councils formed in urban areas just before World War II to enable DCs to keep in closer touch with African populations lest they become "detribalized," a chronic fear in an administrative system that took tribal units and identities as a given. Immediately after the war with much prodding by Stewart Gore-Browne provincial councils were set up, embracing both rural and urban populations. The provincial councils nominated 25 representatives to the territory-wide African Representative Council, with four more appointed directly by the paramount chief of Barotseland in acknowledgment of the region's special status. By the early 1950s the territory-wide council elected two African members for Legco, the Legislative Council. It was a very indirect system, always under the thumb of colonial officials, and relying on appointment rather than election at the primary level. Like the Lozi Katengo, the councils were strictly advisory, serving, as one historian, writes, rather like "a formalised *indaba*,"[68] an indigenous assembly of adult males. Even so, *litunga* Mwanawina was so suspicious of the African Representative Council that he instructed the Lozi delegates to play a purely passive role.

The *litunga* was quite right to see the councils as a veiled challenge to the "hallowed doctrine of indirect rule."[69] At the same time they looked like nothing to be seen in England. Nevertheless, for all the checks on their authority, it was impossible to insulate them from the political currents. Kaunda had gained a seat on the council of Western Province when he was living on the Copperbelt, and in 1951 the two Africans elected to the Legislative Council belonged to the ANC. At all levels, the councils voiced their opposition to the impending Federation of Rhodesia and Nyasaland. Members could not understand why, having brought them into existence, the British government could so blithely ignore their sentiments. As a representative warned in 1953:

> … in the past we have had the Secretary of State for the Colonies as our guardian in every sense of the word, but once we realize that we are not regarded as a protectorate any more everyone is likely to do his own will. Even fowls, if you have kept a crate of fowls, and they are not looked after, they will scatter. To those who are underestimating us by saying "What can they do, it does not matter", I can assure them that even to collect those fowls again it will cost

time and money. Sir, I say that if four men have walked away from the law, the Government will have to send ten askaris [soldiers] to see what is happening.[70]

One can understand his sense of betrayal. The Colonial Office, in African eyes, was supposed to buffer them from the domination of European minorities. In 1923 the then secretary of state for the colonies, Lord Devonshire, declared apropos of Kenya that as far as His Majesty's Government was concerned, "the interests of the African natives must be paramount, and that if and when those interests and the interests of the immigrant races should conflict, the former should prevail." "The Government," he explained "regard themselves as exercising a trust on behalf of the African population ... the object of which may be defined as the protection and advancement of the native races."[71] This doctrine of "paramountcy" was extended by Lord Passfield (Sydney Webb, of Fabian fame) in 1930 to cover all settler colonies. At the time it created a furor among Northern Rhodesian whites until they saw that governors were largely ignoring it.

Creech Jones of course realized that colonies such as Northern Rhodesia with sizeable European populations posed a particular problem in any attempt to impose a uniform colonial policy on Africa. For these settlers, progression to self-government was synonymous with white self-government of the kind Southern Rhodesia had enjoyed since 1923. This was not at all what the framers of the Local Government Despatch had in mind, and yet the secretary of state had vetoed amalgamation but suggested federation as an alternative. Why?

When Creech Jones toured Northern Rhodesia in 1949, he saw firsthand how profound was African distrust of Southern Rhodesia and of Federation. He assured Africans that the British government would do nothing without consulting them fully: "We shall honour the responsibilities we have entered into."[72] In other words he reiterated traditional policy. Behind the scenes, Andrew Cohen argued that with the right sort of constitutional protections federation could co-exist with his masterplan of gradual democratization from below. He seems to have believed, "naively," as his biographer comments, "that better constitutions can improve human nature. By conceding considerable local authority to the white minority he hoped at best to persuade them to share power with the black majority; at worst, to stop the spread of apartheid from South Africa into the British dependencies. It seemed better to Cohen to make sure of half a loaf of political rights for Africans now than to wait for the settlers' repeatedly threatened unilateral declaration of independence which would leave the Africans with none."[73]

The Nationalist victory in South Africa in 1948 had indeed cast a long shadow. Godfrey Huggins and Roy Welensky knew well how to play on the fear that Southern Rhodesia would look southward if the Colonial Office blocked any closer union with the northern territories. Cohen persuaded his Labour colleagues to accept federation, trusting all too much in the reassurances offered to Africans. Possibly he believed the talk of "partnership" emanating from Salisbury, a term shrewdly lifted from Creech Jones's own speeches about the new relationship to be forged with native peoples. Ultimately he succeeded in selling the idea of federation because all the affected parties—except the Africans— could fit it into their own particular Procrustean beds. The governing elite of Southern Rhodesia would get their hands on the mineral wealth of the Copperbelt and enjoy a larger stage for their political ambitions. Cohen counted on federation to strengthen this elite and enable it to sell more liberal racial policies to its diehard white electorate. The British treasury looked with relief to the ending of annual subsidies to keep the poverty-stricken Nyasaland afloat. The government of Nyasaland, ruling over more Africans than either of the other territories, saw in federation the likelihood that more money would become available for development, leaving the colony less dependent on migrant labor. White settlers in both Nyasaland and Northern Rhodesia wanted to shake off colonial rule and "join a club which would make them feel less of an isolated minority and seemed to guarantee them a place in central Africa for ever."[74] The most reluctant party to the match was the colonial government of Northern Rhodesia which wondered how it would be able to continue to safeguard African rights. Ironically, Creech Jones began to distance himself more and more from federation as the mantra of "partnership" became more strident and less believable. In the end, he and his fellow Fabians were its most outspoken opponents.

By the time federation took final shape, however, he had lost his seat in Parliament, Labour was out of office, and Cohen had been "exiled" to Uganda. The new Conservative colonial secretary, Oliver Lyttelton, was a Tory of the old school with a belief in Empire that was not universally shared even in his own party. He dismissed African opposition to federation as the grumbling of a few malcontents. How could the mass of illiterate Africans object, he argued, to something for which their languages had no word? He worried much more that the Southern Rhodesian (white) electorate might prefer union with South Africa or independence as a separate state. To win them over, he was willing to scale back the original provisions for African representation in the federal legislature and on the African Affairs Board, which had the power to refer any federal laws it considered discriminatory to London It was enough to satisfy the Rhodesian prime minister, Godfrey Huggins, although he grumbled that the African Affairs Board was "a frightful waste of money and manpower . . . a little piece of Gilbert and Sullivan." Huggins assured his constituents that they need not trouble themselves about British mutterings about the primacy of African interests, explaining that the British "suffer from a kind of unctuous rectitude and apparent hypocrisy which is disliked by foreigners and their overseas kinsmen."[75] Perhaps he was particularly annoyed by the "grave doubts" expressed by the Archbishop of Canterbury in the House of Lords debate about federation, and the prelate's "anxiety for a good long time to come to know how in fact it will work out."[76]

Colonial Service officers in the field were informed about federation by circular letter. One DC, Robin Short, refused to disguise his bitterness that the British government had totally ignored reports from its "men on the spot." He branded federation a "gigantic miscalculation which worked against the unanimous opposition of the complete African population."[77] When the British Cabinet approved it on March 24, 1953, "it was as though a great tree had fallen. True imperialism had crashed to the ground, to give place to something different. What it was time would tell, but it was not what we had known and served. Economics had been preferred to human beings."[78] He and many of his fellows had "the tact and decency . . . to refrain from publishing or even mentioning those offending documents."[79] What purpose could it serve other than to play into the hands of agitators? He rejected Colonial Office arguments that without federation, Southern Rhodesia would be thrown into the arms of South Africa, insisting that there were plenty of other means to ward off "Dr. Malan [the South African prime minister] on the Zambezi."[80] Real partnership Short approved of, but it would always be a sham in the federation as presently constituted.

In the face of such sentiments, it is not surprising that Welensky blamed colonial officers for generating needless fears in the African population. Had they supported federation, it would have been enough to reassure Africans since the officers stood in the position of "mother and father"[81] to the natives. Instead, it became a pitched battle: White settlers railed against "upper class civil servants with Oxford accents and 'Thirds' from Balliol" who posed as "the African's chosen champions."[82] Officials for their part harped on settlers' "immaturity" and the perils of entrusting political power to a small, self-interested clique. No other event threw into sharper relief the "chameleon effect,"[83] the tendency of colonial officers to identify fiercely with the interests of their colonies. Trusteeship was no idle word.

In letters to the *Times,* Margery Perham also warned of the likely consequences of federation. She was not ready to buy the "kith and kin" argument—that Britain's first loyalty was to the white settlers with whom she shared blood and heritage. She bristled at Welensky's recent references to imperial restrictions as "museum pieces" of "little moment"[84]; on the contrary, if the British government waffled on its obligations, "we risk losing the greatest asset we have in the continent—the confidence of Africans."[85] To those who maintained that Africans were incapable of understanding the issues, she responded that although "this may well be true of the actual Federation proposals, ... they can distinguish clearly between the relatively disinterested rule of a distant imperial Government and that of the local white community whose position in some vital matters conflicts with their present interests and future hopes." Africans also see through the seductions of economic benefits: "People who feel their human dignity injured cannot be soothed by material palliatives."[86] South Africa provided evidence enough of that.

Opponents of federation did not propose "either that the Africans are now ready to play their full part in a democratic government or that the Europeans are politically inferior to themselves. It is just because Africans are politically unready that power over them should not be transferred to a group of people who, however high their individual merit, together represent a small racial minority of employers and large landowners."[87] Perham was far too aware of the tumult beginning to bubble up in other parts of the continent not to foresee that a federation dominated by the white minority could catalyse similar movements where they did not now exist. "The risk of disorder is one that no one can estimate .... It is not inconceivable," she cautioned, "that something very like the Ulster dilemma might emerge in Central Africa."[88] Since one day power must inevitably pass to the "immense African majority,"[89] it was for the British government to decide whether this happened peacefully or through violence.

Perham was prescient on both counts. British support for federation did cost her the loyalty of her Central African subjects and before long it did lead to just the violence and repression she hoped could be avoided. The last shred of loyalty evaporated in 1957 with the passage of the Constitution Amendment and the Federal Franchise Bills whose combined effect was to devalue African representation in the Federal Assembly and guarantee that the white minority could take the

Federation in any direction it wanted when the appointed time came for review in 1960. For the first and last time, the African Affairs Board, a standing committee of the Federal Assembly that served as the protector of African interests under the federal constitution, used its right of appeal to the British Parliament to block the bills. After a lengthy debate, the Conservative government easily won the vote, thereby declining to set aside the actions. Conservatives accepted the argument that because the enlarged assembly would contain more Africans than its smaller predecessor, it meant an advance for Africans. As the commonwealth secretary explained: "The Federal government did let more Africans in on the act; not enough in our view, but they made progress; and so we did make some concessions."[90] He glossed over the fact that under the complicated system of separate electoral rolls, most of the new Africans would be entirely dependent on European votes and that they would still be less than a fifth of the total. John Moffat, the chairman of the Board, resigned in anger. The Board ceased to exist in anything but name and with it ended any faith in Whitehall on the part of moderate Africans.

Governor Benson of Northern Rhodesia was just as troubled and considered resigning himself. Upon receiving a telegram announcing the British government's decision, his "reaction was one of absolute profound shock. I was shattered by it. It seemed to me that that was probably the end of Federation."[91] As he wrote an old friend in the Colonial Office, "You know it is wrong and I know it is wrong and what is more our masters know that it is wrong. But they don't give a damn."[92] Benson had good reason to feel betrayed. He had been a fervent believer in federation even before he moved into Government House in 1954, advising Huggins that dominion status was a sure bet if he would only woo Africans with the promise of genuine partnership. Huggins, and Welensky after him, ignored his advice. Their dominion was going to be a white one, pure and simple; the only Africans allowed in the door would be a hand-picked few from the minute indigenous bourgeoisie. When Benson protested their policies to the colonial secretary, Alan Lennox-Boyd, in 1956, his secret memorandum was not just ignored, it was leaked to the Commonwealth Relations Office and thence to Benson's adversaries in the federal government who exploited it in their campaign against meddling by colonial administrators. Lennox-Boyd's sympathies were, in fact, entirely with Welensky, so much so that when he toured the region in the opening days of 1957, he announced that federation had come to stay. "It is good for you," he told Africans, "and you must accept it."[93] On his way back to London, he declared at a press conference in Johannesburg: "I met many settlers who, if anything, have more right to live in the Rhodesias and Nyasaland than many of the Africans."[94] Not surprisingly, Welensky approved of the Colonial Secretary: "I liked and trusted Lennox-Boyd."[95] Not a comment he would ever make about Benson.

Caught between the intransigence of European politicians in both Salisbury and Lusaka, the growing militancy of African nationalism, and a Colonial Secretary with his head in the sand, Governor Benson was in an impossible position even before his ill-fated constitutional revisions for Northern Rhodesia saw the light of day.

1959. Constitution-crafting has been overtaken by events. Ironically, from Whitehall's perspective, while all eyes have been focused on the Northern Rhodesian constitution and the upcoming review of the Federation, Nyasaland, the poor relation, is suddenly upstaging the other players and forcing the pace of change. The reverberations will in time be felt in the farthest reaches of Barotseland along with the rest of Central Africa.

Just before returning to Nyasaland after an absence of 42 years (in South Africa, the United States, the United Kingdom, and, most recently, Ghana), Dr. Hastings Kamuzu Banda warns Lennox-Boyd, the colonial secretary, "I go back to break up your bloody Federation." Lennox-Boyd in his turn warns Banda, "This may very well end in your detention."[96] Both have carried through on their threats. Attired in a business suit draped with the skin of a civet cat, Banda lands at the Chileka airdrome on July 6, 1958 to a tumultuous welcome. He is hailed as "our Mahatma," "our Messiah," the "Saviour" who will lead his people out of bondage. His return galvanizes the Nyasaland African National Congress; enormous crowds turn out to meet him although, paradoxically, the messiah has been in exile so long he does not speak Chinyanja, the *lingua franca* of the country, and everything he says has to be translated. Demands mount for an end to alien rule—and an end to forced compliance with government anti-erosion and veterinary regulations (which seem equally oppressive to the largely agrarian population). At the same time, the rhetoric of his more incendiary followers turns menacingly anti-federation and anti-European. Banda himself disavows violence and blanket condemnations of Europeans. It is politicians and supporters of federation, "the politicians at Zomba," who are the enemy, not civil servants or even police. In other speeches he insists that "white men ... are our friends some of them, and some of them are very good and very nice."[97]

In negotiations with the territorial administration, he makes it clear that Congress will accept nothing less than an African majority in the Legislative Council. His strategy is to force a showdown, defying the government by holding more and more meetings without obtaining the required permit—not that he could have complied with the letter of the law in any case, since many of the meetings are spontaneous outbursts rather than planned assemblies. Still, the Nyasaland government hesitates to use more than minimal force against increasingly violent protesters or to oblige Banda with the arrest he seems to be courting ("interesting," notes one observer "that the Europeans always claim that Africans use violence whereas they use force.")[98] Under pressure from Welensky to declare a state of emergency, Governor Armitage holds firm. He counts on new constitutional proposals due any moment from Whitehall to keep the pot from boiling over.

Then abruptly the governor blinks. He gives in to Welensky and calls in federal troops (that is, European Territorials from Southern Rhodesia) to help keep order. Banda can now claim with some justification that "the government of this country is only a puppet in the hands of the European settlers of Southern Rhodesia."[99] He refuses any longer to condemn violence. Angry demonstrations escalate throughout the country, security forces retaliate with gunfire and the first Africans are killed. The governor requests that Lord Perth postpone his visit and declares the state of emergency so fervently desired by Welensky. In the pre-dawn of March 3, 1959, four hours after the declaration, security forces carry out "Operation Sunrise," arresting hundreds of African National Congress leaders, including Banda. Over the next few months some 1,346 Africans are detained, not the 180 Armitage had initially announced. It is getting harder to dismiss the nationalists as an unrepresentative minority of trouble makers when they include the most highly educated and articulate members of the territory, including 34 of the 35 Nyasalanders with university degrees. Banda himself is spirited away to a prison in Gwelo, Southern Rhodesia, and the other main leaders are jailed outside the territory.

To the House of Commons, Lennox-Boyd justifies the state of emergency with the revelation that he himself has "seen information that made it clear that plans had been made by Congress to carry out widespread violence and murder of Europeans, Asians and moderate African leaders; that in fact, a massacre was being planned."[100] His deputy, Julian Amery goes even farther, conjuring up images of Mau Mau and warning ominously of a "bloodbath."[101] Governor Armitage is stunned, having made no mention of a massacre or murder plot in his announcement of the emergency; his aim is simply to put an end to the disturbances and shield African civil servants against possible reprisals. Europeans he considers quite capable of looking out for themselves.

Not surprisingly, the arrests touch off further waves of disturbances; it becomes impossible to distinguish between acts of legitimate protest and opportunistic hooliganism. All told, 51 Africans are killed by security forces, most of them by gunfire, a few by bayonet or baton. At least 79 are wounded—the exact number is not known because some are afraid to request medical treatment for fear of arrest. Half a dozen Europeans and Africans are injured by protesters, several seriously. The severity of the reaction and the apparent brutality of the security forces immediately provokes an outcry in Great Britain. Why were federal troops dispatched? Why were so many Africans killed in political demonstrations? It does seem odd that the governor of Nyasaland and the colonial secretary are telling two different stories about the events leading up to the Emergency and the resort to violent repression.

Prime Minister Macmillan is forced to calm the storm by appointing a commission of inquiry, headed by the respected Conservative jurist, Patrick Devlin. The commission immediately spends five strenuous weeks in Nyasaland, hearing evidence from almost 2,000 witnesses. It combs through a mountain of memoranda and government documents. In record time, it presents its draft report to the British government. Even though the commission vindicates the state of emergency, its findings are damning. It condemns the police and security forces for using unnecessary force and for the punitive spirit in which houses have been burned, ordinary farm implements confiscated, and assemblages dispersed by any means necessary.

Its harshest comment comes on the very first page, explaining why all of the commission's interviews had to be conducted in private: "Nyasaland is—no doubt only temporarily—a police state, where it is not safe for anyone to express approval of the policies of the Congress party, to which before 3rd March 1959 the vast majority of politically-minded Africans belonged, and where it is unwise to express any but the most restrained criticism of government policy."[102] The report's final sentence raises the troubling question of "whether sound administrative reasons can justify breaches of the law."[103] Above all, the report reminds the government that the core of the problem is not Banda's return to Nyasaland but its refusal to acknowledge the depth and breadth of anti-federation sentiment that even its own administrators have been warning about, Cassandra-like, for years. "Opposition to Federation was there," the commission declares, "it was deeply rooted and almost universally held."[104] Even among the chiefs, they had not been able to uncover a one who favored federation.

The prime minister is furious with the report and with Devlin. "I have … discovered," he sputters in his diary, "that he is (a) Irish—no doubt with Fenian blood that makes Irishmen anti-Government on principle. (b) A lapsed Roman Catholic. His brother is a Jesuit priest."[105] Macmillan even hints that Devlin is out for revenge because he has been passed over for Lord Chief Justice. Still, a general election is looming later in the year and damage control is a top priority; otherwise the report "may well blow this government out of office."[106] After considerable pressure, Devlin agrees to scrap the particularly critical summary lodged in appendix one but holds firm to the rest. At the same time, leading members of the government huddle at Chequers, the prime minister's country estate, to produce a "counter-blast,"[107] a dispatch issued in Governor Armitage's name and intended to undermine the credibility of the Devlin Report. To protect the colonial secretary, the hapless governor has to declare that the main reason for declaring the state of emergency was indeed the murder plot Lennox-Boyd referred to and to cite verse and chapter of a secret meeting held in the bush by extremists, which at the time he and others dismissed as little more than overheated rhetoric, reported by informers of doubtful reliability.

The Devlin Report and response to it are made public simultaneously on July 23, 1959. In the meantime, the government has had to defend itself against another equally damaging revelation. On March 3, 1959, the same day the state of emergency was declared in Nyasaland, 11 prisoners died in Hola, a camp for "hard-core" Mau Mau detainees in Kenya, and 20 others were severely injured. Initially the governor of Kenya attributed their deaths to contaminated water, but it soon became impossible to deny that they had died from beatings by warders who were forcing them to work on an irrigation project at the camp. Further, the beatings were, it turned out, part of a more general get-tough policy developed to deal with the remnants of Mau Mau who had resisted "rehabilitation" after the insurgency had been put down.

Dismay and shock over Hola and Nyasaland are not limited to the opposition party. When the two topics come up for debate on successive days in late July, no one is surprised when the fiery Labour MP Barbara Castle, "'trembling so much from anger' that she could barely articulate the facts of the case," runs through a "catalogue of incompetence and deception,"[108] showing that Hola was no aberration. Much more damaging is the intervention by Enoch Powell, a former Conservative treasury minister. Using the government's own exculpatory White Papers, he demolishes the attempt to lay the blame solely on rogue camp officials. Hola was in essence, he argued, "a great administrative disaster," and responsibility goes right up the chain of command in Kenya, to the governor himself for countenancing practices that would never be condoned in Britain. He concludes:

We cannot say, "We will have African standards in Africa, Asian standards in Asia, and perhaps British standards here at home." ... We cannot, we dare not, in Africa of all places, fall below our own highest standards of responsibility.[109]

For the first time ever, it looks as if Africa may topple a government. But Macmillan and his front-benchers prove more adroit than their Labour opponents. The final debate is deliberately scheduled to run late into the night, much too late for anything embarrassing to make it into the morning newspapers. When the vote is taken, the government carries the day, Parliament recesses, and everyone repairs to the Scottish moors for the grouse-shooting season. No one senses that "we [have] crossed a watershed."[110]

Lennox-Boyd offers to resign over Nyasaland and then again over Hola. Macmillan refuses to accept the resignation for fear his whole government will come tumbling down. Ironically, the colonial secretary has all along planned to announce his retirement from politics in early March— to become managing director of a brewery instead of an empire (his wife is an heir to the Guinness fortune). Then the string of colonial disasters strike. Macmillan insists Lennox-Boyd keep his long-term intentions to himself and brazen out the storm by standing in the general election in October. Both he and the Conservatives are returned with resounding margins, but Lennox-Boyd is no longer secretary of state for the colonies. He is translated to the House of Lords and replaced by the minister of labour, Iain Macleod.

Macleod and Lennox-Boyd, like Nkumbula and Kaunda, are a study in contrasts. The most striking thing about Lennox-Boyd is his height. At 6'5" he towers over most of the world, so much so that in early 1952 when he was second-in-command at the Colonial Office to the almost equally tall Oliver Lyttelton, Churchill transferred him to the Ministry of Transport because, he explained, "I can't have my two tallest ministers, 12 foot nine inches of you, being wasted in the same department."[111] Thanks to his wife's wealth, Lennox-Boyd can afford to entertain visitors from all corners of the Empire lavishly and does so with a disregard for color or rank that disarms his guests and shocks some of his colleagues. For Lennox-Boyd colonial affairs have been the enduring passion of his life; his five years as colonial secretary (1954–59) are "Paradise enow,"[112] the culmination of his highest aspirations.

Macleod has taken little interest in colonial questions heretofore. At the time of his appointment in October 1959, he has never set foot in a British colony and has met hardly any of the leaders with whom he will have to deal and with whom Lennox-Boyd is on such cordial, even intimate terms. His modest Chelsea flat is no match for the opulence of Chapel Street. When he does entertain, his wife does the cooking. He lacks Lennox-Boyd's gift of charming friend and foe alike; some even find him abrasive and intolerant of opposing views. He is a shortish, balding Scot with a passion for bridge that he no longer has time to indulge. But the new secretary is undeniably brilliant, a spell-binding orator, and ambitious. Not a few think he may be the next prime minister. Hola and Nyasaland have jolted him, just as they have jolted the party and the public. Unfettered with the bred-in-the-bone imperialism of his predecessor, Macleod may be just the man to rethink the leisurely transfer of power that has so long dominated Colonial Office planning. For, whatever his bluster about the Devlin Commission, Macmillan realizes that it is time to "get a move on."[113] Africa, he realizes, is "like a sleeping hippo in a pool; suddenly it gets a prod from the white man and wakes up; and it won't go to sleep again."[114] Maybe the timetable for independence will have to be scaled back to a decade rather than a generation in some of the more "mature" colonies.

Macleod cheerfully acknowledges that he knows next-to-nothing about Africa—"a very considerable advantage" since it leaves him free of "preconceived ideas."[115] He turns to academics far more than his predecessors and to other sources of information such as David Stirling, founder and head of the Capricorn Africa Society, now sadder and wiser about the "multiracialism" of the Federation. Macleod is less concerned than Lennox-Boyd that speeding up the pace of constitutional change will threaten economic development by scaring off whites and outside investment; white settlers no longer have his ear to the extent they did with his immediate predecessors. Above all, he and his allies are ready to consider African nationalist leaders as part of the solution, not simply as the problem. Perhaps he has taken to heart Margery Perham's warning that "at least north of the Zambesi and east of the Luangwa, it is too late to impose a political Kariba dam upon the flood of African nationalism."[116]

Without a precise blueprint for decolonization, he is guided by what he terms "the criterion of the lesser risk:"[117] balancing the risks of moving quickly in Africa with those of moving too slowly. If he fails, he is fully aware that the result may be terrible bloodshed. In his first speech to the Commons, he notes that "there is a state of emergency which has lasted for seven years in Kenya; there is a state of emergency which has lasted for seven months in Nyasaland; there are persons in Northern Rhodesia living in restriction by order; and there is rule in Malta by the Governor instead of by normal processes. Here clearly are my first tasks."[118]

No doubt his "criterion of the lesser risk" also applies to the home front, to the political fall-out for the Conservatives of another Hola or another report labelling a British colony a "police state." He wants to make sure there are no more skeletons lurking in the Colonial Office cupboard and is shocked by Lennox-Boyd's confidential revelations. Amused by his naiveté, the former colonial secretary replies: "Well if you can apply the canons of the cloister to a battle in tribal Africa, good luck to you."[119] At the same time Macleod is all too aware that the settler colonies have strong supporters in the Empire-wing of his own party. Partisans of federation have hired Voice and Vision, a top-drawer public relations firm, to carry out a sophisticated lobbying campaign, bankrolled by the federal government. On the other hand, the "kith and kin" colonies are no longer as monolithic as they once were. Some mining and other commercial interests see the handwriting on the wall and are beginning to hive off from the white settler-farmers and reach out to African nationalist movements as the wave of the future.

The Federal Review Conference is scheduled for 1960. Belatedly the government realizes that it has trapped itself between a rock and a hard place. It has virtually committed itself to independence for the Federation at this time or shortly after, while simultaneously pledging not to alter the protectorate status of the two northern territories without the consent of their inhabitants. In mid–March 1959, while Nyasaland is still in turmoil, Macmillan's cabinet decides on a tried and true device: the appointment of a royal commission "to dispel widespread ignorance of the purpose and working of the Federation."[120] As soon as he gets wind of it, Welensky smells a rat. All the Africans have to do, he mutters, is to riot and the British government sends out a commission to "decide whether or not they were right."[121] Its real purpose, he suspects, will be to put the Federation "on trial."[122] It will have to include Labour members, and the Labour Party by now is solidly against federation.

In the months that follow there are seemingly endless negotiations between Salisbury and London. Initially Welensky tries to talk the government out of any commission at all, then to influence its composition and whom it will talk to (no political detainees, please), and finally to insist that the topic of secession must be off-limits. Before long he comes to distrust Macmillan profoundly; he refers to one personal message from the prime minister as "soothing as cream and as sharp as a razor." Macmillan is so confident in his charm and persuasiveness, Welensky concludes, that he "succumbed to his own enchantment and believed that I was as much under the spell as he was."[123] (In his memoirs,

Macmillan more blandly insists that he "liked and respected" Welensky and that "his heart was in the right place,"[124] whatever that might mean.) Nor is Welensky happy to see Lennox-Boyd replaced by Macleod, whom he finds "a new and disconcerting opponent," "a very difficult man to get on terms with and to understand. I doubt if we ever talked the same language."[125] Nonetheless he can still count on powerful Whitehall allies such as Lord Salisbury (who dismisses Macleod as "too clever by half"[126]) and Lord Home, the commonwealth secretary. Yet again "the Colonial Office and the Commonwealth Office are at daggers drawn."[127] Grudgingly he accepts the commission when he secures a promise from Macmillan that secession of any of the territories will be a tabooed subject.

To head the commission, Macmillan turns to a "silver-tongued lawyer and skilled arbitrator,"[128] his old friend and fellow Oxonian, Lord Monckton. But the Labour Party proves as obdurate as Welensky. It refuses to participate unless secession *is* a permissible topic—or even, near-blasphemy, the liquidation of the Federation altogether. Finally Macmillan persuades Lord Shawcross, an ex-Labour minister and friend of Monckton's, to join the team by assuring him privately that the commission will be free to recommend anything it wants, not excluding secession. The prime minister is playing a dangerous game.

The commission assembles at the Victoria Falls Hotel on February 15, 1960. Its charge is to gather information "to advise the five Governments, in preparation for the 1960 Review, on the constitutional programme and framework best suited to the achievement of the objects contained in the constitution of 1953, including the Preamble."[129] Over the next three months it fans out over the Federation territories to study conditions first hand, dividing into three separate parties to maximize the amount of ground it can cover. In Northern Rhodesia both UNIP and the ANC boycott the commission, suspecting that its purpose is to whitewash the Federation and clear the way for its independence later in the year. Many of their followers are too intimidated to meet with the commissioners, but even so it is impossible to miss the depth of dissatisfaction among the African population with the Federation as now constituted.

Many district officers are pleasantly surprised by news of the commission. Tired as they are of the "bullying tone from Salisbury," they had become resigned to federation as "part of the fixed order of things, imposed in ignorance and folly, but to be lived with as a disagreeble necessity." They are just as bothered by the nationalists' threats of violence and boycotting, determined not to let "a few irresponsible, unemployed riff-raff [silence] by fear what the great mass of Africans had to say through their Chiefs and Councils." And of course, they want to put on a good show for their visitors. In Mwinilunga in the far northwest, "the Chiefs, in full ceremonial robes and head-dresses, caught the imagination of the Commissioners, and they were listened to with close attention."[130]

In Kalabo the visit of the "Monkey Men" has been preceded by the arrival of bulky packets of information sent out to everyone in the District who can read and to important people who can't, asking if they would like to give evidence. This occasions considerable interest. As the cadet notes, even in so remote a spot, the word "Federation" has become a term of abuse for many—a politicization due perhaps to the Zambia men detained in the village. The relevant third of the commission is due on March 5. All told, about 160 people will descend on the *boma,* including pilots, secretaries, etc.—thank goodness they are not spending the night—and the *mulena mbowanjikana* will be coming for the weekend along with a host of chiefs and *indunas.* The DC wants to hold a tea party and mobilizes the whole staff in a frenzy of preparation. The cadet finds it all a bit too much and the DC insufferably self-important. Much better to see the place in its normal state, not gussied up beyond all recognition. Then the DC thanks the cadet warmly for his heroic efforts and all is forgiven.

In a sense Prime Minister Macmillan has upstaged the Monckton Commission with his own trip to Africa in the opening days of 1960. Billed as the sequel to his Commonwealth tour of two years before, it actually has a different agenda, namely to signal the belated importance the continent is assuming for the Conservative government. It is the first visit ever to Africa by a British prime minister. After a somewhat rocky start in Ghana (where his most enthusiastic welcome comes from the colorful "mammies" who dominate the market: "They all seemed large, jolly, exuberant—and rich. I am told that they are all very powerful—and I can well believe it."),[131] the reception improves in Nigeria, which is looking ahead to independence later in the year.

When Macmillan lands in Salisbury, the atmosphere is frosty because of an off-the-cuff remark he made in Lagos that the people of Northern Rhodesia and Nyasaland "will be given an opportunity to decide on whether the Federation is beneficial to them,"[132] a remark quickly seized upon by the press and widely reported. To make matters worse, Lord Shawcross, the Labour recruit to the Monckton Commission, has indiscreetly told a television interviewer in Britain that he would feel quite free to advocate the break-up of the Federation if it should come to that. Welensky has hardly been mollified by a massive dose of Macmillan charm when he receives a report of a bugged conversation between the still imprisoned Banda and his British lawyer, Dingle Foot. In the secret recording, Welensky hears Foot trying to persuade Banda to give evidence to the Monckton Commission when it arrives, assuring him that Macleod is in fact anxious to release him from jail as soon as it can be done.

Macmillan's last stop is South Africa. On February 3, 1960 he addresses both houses of Parliament in Cape Town on the Golden Wedding anniversary of the Union of South Africa. The speech is a *tour de force*, perhaps the finest of his career, although few are aware of the physical price it exacts from the speaker (who becomes physically ill before major speeches). So much does it dazzle its hearers with its historical sweep and praise of all that has been accomplished in the country, that at first they hardly catch the critique of apartheid and the warning of things to come embedded in its velvety rhetoric. Comparing African nationalism with the Afrikaner nationalism now triumphant in the Union, he declares:

> The most striking of all the impressions I have formed since I left London a month ago is of the strength of this African national consciousness. In different places it make take different forms, but it is happening everywhere. The wind of change is blowing through the continent, and, whether we like it or not, this growth of national consciousness is a political fact. We must all accept it as a fact, and our national policies must take account of it.
>
> Of course, you understand this better than anyone. You are sprung from Europe, the home of nationalism, and here in Africa you have yourselves created a new nation. Indeed, in the history of our times yours will be recorded as the first of the African nationalisms.... [133]

The "wind of change" phrase is not original. Lord Home used it months before, and Macmillan himself floated it in a speech at a banquet in Ghana a few weeks earlier. Hardly anyone noticed at the time. But, then, Ghana has already been independent for going on three years. So little do white South Africans grasp the import of his speech that they cheer him the next day as he drives through the streets of Cape Town, "looking unchangeably imperial," [134] and serenade him and Lady Dorothy with *Auld Lang Syne* and *God Save the Queen* as they board their ship for the homeward voyage.

Macmillan's progress through Africa has been a staple of BBC news, re-transmitted every evening by the Federal Broadcasting Corporation. In Kalabo quite a few people have the cheap saucepan radios, but there is little reaction to the Prime Minister's stopover in Lusaka, even though he meets there with the paramount chief of Barotseland, or to the "wind of change speech" in South Africa. As for Macmillan, he seems to have been more impressed by the "beauty of Government House with its strange garden and aviary"[135] than by the paramount, the only chief in the territory to manage an audience. It is hard to imagine that Mwanawina for his part doesn't seize the chance to remind Her Majesty's Government of Barotseland's direct connection to the Crown and its aloofness from the sordid political clamor of the moment.

On the long journey home aboard the *Capetown Castle,* Macmillan jumps into what he sees as one of the most challenging political contests of his career, the race to become chancellor of Oxford University, a lifetime post always held by a public figure. His sponsor and campaign manager is Hugh Trevor-Roper whom Macmillan had appointed Regius Professor of Modern History two years earlier in preference to a more left-leaning historian (and who dismisses Africa as a continent without history, only the "unrewarding gyrations of barbarous tribes in picturesque but irrelevant corners of the globe."[136]) Any Oxford graduate is eligible to vote on payment of the sum of £5 to upgrade his degree from B.A. to M.A. The election is full of "venomous intrigue and lobbying."[137] As the *Daily Express* observes, "even Tammany Hall was never like this!"[138] Macmillan contrives to run as the "anti-Establishment" candidate and wins, thanks to an open bar in Balliol College and a special train-load of recently minted Oxford M.A.s who come up from London to vote. On May 1, 1960 he is installed and delivers a speech half in English, half in Latin. What makes the job so appealing, he admits, is the patronage, the chance to spread honorary doctorates among his friends and supporters: "I rather enjoy patronage; at least it makes all those years of reading Trollope seem worthwhile."[139]

EPILOGUE

I never resented Alan Lennox-Boyd, who put me inside; in a way it was rather helpful to me. But I have always loved Iain who let me out.

—Dr. Hastings Kamuzu Banda (1970)

When the rulers begin to doubt the moral validity of their rule and the subjects absorb this new doubt, the game is up.

—Margery Perham (1960)

It has been said that the epitaph of the white man in Africa will be: He allowed his intelligence and his conscience to become blunted by colour prejudice, and did not realize it until too late.

—Doris Lessing (1956)

The world is not divided into compartments like a train, with first-class, second-class and so on. We are travelling together as equal passengers on the dangerous journey of life.

—Kenneth Kaunda (1964)

Kalabo. 1999. The *boma* is dilapidated. No messengers sit on the verandah, dozing in the sun until they are needed. Gone are the spreading jacaranda tree and the mangoes and lemons and limes. There are no more flower gardens or grassy lawns stretching down to the crocodile-infested river; in fact, there are almost no crocodiles left in the Luanginga. But two weathered one-way signs still mark the overgrown roundabout, and with a little grubbing one can clear away the old pipe that fed the fountain. If anything, there is even less traffic to operate it for. A rusted red pontoon boat has keeled over on its side in the harbor. A little way up, there are hulks of equally rusted trucks and heavy equipment, gifts from donor agencies, now mechanical orphans no one much cares about. Half-built houses of brick languish open to the sky and the elements, a tangle of thorny weeds pushing up through their rubbish-strewn floors.

There are still no all-weather roads in the District although a tarred and much-potholed road now connects the provincial capital at Mongu, on the eastern edge of the floodplain, with the national capital, Lusaka, and with Senanga to the south. A pontoon ferry across the Zambezi makes Libonda more accessible during the dry season, but barges no longer ply the Zambezi and the lower reaches of the Luanginga. A more modern airfield has been built several kilometres out of town, but the plucky little Beavers have disappeared from the sky, leaving Kalabo more cut off from the outside world than it was 40 years ago—it takes nine bruising hours by four-wheel drive to cover the less than 50 miles from Mongu when the ferry is running, and the trip is impossible during the months when the flood closes the ferry down. Then, as in Lewanika's time, the only way to get there is by boat. The Lozi are still at home on the water, plying the river and its branches in their shallow canoes.

The annual ritual of the *kuomboka,* on the other hand, not only survives, it has become one of Zambia's main tourist attractions. This is all the more remarkable since the exact date of the ritual can never be predicted very far in advance and it is not easy to reach Barotseland. Nevertheless, tourists and television crews flock to Limulunga from Mongu to see the royal barges and the buzzing flotilla of smaller craft swarming behind them; *kuomboka* T-shirts sell like hotcakes. The Germans have built a brand new museum devoted to Lozi arts in Limulunga. A new Seventh Day Adventist Church of brick is rising in Lealui; otherwise the capital has changed hardly at all, perhaps because of its isolation, perhaps because the royal family prefers it that way. Ilute Yeta IV has been *litunga* for more than 20 years, but his health is beginning to fail. He still wears the uniform made for Lewanika at the coronation of Edward VII.

No one in Barotseland goes to the gold mines in South Africa anymore. The minister of labor closed down Wenela's operations in Kalabo in 1966 as part of the government's policy of distancing itself from apartheid South Africa. The sawmills at Mulobezi took up a little of the slack, but these too have closed, so that unemployment is a major problem in Barotseland. Even if the Copperbelt were not Bemba territory, it has also been severely depressed for decades and employs only a small number of those who used to go south. Local agriculture continues to stagnate and there has been no development, either of industries or of infrastructure. There is little to keep young people from drifting to the cities.

What memories linger from "the time of Welensky," as the pre-independence period is commonly referred to? Older people remember "Robbie" (Rob Hart) and "Jappie" (Dick Japp) and the DC, although only by his Lozi name, "Kawayawaya." They are delighted that the "Little Frog" (Mike Japp) still speaks SiLozi fluently. They recall the DC's boundless energy, the canal digging, the road building, and the horse racing, but their fondest memory is of the regatta, that unique blend of *kuomboka* and English church fête—people still talk about it 40 years on. Alas, it never became the annual event the DC had hoped for because by the next August (1960) he was gone, and his successor frowned on such frivolous doings.

Two months after his Cape Town speech, Prime Minister Macmillan commented in a television broadcast: "I spoke of the wind of change that was blowing through Africa. But that's not the same thing as a howling tempest which would blow away the whole of the new developing civilization. We must, at all costs, avoid that."[1] A tempest is nevertheless what he got. Ironically, the only place the wind of change did not reach was South Africa. At just about the same time as the broadcast, 62 South Africans were being shot down in Sharpeville and a state of emergency was declared, 1,700 people were detained, and political advance was snuffed out for another 29 years. In Central Africa, however, change came with bewildering speed.

The Monckton Commission Report was made public in October 1960. It pulled no punches about the failure of the Federation to overcome African fears and the impossibility of maintaining it in its present form. A whole section was devoted to the topic of secession, suggesting ways in which this option could and should be incorporated into any future constitution. On the other hand, the report commented sadly, "to break [the Federation] up at this crucial moment in the history of Africa would be an admission that there is no hope of survival for any multiracial society on the African continent, and that differences of colour and race are irreconcilable. We cannot agree to such a conclusion."[2] But the best the commissioners could offer was a redesigned association, tinkering with some of the most egregious shortcomings of the old one, and more liberal constitutions for the member states. As one of Welensky's parliamentary allies wrote him, the report "came as a shock to nearly everyone but the fact that it was a predominantly right wing commission and that the report was virtually unanimous has undoubtedly made a great impression. Most people take the view that although the Federation has been an overwhelming economic success, it has been a political failure and that there is now little hope in preserving it in its present form or indeed in any form unless the black Africans are persuaded to agree."[3] After the Commons debate, the same correspondent put the matter more bluntly: Federation "had had it."[4]

In fact, federation had not quite had it. The much heralded review conference in December 1960 was a non-starter. Macmillan was amazed that the conference was the first time the federal prime minister had even met Kenneth Kaunda, leader of the United Independence Party (UNIP), Dr. Banda, or other nationalist leaders. However, no one could agree about anything. Kaunda demanded that the Federation be dissolved, Banda called for secession, and Joshua Nkomo, the newly prominent Southern Rhodesian nationalist, demanded universal suffrage and a born-again federation of liberated African states. Welensky attacked the nationalist battle cry "Africa for the Africans" as "a tragically irresponsible slogan,"[5] a pure grab for power. After walk-outs and boycotts, the conference was adjourned, never to resume.

Nonetheless, the Federation limped on during another three years of tortuous negotiations and slide-rule constitutions for its constituent parts. Macleod tried to navigate through the Scylla of European demands for continued domination or at least parity and the Charybdis of African demands for one man, one vote. Nyasaland was expendable. It had only seven or eight thousand Europeans, the largest African population of the three territories, and few resources. Once Banda was freed on April 1, 1960, it was just a matter of time until the country moved to African rule and secession. Northern Rhodesia, however, was a different matter with its mineral wealth and European population of 72,000. Both Welensky and the Conservative back benchers were prepared to fight Macleod to the death to stave off majority rule there and hold onto some sort of federation of the two Rhodesias. At successive points in 1961, the British government seriously feared first a European *coup d'état* in Salisbury or Lusaka and a declaration of independence on the part of Welensky, then, an African uprising which, Kaunda had warned, "by contrast would make Mau Mau a child's picnic."[6] If the prospect of bringing in British troops to subdue Africans was appalling, it would be even more appalling in some eyes to bring them in to subdue Europeans.

Macleod's gamble that the release of Banda would prevent rather than provoke bloodshed had paid off. The cardplayer's instincts brought him through the non-stop African crises that followed, but in the end his stubborn insistence that the danger of moving too slowly was greater than the danger of moving too quickly cost him Macmillan's support. To the prime minister Mcleod was in the end the quintessential "Highlander ... easily worked up into an emotional mood."[7] Perhaps too optimistically, Macleod had hoped to be the "last Colonial Secretary," guiding his still numerous imperial progeny safely to independence and into the sheltering arms of the Commonwealth. This was not to be. In October 1961, he was replaced by Reginald Maudling. To Macmillan's surprise, Maudling turned out to be just as troublesomely "African" as Macleod (*"plus royaliste que le roi"*[8] was Macmillan's exasperated verdict) and lasted only five months.

Finally, the government created a special post for Central African affairs, solving at long last the dilemma created by the conflicting jurisdictions and loyalties of the Colonial and Commonwealth Relations Offices. It had long been apparent that the two were "running on parallel lines which do not meet at any point."[9] At the end of March 1963, "Rab" Butler, in charge of the new office, sounded the death knell of federation by affirming that all the member territories had the right to secede. In fact, it required three agencies to drive the stake into the federal heart: the CO, the CRO, and Butler's Central African Office. Lennox-Boyd, now Viscount Boyd, wrote Welensky: "I can hardly find words to express my feelings of shame and distress at the events of the last weeks which are the culmination of a long period of disastrous surrenders."[10] As another minister put it, "we British have lost the will to govern."[11] With his customary bravura, Welensky declared that "the most hopeful and constructive experiment in racial partnership that Africa has seen in our time has been wantonly destroyed by the Government which only ten years earlier gave it its impetus."[12]

Kaunda later claimed that his Mau Mau threat had been misunderstood. "As far as I was concerned Mau Mau meant not only a massacre of white people by black people, but also a massacre of blacks by whites."[13] In fact, many more Africans than Europeans *had* been killed during the Mau Mau emergency in Kenya. As tensions grew, Europeans in Northern Rhodesia were openly stocking up on weapons. UNIP-inspired violence flared up sporadically. In mid-1961 Cha-cha-cha erupted, the "dance of freedom" that mobilized men, women, and children all over the country. Armed units of the Northern Rhodesian police and white troops of the federal army were brought in, Special Branch plainclothesmen became fixtures at UNIP political meetings, and informers infiltrated the party. Demonstrations were banned and hundreds of activists were jailed. Although Kaunda continued to deplore violence publicly, it was not clear whether he could or really wanted to enforce non-violence upon his followers. UNIP had raised expectations with the unmet promise of "Independence by October" in 1960; now he risked losing out to more radical rivals if he could not deliver *kwacha,* the new dawn, in the near future. He was "like a man riding a bicycle," commented a Colonial Office observer, and "had to keep up the impetus to stay in control of the machine."[14] But he was quite right about one thing: In the disorders that escalated in mid-1961, more Africans than Europeans met their deaths. Thirty-two Africans were killed by federal forces, while no Europeans died, although a year earlier a young white woman had been murdered and her children injured by a mob who burned her car after the police broke up a political meeting in Ndola.

Ultimately UNIP's unrelenting pressure and its mushrooming strength throughout all parts of the territory and among all segments of the African population during 1961 forced Britain to speed up the pace of constitutional change and announce new elections for the following year. Whitehall still clung to a system of multiple franchises and weighted voting that was intended to increase the number of African voters and at the same time force parties to go beyond a purely racial constituency but that, like the 1958 Benson constitution, was difficult to understand and even more difficult to implement. Kaunda had tried hard to recast UNIP as a "multiracial" party in an appeal to white voters. He brought in "new men" as candidates who would be less threatening than better known activists, and campaigned on issues that would reassure Europeans about their place in the independent nation to come. A few mavericks such as Gore-Brown, Merfyn Temple, and the very useful lawyer, James Skinner, had rallied to UNIP early on, but Europeans overwhelmingly supported the UFP, as much out of fear as enthusiasm. As a defeated candidate of the newly formed Liberal Party exclaimed, "They would have voted for a cow" as long as it had the UFP label.[15] During the election the UFP formed a secret alliance with the ANC. (There were even overheated fantasies about joining up with the break-away province of Katanga to the north in a grand scheme of union presided over by Nkumbula and Moïse Tshombe, with plenty of whites pulling strings behind the scenes.) When Kaunda and his backers learned of this, they lambasted the sheer cynicism of the deal since the two parties had nothing in common except the desire to block a UNIP victory and share power among themselves; with no hope of winning on his own, Nkumbula had simply sold himself to the highest bidders—Welensky and Tshombe.

In the end, voting in the October 1962 elections was largely along racial lines; people "voted with their skins."[16] Although they voted in many cases for candidates of the opposite race, they favored the *parties* identified with their own race. The results were so evenly divided between UFP and UNIP that the ANC held the balance of power. It was gall and wormwood for Kaunda to play suppliant to Nkumbula, and far from easy for Nkumbula to decide where his own and ANC's future lay. The two met finally in London, joining in a marriage of convenience to demand a new constitution before 1963 was out and agreeing to work together in the interim. For the first time, therefore, African parties held a majority, if only of a single seat, in the legislature and divided the ministerial posts between UNIP and ANC. "By any standard," commented a historian who had watched events unfold firsthand, "the Territory's political metamorphosis had been phenomenal"[17] in the less than two years since Kaunda had been released from prison.

Nevertheless, Kaunda pressed for new elections before the end of 1963. Nkumbula wanted to delay them because his party was in total disarray and his own leadership under fire. In the event, Kaunda came close to his target date. Elections were held in January 1964, only fifteen months after the previous one, this time with only minimal requirements but with reserved seats for Europeans. UNIP mounted a formidable registration campaign, frightening some of the chiefs who feared that they would be the losers in a UNIP-dominated government. There were outbreaks of violence in many parts of the country leading up to the polls, but the result was a foregone conclusion in spite of rumors of plots to sabotage the election.

And so it happened. UNIP won an overwhelming percentage of the African vote and the support of almost a third of the country's Europeans. In late January 1964 the governor invited Kenneth Kaunda to serve as prime minister of Zambia and to form a government. Kaunda was not quite 40 years old. Independence followed nine months later under still another constitution, this one based on full universal suffrage and a presidential form of government. In the space of five years the territory's African electorate had exploded from exactly eleven voters to nearly a million and a half. Contrary to the apocalyptic predictions of some white politicians, there was no mass exodus of Europeans.

When the DC returned to Barotseland in May 1963, a year and a half before independence and three years after he had left Kalabo, the world had turned upside down. He was now stationed with his new wife in Sesheke, in the southern part of the province. From their verandah they could look westward across the Zambezi and watch storm clouds gathering in all their terrifying tropical majesty during the rainy season.

But storm clouds of another kind were also gathering. Here, as everywhere else in the country, security was the overriding concern. "For years past district annual reports have described years of change and have with pride detailed the advances made," he wrote. "In 1963 the changes were thrust on the district at such a pace, with such far reaching effects, that our only pride can be in having maintained law and order during the period, and having carried out the many difficult tasks laid on us."[18] There was a steady stream of provocations: riots, intimidation, fights between UNIP and ANC Youth Brigades, lawlessness masquerading as political protest—"popular crime with public support."[19] Furthermore, the "clientele" of the Sesheke prison "has shown signs of a growing sophistication."[20] No longer could they be counted on to lock themselves up when the warden was too tipsy to do so. Nor could messengers cope with the increasing demands of law enforcement or DCs handle the mounting judicial case load and still keep up with their other duties. Touring was a prime casualty.

On top of all that, there was friction with the Portuguese across the Angolan border, in contrast to the pleasant relations the DC had enjoyed in Kalabo with his Portuguese counterpart. Sesheke's location made it a particularly volatile spot. Just across the Zambezi was Katima Mulilo, site of the only hospital for the district and split down the middle between Northern Rhodesia and the Caprivi Strip, administered by South Africa under a United Nations mandate. The eastern Caprivi, earlier known as "Criminals' Corner," was fast reverting to its old self, with the added spice of illicit political comings and goings. A case in point: just before the Victoria Falls conference that officially dismantled the Federation and distributed the remains, the Katima customs post was burned down by skilled arsonists. The DC suspected that it was the work of the UNIP Youth Brigade.

Shorthanded as the *boma* was, the only hopeful development was the incorporation of the first Africans into the administrative and specialist services. The DC could rely on two African district assistants, along with one European DO, and a veterinary assistant who seemed to know every cattle owner in the district by name. The other bright spot was the construction of a new squash court with funds from the "goat bag" (officially, with "a lottery grant").[21] The men involved in building it were baffled about why anyone would want such an odd room, with no windows and no roof. They were told it would be used for "orgies," a word they did not recognize. As soon as a translation got around, work was completed in record time.

A top priority of the *boma* officers was registering voters for the general election in early January 1964. Considering that the average voter had to walk between 10 and 15 miles to get to a registration center, the fact that 88 percent of those eligible did register was "a vivid demonstration of the political consciousness of the villager and belies the often heard theory that African Nationalism is an expression of the will of an articulate few."[22] The DC contrived to work out a fragile *modus vivendi* with the local officials of UNIP that had won "universal support in the district."[23] Locally, UNIP supporters forced a show of strength with the Mwandi *kuta,* the Native Authority in Sesheke District, and there were some ugly moments between individual nationalists and the *boma* as well, playing on the building tensions and the shorthandedness of *boma* personnel. In one face-off a particularly belligerent fellow forced his way into the DC's office brandishing a heavy metal walking stick made from a brass bedstead; the DC grabbed it, hit him over the knuckles, and punched him. It was probably a deliberate provocation, but, like his earlier confrontation with the nationalists exiled to Kalabo, the episode would soon come back to haunt him.

UNIP had swept the province in the 1962 territorial elections, holding out promises of such economic plums as a railway line from Mongu to Lusaka (which might have won even Lewanika's vote). The next year the party captured all 25 seats in the Barotse Katengo Council that was now entirely elective by order of the central government. Its members made no bones about their intention to reform the Barotse Native Government and to undermine the position of the traditionalists. There was indeed no love lost between UNIP and the BNG. The nationalists had not forgotten the paramount chief's support of federation, his successful campaign to ban UNIP from the province in the early sixties, his imprisonment of UNIP organizers, and his threats of secession. In 1961 Mwanawina had flown to London to receive his knighthood directly from the Queen. He used the occasion to demand that Iain Macleod allow Barotseland to secede and form an independent state of its own. Macleod refused because of his unwillingness to provoke Kaunda and the nationalists, but he did offer the usual set-speech about honoring Barotseland's special status. He also recognized the title *litunga,* rather than paramount chief, belatedly undoing the demotion effected by the British South Africa Company a half-century earlier. Predictably, the compromise satisfied neither the *litunga* nor the nationalists. Furthermore, the knighthood ceremony had been something of a diplomatic blunder: A Lozi ruler was never supposed to speak directly to anyone, only through his *ngambela,* but the latter had not been invited to Buckingham Palace for the occasion. No one had thought to consult Gervas Clay, who had accompanied the *litunga* to London and who was an old Barotse hand, about matters of protocol.

As independence approached and UNIP's power increased, the situation became more urgent. The Barotse elite stepped up the secession campaign. Rumors abounded that the campaign was being covertly funded by the Federation, by South Africa, even by Portugal (which feared that the nationalist tide would swamp its African colonies). There were defections even within the royal family, however. Princess Nakatindi, the *litunga's* niece, was a staunch UNIP supporter (allegedly miffed because she was passed over in 1959 for the Nalolo chieftaincy), and appeared on the platform with Kaunda at public meetings. The majority of Lozi working in the towns along the line of rail, too, opposed the Lealui clique as "old fashioned and reactionary"[24] and supported the Barotse Anti-Secession Movement. They warned that if Barotseland were allowed to secede, the "chaos and discord"[25] that would follow would be even worse than that attending Katanga's secession from the Congo. So convoluted were Barotse politics, however, that before long the UNIP members elected to the Katengo Council became just as avid champions of Barotse separatism as the traditional elites, albeit in their own fashion. "Attempting to be both Lozi patriots and Zambian nationalists,"[26] they wanted to be part of an independent Zambia but to have Barotseland's special status left inviolate.

The Barotseland problem threatened to derail the whole timetable for independence. The most bizarre twist came when a secret South African envoy proposed to invade Barotseland from Katima Mulilo, free it from Zambia, and add it to South Africa's collection of Bantustans. This was too much even for the *litunga;* instead he lobbied hard to get Barotseland's special status enshrined in the Zambian constitution. Kaunda categorically refused. Finally, he and *litunga* Mwanawina signed a separate document, the Barotseland Agreement of May 1964, which replaced all earlier agreements between Britain and the Lozi. It provided that Barotseland would become an integral part of Zambia and recognized the *litunga* as "the principal local authority for the government and administration of Barotseland,"[27] listing the areas over which he would continue to have jurisdiction (land, forests, fishing, game, trees for canoes, etc.). Effectively, however, he had lost his independent treasury and most of the power formerly exercised by the Native Authority. Henceforth he and his province would have to go hat in hand to Lusaka for anything they wanted. Ironically, the very success of the Lozi elite in dealing with European colonialists had lulled them into a complacent resistance to change. The "living museum" was ill prepared to deal with the modern state.

President Kaunda and most of his cabinet descended on Lealui in March 1965 for the *kuomboka* ceremony. He and his wife joined the *litunga* on the royal barge and relations seemed cordial (see figure 21). There were still grounds for hope that Barotseland would do well under Zambia's transitional development plan.

As October 24, 1964 approached, enthusiastic patriots outfitted themselves in "*kwacha* cloth"—cloth celebrating independence with a portrait of Kenneth Kaunda and the motto "Freedom and Labour." Schoolchildren throughout the country were drilled in the new national anthem, sung to the tune of *Nkosi, Sekelel' iAfrika* (originally composed as the hymn of South African liberation). Leaders of newly independent states in Africa and Asia sent warm messages, and the Princess Royal came from Britain as the representative of her niece, Queen Elizabeth II. Colorful ceremonies climaxed in a state banquet and dance, with President Kaunda squiring his royal partner onto the dancefloor in the great ballroom of the capital. At midnight the Union Jack came down, the Zambian flag went up: red, black, and orange bars on a background of green with the African fish eagle in the corner. There was a blaze of fireworks to mark the beginning of the new era as Kaunda took the oath of office in a stadium thronged with 30,000 delirious Zambians. On becoming a government minister, he and Betty had moved from their cramped, two-room house in Chilenje into a mansion once owned by the British South Africa Company; now they settled into Government House with their nine children. Twins had been born to them early in the year of independence—an ambiguous, even inauspicious event in many cultures but one welcomed with joy by the Kaundas for whom *ShiMpundu* and *NaMpundu,* father and mother of twins, became titles of honor.

Colonial officers found themselves an "extinct species."[28] The DC was branded a *persona non grata* by the new government and went home with his wife in April 1964 to start life over again in Britain at the age of 35. He left behind an infant son, laid to rest in a Lusaka churchyard. True to his love of building, he became the father of the "self-build" industry in England—complete instructions on how to build your own home and a cornucopia of plans to choose from. Other officers became solicitors, judges, airline pilots. Still others stayed on at the urgent invitation of the new government, desperately short of trained administrative personnel.

Cadet Salmon (no longer a cadet) remained until 1968. When Wenela was closed down, the Japps moved to Katima Mulilo (the Caprivian side) and eventually to Mozambique, before retiring to South Africa, not far from the Harts. Squire Davis went to England, having entrusted his coffin to Dick Japp. He found it impossible to adapt and ended his days in Papua New Guinea. The coffin is still in Dick's garage. Mrs. Dempster returned forlornly to Switzerland where she felt a total stranger.

Father Bruno is the only one of the Kalabo Europeans left in Zambia, and he intends to finish out his life there; Northern Ireland has become a foreign country for him as well. Gervas Clay, on leaving the Service, devoted himself to the Boy Scout movement his father-in-law had founded. His wife Betty said it was only to use up all those shorts from Africa. Meanwhile, she continued to tour the world on behalf of the Girl Guides until well into her eighties. *Litunga* Mwanawina died in 1968 and was replaced by Godwin Mbukusita Lewanika, the first president of the ANC, later a minister of the federal government and arch agitator for Lozi secession. As for the Queen Mother, she would still retain "many happy memories" of her visit to Barotseland in her 102nd year.[29]

After the demise of the Central African Federation, Sir Roy Welensky, the "Bad Fairy of Africans' imagination,"[30] found himself faced with a choice between his loyalty to the British Commonwealth and his loyalty to Ian Smith's Rhodesia, a Rhodesia even more blatantly racist than it was during Federation days. However bitter his feelings of betrayal at the hands of Macmillan and Macleod, he chose Britain. When Rhodesia's settler-dominated government made its Unilateral Declaration of Independence in 1965, throwing down the gauntlet both to African nationalism and to Great Britain, Welensky moved to London. He was invited by President Kaunda to attend the celebration of Zambia's tenth anniversary in 1974, but was not able to visit the country till the next year. What struck him most, he reported, was how visible Zambian women had become. Not only were they driving cars, they were also serving as administrators and managers. Unexpectedly, Welensky became, as a former DC put it, "a more attractive figure in defeat than when he rode on the crest."[31]

Margery Perham was made a Dame in 1965, not in the Order of the British Empire but in that of St. Michael and St. George, the Colonial Service order of chivalry. Iain Macleod died suddenly of a heart attack in 1970. One of the first to send condolences to his widow was Dr. Banda. Macleod never became prime minister; the Empire-wing of his party could not forgive the tempos of change he orchestrated in East and Central Africa, and the charge of "too clever by half" struck too deep. Possibly it was some consolation that a generation of Malawian boys were named Iain.

And Kenneth Kaunda, former agitator, now head of state? Zambia had been born, as he said, "with a copper spoon in its mouth"[32]— fittingly, a copper chariot drawn by two eagles had swept through the stadium during the independence festivities. While prices remained high, this resource translated into massive reserves of foreign exchange and ambitious education and development programs under the rubric of Kaunda's "African humanism." Then the world copper market collapsed soon after the government nationalized the industry in 1970, and Zambia experienced the full misery of its reliance on a single commodity. The government had also kept a tight rein on farming by retaining the old colonial marketing boards and an impenetrable maze of regulations. The result was that the country, once more than self-sufficient agriculturally, became a net importer of food. As one of the "frontline states," Zambia supported liberation movements in southern Africa and sanctions against South Africa and Rhodesia, but the cost was high (Rhodesia had ended up with the lion's share of federal assets and with the switches to the Kariba Dam). Zambia's landlocked position made it dependent for exports and imports on both Rhodesia and Portuguese Mozambique. To break this hold, the Chinese constructed a railroad to the coast in Tanzania as part of their push for political influence in Africa, but the project was enormously expensive, transport costs were steep, and the capacity of east coast ports limited.

Increasingly, Kaunda and UNIP pressed for a one-party state to deal with mounting economic problems, domestic divisions, and inter-national tensions. This was made part of the constitution in 1973 but did little to halt the downward spiral. Political life was increasing marked by riots, assassinations, and detentions. In 1991 the one-party state imploded, a victim of its own weaknesses as well as forces beyond its control. UNIP was defeated at the polls and Kaunda replaced by the labor leader Frederick Chiluba. In a classic demonstration of a revolution devouring its young, Kaunda himself was arrested in 1997 on charges of treason; he was imprisoned, then placed under house arrest. Two years later the High Court declared that he was not even a citizen of Zambia. But Chiluba's government has had no more success in dealing with crushing debt and the austerity policies imposed by the IMF and World Bank, or with political instability and the ravages of AIDS.

UNIP's popularity declined precipitously in Barotseland almost from the moment of independence. The president countered by stripping the *litunga* of virtually all remaining powers. He was just another chief and a dependent one at that. The BNG no longer received its annual subsidy from the British South Africa Company, and, after the expulsion of Wenela in 1966, fees for each recruit sent off to South Africa evaporated as well. The *litunga,* like any other chief, depended on Parliament for his salary and household expenses. The Barotseland Agreement was in tatters but was not formally abrogated until 1969. Humiliation was complete when the region was renamed Western Province. Not surprisingly, opposition to the regime again threatened to boil over. As a gesture of reconciliation, UNIP lured *litunga* Ilute Yeta (Mbikusita's successor) into active politics, giving him a place on the party's central committee. Inevitably, this alienated many traditionalists who felt it was unseemly behavior for a *litunga.* After the re-introduction of a multi-party system, he reverted to his largely ceremonial role.

Dissatisfaction with the continuing marginalization and poverty of Barotseland continued to fester, flaring up once again in an attempted coup at Katima Mulilo in early August 1999, a coup that was clumsily executed and quickly—savagely—put down by the Namibian government. It was carried out by the Caprivi Liberation Army that had close ties to the Barotse Patriotic Front (apparently with funding and training from the Angolan rebel group, UNITA). Their joint aim was to sever the Strip from Namibia and unite it with its Lozi neighbors in an independent state. History was on their side, but perhaps not much else.

"One of the strange things about our presence," reflected a district officer, "was the reluctance with which we appeared to go in and the speed with which we came out."[33] In 1945 Great Britain ruled over 600 million people. British school children had become accustomed to maps where something between a quarter and a third of the world's inhabited land mass was colored red. Twenty years later, little was left beyond "a few small and scattered ports and islands."[34] The Colonial Office itself was abolished the following year. Did the transfer of power occur too quickly in Africa? Or was it long overdue?

In 1960 Margery Perham could still "regret that the white man had not been allowed another fifty years in which to build his civilization in Africa."[35] But unlike Winston Churchill she knew that this was impossible. She also realized that the timetable was no longer entirely in British hands. "Independence," she declared in a BBC broadcast in 1954, "is something that cannot be given, but must be taken. And first it has to be demanded."[36] Demanded it was, ever more urgently. Macleod did not live to write his memoirs. Macmillan did, however, and defended his government's role as midwife of decolonization with a quotation from the nineteenth-century English historian and Indian civil servant, Thomas Babington Macaulay:

> Many politicians of our time are in the habit of laying it down as a self-evident proposition, that no people ought to be free till they are fit to use their freedom. The maxim is worthy of the fool in the old story, who resolved not to go into the water till he had learnt to swim. If men are to wait for liberty till they become wise and good in slavery, they may indeed wait for ever.[37]

He then recalled a conversation with a man who had spent his life in the Colonial Service. When the prime minister asked him whether the people whose destinies he held in his hand were ready for independence, he answered that of course they weren't. They would not be ready for another fifteen or twenty years. What would you advise then? Without a moment's hesitation, the governor replied that they should be given independence at once—as soon as possible. "When I expressed some surprise, he developed an argument which seemed to me, as to him, unanswerable. 'If fifteen or twenty years were to be applied in learning the job, in increasing their experience of local government, or of central administration, why then I would be all for it. But that is not what will happen. All the most intelligent men capable of government will be in rebellion. I will have to put them in prison. There they will learn nothing about administration, only about hatred and revenge.' "[38]

To many officers on the spot, however, Macmillan's version avoided some unpleasant truths about the nature of colonialism. Colonial administration was inherently paternalistic. The Devlin Report had referred to the government of Nyasaland as "a benevolent despotism," adding, "about its benevolence there should be no mistake and the 'despotism' was that of a kindly father and not of a tyrant. Every member of the Government believes that at bottom ... there is a government by consent and would not be happy if he thought otherwise."[39] This applied equally to Northern Rhodesia. As an officer wrote with the clarity of hindsight: "Many of us were far too young and very sure we were right.... We assumed ... that people would understand our motives and would go on to approve of our actions. We assumed, for example, that our concepts of justice would come as a blinding revelation of beauty and excellence whereas, most of the time, I guess that people thought we were arrogant and daft." The Romans had brought good government to ancient Britain, but this made them no less unwelcome to Queen Boadicea. "What she wanted was to be allowed to do it her way and if her ideas on makeup or personal hygiene were smelly to Caesar what the hell business was that of his? And what is wrong with a nice wiggly road once in a while?"[40] The "false god"[41] of indirect rule, too, had important consequences. It resulted in a bias toward "princes and peasants" and an antipathy toward urban peoples and the newly educated class of teachers, clerks, and the handful of professionals—and worst of all, toward nationalist troublemakers; the colonial officer and the anthropologist shared a preference for the timeless Africa of thatched huts and deference to chiefs. The net effect was to freeze things at a moment in time. Native authorities did not have to change because they were buttressed by the British government itself. But by the later 1950s many "men on the spot" who worked daily with indigenous authorities realized that indirect rule "was going nowhere," in the DC's words. "However, to voice such a heresy would have been disastrous to one's career, and as we all liked what we were doing, we dismissed it from our minds."[42] In any case, there was no provision in the administrative hierarchy for the views of the district officer to be heard. Perhaps more could have been done to develop democracy on the grassroots level. Simply grafting a bit of democracy onto local authorities did not work.

Another failing of the colonial administration was to ignore basic techniques of modern management. The idea that "information about confidential policy, trends accepted as inevitable, or hidden agendas" should be shared had not occurred to those in charge of British colonial Africa in the 1950s. On the contrary, "there was deliberate misinformation as far as middle rank officers were concerned, like being assured by superiors that Macmillan's Wind of Change speech was 'just for the Americans' "—just as those involved in suppressing Mau Mau "were assured that we had gained a generation's breathing space before any further consideration need be given to self-determination."[43] In fact, Kenya became independent almost a year before Northern Rhodesia.

While it was an object of faith that one day the colonial state must wither away, it was not going to happen very soon so that one could take one's time in preparing for the transition. One could count on the pace of the African ox. In due time, however, Africans would have to be brought into all branches of the administration, and to this there was a great deal of resistance and much talk about maintaining standards, waiting until there was a generation of university graduates, and so forth and so on. At bottom, confessed a former DO, "those of us who were on the spot [were] guilty of something very close to racism if not the real thing. There was a powerful reaction against the idea that the cream of the

African civil service should finish up as full-blown District Officers
with all the powers including that of the magistracy."[44] In India, at
independence in 1947, over half of the Indian Civil Service was Indian.
In Northern Rhodesia the first handful of Africans were not admitted to
the Colonial Service until the late 1950s. At independence only one, an
education officer, had reached the higher levels. "Perhaps the most serious problem of the transfer of power were due," Margery Perham
declared, "to Britain's tardiness in opening the civil service to Africans."[45]

Even the term "transfer of power" may suggest something altogether
too orderly and intentional. Was it guided by Whitehall as part of a comprehensive process or was it only a series of reactions to crises, a policy
of expediency dictated by domestic politics as much as by any philoso-
phy? Would African nationalism have gotten anywhere without periodic
bursts of violence and the threat of more to come? Some thought so and
concluded sadly that it left as its legacy, "an understanding that power
comes from the manipulation of mobs. It was a poor legacy."[46] The
problem was that those most experienced in organizing the masses and
bargaining with the colonial state and its masters had little training in
statesmanship. Most nationalist leaders *were* graduates of the "University
of Territorial Prisons," not schools of administration, and virtually none
of them came up through the ranks of local government, as Cohen's
blueprint had anticipated. When Kenneth Kaunda took over in 1964,
observed Father Bruno, it was much "as if Guy Fawkes had succeeded in
blowing up the houses of parliament and getting rid of the old government."[47] The problem was what to do next.

The colonial era in Central Africa lasted only threescore years and ten,
the biblical span of a single human life. When twilight came, it was brief,
as African twilights are. What British rule accomplished, it did on a shoestring; what it didn't accomplish was partly because the shoestring was
ludicrously short measured by any standard—at one point the budget for
all of Northern Rhodesia was said to be roughly equivalent to the
annual street-cleaning bill for the city of Glasgow. In the end it was
the "little minds" of the British Treasury that made policy as much as the
Colonial Office, the "Cinderella amongst government departments."[48]
For Barotseland over the last 40 years the Zambian treasury has been just
as unforgiving.

What about the future? A story from American history is perhaps
instructive. Benjamin Franklin spent the long months of the United
States constitutional convention of 1787 gazing at the sun emblazoned
on the back of the presidential chair without being able to decide
whether it was rising or setting. When the document was at last signed,

he announced that he had "the happiness to know that it is rising and not a setting sun."[49] Lozi, like other Zambians, may have pondered the same question about their own post-colonial world. But when asked if life is better now for the people of Kalabo, a Lozi businessman whose career began by learning construction at the side of the DC, answered without hesitating, "Yes, because we don't have the white man running things."[50]

NOTES

Prologue

1. Foreword to Terence Gavaghan, *Of Lions and Dung Beetles: A "Man in the Middle" of Colonial Administration in Kenya* (Ilfracombe, Devon: Arthur H. Stockwell, 1999), 8.
2. John Lonsdale, "Kenyatta's Trials: Breaking and Making an African Nationalist." In Peter Coss, ed. *The Moral World of the Law* (New York: Cambridge University Press, 2000), 199.
3. Foreword to Gavaghan, *Lions and Dung Beetles*, 7.
4. Wole Soyinka, *A Dance of the Forests* (Oxford: Oxford University Press, 1963), 39.

Introduction: Barotseland

1. Quoting *Hamlet* IV, v, 78.
2. François Coillard 1889, quoted in Mutumba Mainga, *Bulozi under the Luyana Kings: Political Evolution and State Formation in Pre-colonial Zambia* (London: Longman, 1973), 175.
3. Edward C. Tabler, *Trade and Travel in Early Barotseland: The Diaries of George Westbeech, 1885–1888, and Captain Norman MacLeod, 1875–1876* (Berkeley: University of California Press, 1963), 50–51.
4. Colonel Colin Harding, *Far Bugles* (Croydon: H. R. Grubb, 1933), 136.

Chapter One   Kalabo: The View from the *Boma*

1. David Livingstone, *African Journal, 1853–1856,* ed. I. Schapera. 2 vol. (Berkeley: University of California Press, 1963), 2: 273.
2. A. H. M. Kirk-Greene, *Britain's Imperial Administrators 1858–1966* (London: Macmillan, 2000), 161.
3. A. H. M. Kirk-Greene, "The Thin White Line: The Size of the British Colonial Service in Africa." *African Affairs* 79: 314(1980), 25–44.
4. V. W. Brelsford, "The Boma Messenger and his Uniform." *Northern Rhodesia Journal* 2: 3(1954), 34–42.
5. Kalabo District Tour Report No. 4/1955.
6. Resident commissioner's Minute No.1 to Kalabo District Tour Report No. 4/1959.

7. David Livingstone, *Missionary Travels and Researches in South Africa* (New York: Harper, 1859), 223.

8. Resident commissioner's Minute to Kalabo District Tour Report No. 7/1958.

9. John Smith, *Vet in Africa. Life on the Zambezi 1913–1933*, ed. Tony Bagnall Smith (London: Radcliffe Press, 1997), 264.

10. Kalabo District Tour Report No. 11/1958.

11. DC's Minute No. 4 to Kalabo District Tour Report No. 11/1958.

12. DS, letter of September 6, 1959.

13. Kalabo District Annual Report, 1958, 4.

14. Smith, *Vet in Africa,* 264.

15. Ralph Furse, *Aucuparius: Recollections of a Recruiting Officer* (London: Oxford University Press, 1962), 221.

16. Ibid., 259.

17. Quoted in Ibid., 4.

18. Lord Lloyd, quoted in Charles Jeffries, *Partners for Progress: The Men and Women of the Colonial Service* (London: G. Harrap, 1949), 19.

19. Margery Perham, *The Colonial Reckoning* (New York: Alfred A. Knopf, 1962), 154.

20. L. H. Gann and Peter Duignan, *The Rulers of British Africa 1870–1914* (Stanford: Stanford University Press, 1978), 51.

21. Randal Sadleir, *Tanzania: Journey to Republic* (London: The Radcliffe Press, 1999), 57.

22. R. E. Wraith in A. H. M. Kirk-Greene, ed., *The Transfer of Power: The Colonial Administrator in the Age of Decolonization* (Oxford: University of Oxford Inter-Faculty Committee for African Studies, 1979), 104.

23. Emily Bradley, *Dearest Priscilla* (London: Max Parrish, 1950), 112.

24. Joan Alexander, ed., *Voices and Echoes: Tales from Colonial Women* (London: Quartet Books, 1983), 32.

25. Bradley, *Dearest Priscilla,* 84.

26. Author interview with Betty Clay, August 1, 1996.

27. David Taylor, "An Aimless Waffle for Fi," unpubl. ms.

28. Northern Rhodesia, *African Affairs Annual Report*, 1957, 87.

29. Quoted in DS, letter of October 4, 1959.

30. The winner produced a three-meter high wooden statue of a figure wearing the traditional wrapper around his waist: He has one hand on the handle of a shovel, the other on his hip. The statue stood on a plinth in Kalabo until it was swept away in the 1963 flood.

31. Kalabo District Tour Report No. 2/1960.

32. Kalabo District Tour Report No. 6/1960.

33. Kalabo District Tour Report No. 4/1957.

34. Kalabo District Tour Report No. 4/1957.

35. Kalabo District Tour Report No. 13/1957.

36. Quoted in Laurel Van Horn, "The Agricultural History of Barotseland, 1840–1964," in Robin Palmer and Neil Parsons, eds., *The Roots of Rural Poverty in Central and Southern Africa* (Berkeley: University of California Press, 1977), 164.

37. Quoted in Peter Fraenkel, *Wayaleshi* (London: Weidenfeld & Nicolson, 1959), 105.

38. Ibid., 107.

39. Uganda-Sudan Diary, February 21, 1938, quoted in Wm. Roger Louis, "The Coming of Independence in the Sudan," in Alison Smith and Mary Bull, eds., *Margery Perham and British Rule in Africa* (London: Frank Cass, 1991), 137.

40. Margery Perham, *Lugard*, 2 vols. (London: Collins, 1956), 1: 137.

41. Northern Rhodesia, *African Affairs Annual Report*, 1960, 77.

42. David Taylor, pers. communication to the author.

43. Northern Rhodesia, *African Affairs Annual Report*, 1960, 77.

Chapter Two   Libonda: The View from the *Kuta*

1. John Smith, *Vet in Africa: Life on the Zambezi 1913–1933,* ed. Tony Bagnall Smith (London: The Radcliffe Press, 1997), 187.
2. Kenneth Bradley, *Once a District Officer* (New York: St. Martin's Press, 1966), 15.
3. Quoted in Robert Heussler, *Yesterday's Rulers: The Making of the British Colonial Service* (Syracuse: Syracuse University Press, 1963), 82.
4. See A. H. M. Kirk-Greene, "The Thin White Line: The Size of the British Colonial Service in Africa." *African Affairs* 79: 314(1980), 26, n.3.
5. Ibid., 42.
6. Codrington quoted in W. W. Brelsford, *Generation of Men: The European Pioneers of Northern Rhodesia* (Salisbury: The Northern Rhodesia Society, 1965), 94.
7. Lugard, *The Dual Mandate,* quoted in Charles Allen, *Tales from the Dark Continent* (New York: St. Martin's Press, 1979), 41.
8. Kirk-Greene, introd. to Allen, *Tales,* xiv.
9. Kalabo District Tour Report No. 2/1959.
10. Quoted in Mutumba Mainga, *Bulozi under the Luyana Kings: Political Evolution and State Formation in Pre-colonial Zambia* (London: Longman, 1973), 43.
11. Kalabo District Tour Report No. 5/1960.
12. Author interview with Gervas Clay August 1, 1996.
13. David Livingstone, *Missionary Travels and Researches in South Africa* (New York: Harper, 1859), 272.
14. Kalabo District Tour Report No. 6/1957.
15. Kalabo District Tour Report No. 10/57.
16. Kalabo District Tour Report No. 3/1957.
17. Kalabo District Tour Report No. 4/1958.
18. Kalabo District Tour Report No. 8/1959.
19. Ibid.
20. Kalabo District Tour Report No. 9/1959.
21. Ibid.
22. David Livingstone, *Livingstone's Private Journals, 1851–53,* ed. I. Schapera (Berkeley: University of California Press, 1960), 209.
23. Ibid., 209.
24. J. P. R. Wallis, ed., *The Barotseland Journal of James Stevenson-Hamilton 1898–1899* (London: Chatto and Windus, 1953), 210.
25. Kalabo District Tour Report No. 4/1960.
26. Kalabo District Tour Report No. 4/1955.
27. Kalabo District Tour Report No. 4/1956.
28. Kalabo District Tour Report No. 5/1956.
29. Kalabo District Tour Report No. 1/1957.
30. Kalabo District Tour Report No. 10/1957.
31. Kalabo District Tour Report No. 7/1958.
32. Kalabo District Tour Report No. 11/1959.
33. Minute No. 4, Kalabo District Tour Report No. 9/58.
34. Kalabo District Tour Report No. 5/1959.
35. Kalabo District Tour Report No. 5/1959.
36. Kalabo District Tour Report No. 3/1960.
37. Livingstone, *Private Journals,* 210.
38. C. G. Trapnell and J. N. Clothier, *The Soils, Vegetation and Agricultural Systems of Northern Rhodesia* (Lusaka: Government Printer, 1937), quoted in David U. Peters, *Land Usage in Barotseland* (Lusaka: The Rhodes Livingstone Institute, 1960), 20.

39. Livingstone, *Private Journals*, 210.
40. Northern Rhodesia, *African Affairs Annual Report*, 1955, 99.
41. James Johnston, *Reality versus Romance in South Central Africa* (Chicago: F. H. Revell, 1893), 164.
42. Thomas Gray, quoted in Kalabo District Tour Report No. 10/1957.
43. Northern Rhodesia Ministry of African Education, *Triennial Survey 1958–1960*, 29.
44. Kalabo District Tour Report No. 3/1959.
45. Kalabo District Tour Report No. 3/1956.
46. François Coillard, *On the Threshold of Central Africa* (London: Hodder and Stoughton, 1902), 171.
47. Ibid., 171.
48. Quoted in Major A. St. H. Gibbons, *Africa from South to North through Marotseland* (London: John Lane The Bodley Head, 1904), 269.
49. Peter Fraenkel, *Wayaleshi* (London: Weidenfeld & Nicolson, 1959), 98.

Chapter Three   Salisbury: The View from the Federation

1. Cyril Dunn, *African Witness* (London: Victor Gollancz, 1959), 27.
2. Ibid.
3. Alan Megahey, *Humphrey Gibbs, Beleaguered Governor: Southern Rhodesia, 1929–69* (Basingstoke: Macmillan, 1998), 43.
4. Margery Perham, *The Listener*, June 9, 1960, reprinted in Perham, *Colonial Sequence, 1949 to 1969* (London: Methuen, 1970), 209.
5. Harold Macmillan, "Africa," *African Affairs* 59(1960), 196.
6. Dunn, *African Witness*, 31.
7. Quoted in Brian Lapping, *End of Empire* (London: Granada, 1985), 476.
8. Quoted in Garry Allighan, *The Welensky Story* (Cape Town: Durnell, 1962), 104.
9. Quoted in Dunn, *African Witness*, 59.
10. Gerald Sayers quoted in Philip Murphy, *Party Politics and Decolonization* (Oxford: Oxford University Press, 1995), 171.
11. Prosser Gifford, "Misconceived Dominion: The Creation and Disintegration of Federation in British Central Africa," in Prosser Gifford and Wm. Roger Louis, eds., *The Transfer of Power in Africa. Decolonization, 1940–1960* (New Haven: Yale University Press, 1982), 414.
12. Quoted in Richard Hall, *Zambia* (New York: Praeger, 1965), 162.
13. Quoted in Doris Lessing, *Going Home* (London: Michael Joseph, 1957), 185.
14. Elizabeth Colson, *The Social Consequences of Resettlement* (Manchester: Manchester University Press, 1971), 185.
15. Quoted in Kenneth Kaunda, *Zambia Shall be Free* (New York: Praeger, 1963), 72.
16. Quoted in Peter Fraenkel, *Wayaleshi* (London: Weidenfeld & Nicolson, 1959), 208.
17. Quoted in Robert Rotberg, *Black Heart: Gore-Brown and the Politics of Multiracial Zambia* (Berkeley: University of California Press, 1977), 260.
18. Quoted in Dunn, *African Witness*, 10.
19. Quoted in Ibid., 12.
20. Quoted in Allighan, *Welensky Story*, 57.
21. Quoted in Dunn, *African Witness*, 81.
22. Thomas Fox-Pitt to Kenneth Kaunda, June 21, 1957, quoted in Fergus Macpherson, *Kenneth Kaunda of Zambia* (Lusaka: Oxford University Press, 1974), 231.
23. Quoted in Allighan, *Welensky Story*, 219–20.
24. Ibid., 220.
25. Fraenkel, *Wayaleshi*, 190.
26. Allighan, *Welensky Story*, 50.

27. Quoted in Rotberg, *Black Heart,* 173.
28. Ibid.
29. Sir Roy Welensky, *Welensky's 4000 Days* (London: Collins, 1964), 28.
30. Quoted in Rotberg, *Black Heart,* 251.
31. Quoted in Ibid., 272.
32. Quoted in Ibid., 299.
33. Quoted in Allighan, *Welensky Story,* 140.
34. Welensky, *4000 Days,* 55.
35. Ibid., 57.
36. Fraenkel, *Wayaleshi,* 202.
37. Quoted in Luise White, *Speaking with Vampires: Rumor and History in Colonial Africa* (Berkeley: University of California Press, 2000), 302.
38. Kaunda, *Zambia,* 14.
39. Ibid., 22.
40. Dunn, *African Witness,* 66.
41. Quoted in Macpherson, *Kenneth Kaunda,* 111.
42. John Charles Hatch, *Two African Statesmen: Kaunda of Zambia and Nyerere of Tanzania* (Chicago: Regnery, 1976), 86.
43. Kaunda, *Zambia,* 83.
44. Welensky, *4000 Days,* 89.
45. Ibid.
46. Kaunda, *Zambia,* 87.
47. Quoted in Robert Rotberg, *The Rise of Nationalism in Central Africa* (Cambridge, MA: Harvard University Press, 1965), 281.
48. Kaunda, *Zambia,* 140.
49. Quoted in Hall, *Zambia,* 187.
50. A. H. M. Kirk-Greene, "Imperial Administration and the Athletic Imperative: The Case of the District Officer in Africa," in W. J. Baker and James A. Mangan, eds., *Sport in Africa: Essays in Social History* (New York: Africana, 1987), 107.
51. Philip Mason, *Year of Decision: Rhodesia and Nyasaland in 1960* (London: Oxford University Press, 1960), 204.
52. Quoted in Hall, *Zambia,* 188.
53. Quoted in David C. Mulford, *Zambia: The Politics of Independence 1957–1964* (London: Oxford University Press, 1967), 96.
54. Quoted in Macpherson, *Kenneth Kaunda,* 268.
55. Kaunda, *Zambia,* 109.
56. Ibid., 110–11.
57. Ibid., 110.
58. Quoted in Hatch, *Two African Statesmen,* 156.
59. Quoted in Hall, *Zambia,* 189.
60. Kaunda, *Zambia,* 114.
61. Quoted in Macpherson, *Kenneth Kaunda,* 286.
62. Ibid., 293.
63. Quoted in Gerald Caplan, *The Elites of Barotseland, 1878–1969* (Berkeley: University of California Press, 1970), 176.
64. Northern Rhodesia, *Native Affairs Annual Report,* 1958, 79.
65. Ibid., 82.
66. A. H. M. Kirk-Greene, *The Transfer of Power* (Oxford: University of Oxford Inter-Faculty Committee for African Studies, 1979), 12.
67. Northern Rhodesia, *African Affairs Annual Report,* 1955, 91.
68. Quoted in Mulford, *Zambia,* 18.

69. Quoted in Fraenkel, *Wayaleshi*, 102.
70. Northern Rhodesia, *African Affairs Annual Report*, 1958, 80.
71. Northern Rhodesia, *African Affairs Annual Report*, 1959, "Barotseland."
72. Kalabo District Annual Report, 1958.
73. Quoted in Mulford, *Zambia*, 130.
74. Quoted in Hatch, *Two African Statesmen*, 1.
75. Merfyn Temple, preface to Kenneth Kaunda and Colin Morris, *Black Government?* (Lusaka: United Society for Christian Literature, 1960), 2.

Chapter Four London: The View from Whitehall

1. Anthony Sampson, *Anatomy of Britain* (London: Hodder and Stoughton, 1962), 219.
2. Ibid., 218.
3. Ibid., 222.
4. Viscount Boyd, in A. H. M. Kirk-Greene, ed., *The Transfer of Power: The Colonial Administrator in the Age of Decolonisation* (University of Oxford Inter-Faculty Committee for African Studies, 1979), 4.
5. Charles Dickens, *Little Dorrit: The Works of Charles Dickens*, 20 vols. (New York: Books, Inc., 1868), 10: 98.
6. Sampson, *Anatomy*, 230.
7. Viscount Boyd, quoting Sir Harry Johnston, in Kirk-Greene, ed., *Transfer of Power*, 7.
8. Quoted in Ibid., 8.
9. Quoted in A. H. M. Kirk-Greene, *Britain's Imperial Administrators, 1858–1966* (London: Macmillan, 2000), 130.
10. Quoted in Ibid., 140.
11. Quoted in Ibid., 279.
12. Quoted in Ibid., 140.
13. Quoted in R. D. Pearce, *The Turning Point in Africa: British Colonial Policy, 1938–1948* (London: Frank Cass, 1982), 146.
14. Author interview with Murray Armor, July 31, 1996.
15. Baillie Hamilton, quoted in Kirk-Greene, *Britain's Imperial Administrators*, 41.
16. George Orwell, "The Lion and the Unicorn," in *Collected Essays, Journalism, and Letters of George Orwell*, ed. Sonia Orwell and Ian Angus, 2 vols. (London: Secker and Warburg, 1968), 2: 73.
17. Kirk-Greene, *Britain's Imperial Administrators*, 46
18. John Hudson, interview with Diana Wylie August 15, 1999.
19. Quoted in Alison Smith and Mary Bull, eds., *Margery Perham and British Rule in Africa* (London: Frank Cass, 1991), 200.
20. Margery Perham, *Major Dane's Garden* (New York: Africana, 1971), 50.
21. Perham 1938, quoted in Smith and Bull, *Margery Perham and British Rule*, 7.
22. Dent in Smith and Bull, *Margery Perham and British Rule*, 201.
23. Quoted in Kirk-Greene, *Britain's Imperial Administrators*, 226.
24. A. H. M. Kirk-Greene, "Margery Perham and Colonial Administration: A Direct Influence on Indirect Rule," in A. F. Madden and D. K. Fieldhouse, eds., *Oxford and the Idea of Commonwealth* (London: Crown Helm, 1982), 128.
25. Private Diary, November 14, 1943, quoted by Porter in Smith and Bull, *Margery Perham and British Rule*, 87. Brackets indicate uncertain word in the original.
26. Lavin in Smith and Bull, *Margery Perham and British Rule*, 49.
27. Ralph Furse, *Aucuparius: Recollections of a Recruiting Officer* (London: Oxford University Press, 1962), 304.
28. Quoted by Kirk-Greene in Madden and Fieldhouse, *Oxford and the Idea of Commonwealth*, 125.

29. Quoted in Ibid., 124.
30. Leo Amery, quoted in Pearce, *Turning Point*, 8.
31. Speech of 1938, quoted in Ibid., 45.
32. Furse, *Aucuparius*, 304.
33. Sampson, *Anatomy*, 317–8.
34. Quoted in Pearce, *Turning Point*, 17.
35. Lord Samuel quoted in David Goldsworthy, *Colonial Issues in British Politics 1945–1961* (Oxford: Clarendon Press, 1971), 9.
36. J. E. Flint, "Macmillan as a Critic of Empire," in Hugh Macmillan and Shula Marks, eds., *Africa and Empire: W. M. Macmillan, Historian and Social Critic* (London: Temple Smith for the Institute of Commonwealth Studies, 1989), 213.
37. Pearce, *Turning Point*, 4.
38. Chamberlain, quoted in Goldsworthy, *Colonial Issues*, 9.
39. Sir Cosmo Parkinson, *The Colonial Office from Within* (London: Faber and Faber, 1947), 86.
40. Quoted in Pearce, *Turning Point*, 14.
41. Quoted in Ibid., 29.
42. Quoted in Crawford Young, *The African Colonial State in Comparative Perspective* (New Haven: Yale University Press, 1994), 183.
43. Quoted by Kirk-Greene in Madden and Fieldhouse, *Oxford and the Idea of Commonwealth*, 126.
44. Quoted in P. J. Cain and A. G. Hopkins, *British Imperialism: Crisis and Deconstruction, 1914–1990* (London: Longman, 1993), 276.
45. Sir John Shuckburgh, quoted in Pearce, *Turning Point*, 84.
46. Sudan Diary February 22, 1948, quoted by Louis in Smith and Bull, *Margery Perham and British Rule*, 149.
47. *Major Dane's Garden*, 130.
48. Ronald Robinson, "Sir Andrew Cohen: Proconsul of African Nationalism (1909–1968)," in L. H. Gann and Peter Duignan, eds., *African Proconsuls: European Governors in Africa* (New York: Free Press, 1978), 354.
49. Pearce, *Turning Point*, 98. The Kikuyu are a major ethnic group in Kenya.
50. John Maynard Keynes, quoted by Louis in Judith Brown and Wm. Roger Louis, eds., *The Oxford History of the British Empire: The Twentieth Century* (Oxford: Oxford University Press, 1999), 331.
51. Robinson, "Sir Andrew Cohen," 354.
52. Ronald Robinson, "Cohen, A. B." *Dictionary of National Biography 1961–1970*, 228.
53. Robinson, "Sir Andrew Cohen," 355.
54. Goldsworthy, *Colonial Issues*, 52.
55. Robinson, "Sir Andrew Cohen," 356.
56. *African Survey* 1938, quoted in John Hargreaves, "Approaches to Decolonization," in Douglas Rimmer and A. H. M. Kirk-Greene, eds., *The British Intellectual Engagement with Africa* (New York: St. Martin's Press, 2000), 94.
57. Quoted in Robinson, "Sir Andrew Cohen," 358.
58. Quoted in Pearce, *Turning Point*, 172.
59. Philip Mitchell, quoted in Ibid., 151.
60. Quoted in Robinson, "Sir Andrew Cohen," 360.
61. Fenner Brockway letter to the *Manchester Guardian*, July 20, 1946, quoted in Pearce, *Turning Point*, 124.
62. Quoted in Ibid., 181.
63. Harry Franklin, *The Flag-Wagger* (London: Shepheard-Walwyn, 1974), 6.
64. Quoted in Colin Baker, *Sir Glyn Jones: A Proconsul in Africa* (London: I. B. Tauris, 2000), 56.
65. Quoted in Ibid., 55.
66. Speech to Legislative Council, April 7, 1959, quoted in Robin J. Short, *African Sunset* (London: Johnson, 1973), 137.

67. Kalabo District Annual Report, 1958.
68. Richard Hall, *Zambia* (New York: Praeger, 1965), 121.
69. Ibid., 121.
70. Chimkoko quoted in David C. Mulford, *Zambia: The Politics of Independence 1957–1964* (London: Oxford University Press, 1967), 86.
71. Quoted in Pearce, *Turning Point*, 5.
72. Quoted in Robert Rotberg, *Black Heart: Gore-Browne and the Politics of Multiracial Zambia* (Berkeley: University of California Press, 1977), 280.
73. Robinson, "Sir Andrew Cohen," 361.
74. Brian Lapping, *End of Empire* (London: Granada, 1985), 462.
75. Quoted in Ibid., 464.
76. Quoted in Hall, *Zambia*, 156.
77. Short, *African Sunset*, 78.
78. Ibid., 86.
79. Ibid., 87.
80. Ibid., 78.
81. Roy Welensky, *Welensky's 4000 Days* (London: Collins, 1964), 35.
82. L. H. Gann, *A History of Northern Rhodesia* (London: Chatto and Windus, 1964), 240.
83. D. K. Fieldhouse, *The West and the Third World: Trade, Colonialism, Dependence and Development* (Oxford: Blackwell, 1999), 77.
84. Letter, February 26, 1953, reprinted in Perham, *Colonial Sequence* (London: Methuen, 1970), 77.
85. Letter, June 9, 1953, reprinted in Ibid., 79.
86. Letter, February 26, 1953, reprinted in Ibid., 78, 77.
87. Ibid., 78.
88. Ibid., 77–78.
89. Letter, June 9, 1953, reprinted in Ibid., 80.
90. Lord Home, quoted in Lapping, *End of Empire*, 470.
91. Quoted in Lapping, *End of Empire*, 470.
92. Benson to William Gorell Barnes, quoted in Philip Murphy, *Alan Lennox-Boyd: A Biography* (London: I. B. Tauris, 1999), 182.
93. Quoted in Robert Rotberg, *The Rise of Nationalism in Central Africa: The Making of Malawi and Zambia 1873–1964* (Cambridge: Harvard University Press, 1965), 282.
94. Quoted in Fergus Macpherson, *Kenneth Kaunda of Zambia: The Times and the Man* (Lusaka: Oxford University Press, 1974), 216.
95. Welensky, *4000 Days*, 123.
96. Viscount Boyd in Kirk-Greene, *Transfer of Power*, 3.
97. Quoted in *Report of the Nyasaland Commission of Inquiry* (Devlin Commission) (London: HM Stationery Office, July 1959), 42–43.
98. Boris Gussman, *Out in the Mid-day Sun* (New York: Oxford University Press, 1963), 173.
99. Banda to Governor Robert Armitage, quoted in Lapping, *End of Empire*, 479.
100. Speech to the House of Commons, quoted in Lapping, *End of Empire*, 480.
101. Murphy, *Lennox-Boyd*, 207.
102. *Report of the Nyasaland Commission of Inquiry* (Devlin Commission), 1.
103. Ibid., 142.
104. Ibid., 22.
105. Quoted in Richard Lamb, *The Macmillan Years 1957–1963: The Emerging Truth* (London: John Murray, 1995), 237.
106. Quoted in Alistair Horne, *Harold Macmillan*, 2 vols. (Harmondsworth: Penguin, 1989), 2: 181.
107. Macmillan, quoted in Lamb, *Macmillan Years*, 236.
108. Murphy, *Lennox-Boyd*, 200.
109. Quoted in Ibid., 220.
110. Sir Leslie Monson in Kirk-Greene, *Transfer of Power*, 24.

111. Quoted in Murphy, *Lennox-Boyd*, 90.

112. Edward Fitzgerald, *Rubaiyat of Omar Khayyam*, st. 12.

113. Nigel Fisher, *Iain Macleod* (London: Deutsch, 1973), 142.

114. Quoted in Anthony Sampson, *Macmillan: A Study in Ambiguity* (London: Allen Lane, 1967), 181.

115. Interview with W. P. Kirkman, quoted in Robert Shepherd, *Iain Macleod* (London: Hutchinson, 1994), 162.

116. Letter to *The Times*, February 27, 1959, reprinted in Perham, *Colonial Sequence*, 158.

117. See Macleod, "Trouble in Africa," *The Spectator*, January 31, 1964.

118. Quoted in Prosser Gifford, "Misconceived Dominion: The Creation and Disintegration of Federation in British Central Africa," in P. Gifford and Wm. Roger Louis, eds. *The Transfer of Power in Africa. Decolonization, 1940–1960* (New Haven: Yale University Press, 1982), 408.

119. Quoted in Murphy, *Lennox-Boyd*, 210.

120. Macmillan, quoted in Lamb, *Macmillan Years*, 233.

121. Welensky to Home, quoted in Lamb, *Macmillan Years*, 233.

122. Welensky, *4000 Days*, 140.

123. Ibid., 144.

124. Harold Macmillan, *Pointing the Way 1959–1961* (New York, Harper & Row, 1972), 139.

125. Welensky, *4000 Days*, 161–62, 187.

126. Quoted in Sampson, *Anatomy*, 81.

127. Macmillan Diary October 25, 1958, quoted in Macmillan, *Pointing the Way*, 134.

128. Lawrence James, *The Rise and Fall of the British Empire* (London: Little Brown, 1994), 614.

129. *Report of the Advisory Commission on the Review of the Constitution of Rhodesia and Nyasaland* (Monckton Commission) (London: HM Stationery Office, October 1960), 6.

130. All quotations from Short, *African Sunset*, 180–81.

131. Harold Macmillan, "Africa," *African Affairs* 59(1960), 194.

132. Quoted in Sampson, *Macmillan*, 184.

133. Macmillan, *Pointing the Way*, 156–57.

134. Sampson, *Anatomy*, 327.

135. Macmillan, *Pointing the Way*, 147.

136. *The Listener*, November 28, 1963, 871.

137. Sampson, *Macmillan*, 177.

138. *Daily Express*, February 23, 1960, quoted in Horne, *Harold Macmillan*, 269.

139. Quoted in Ibid., 272.

Epilogue

1. Quoted in Anthony Sampson, *Macmillan: A Study in Ambiguity* (London: Allen Lane, 1967), 190.

2. *Report of the Advisory Commission on the Review of the Constitution of Rhodesia and Nyasaland* (London: HM Stationery Office, October 1960), 110.

3. Patrick Wall to Welensky October 17, 1960, quoted in Philip Murphy, *Party Politics and Decolonization* (Oxford: Oxford University Press, 1995), 182.

4. Wall to Welensky November 4, 1960, quoted in Ibid., 183.

5. Roy Welensky, *Welensky's 4000 Days* (London: Collins, 1964), 288.

6. Quoted in Robert Shepherd, *Iain Macleod* (London: Hutchinson, 1994), 221.

7. Diary June 4, 1961, quoted in Harold Macmillan, *The End of the Day* (New York: Harper & Row, 1973), 314.

8. Ibid., 318.

9. Harold Evans, quoted in Shepherd, *Iain Macleod*, 230.

10. Boyd to Welensky April 3, 1963, quoted in Philip Murphy, *Alan Lennox-Boyd: A Biography* (London: I. B. Tauris, 1999), 249.

11. Duncan Sandys, quoted in Welensky, *4000 Days*, 319.
12. Ibid., 363.
13. Kenneth Kaunda, *Zambia Shall Be Free: An Autobiography* (New York: Praeger, 1963), 155.
14. Sir Leslie Monson, in A. H. M. Kirk-Greene, ed., *The Transfer of Power: The Colonial Administrator in the Age of Decolonisation* (University of Oxford Inter-Faculty Committee for African Studies, 1979), 29.
15. Quoted in Richard Hall, *Zambia* (New York: Praeger, 1965), 218.
16. John Charles Hatch, *Two African Statesmen: Kaunda of Zambia and Nyerere of Tanzania* (Chicago: Regnery, 1976), 174.
17. David C. Mulford, *Zambia. The Politics of Independence 1957–1964* (London: Oxford University Press, 1967), 301.
18. Sesheke District, Annual Report for 1963, 1.
19. Ibid., 1.
20. Ibid., 19.
21. Ibid., 15.
22. Ibid., 5–6.
23. Ibid., 1.
24. Northern Rhodesia, *African Affairs Annual Report* 1960, 78.
25. Quoted in Gerald Caplan, "Barotseland: The Secessionist Challenge to Zambia," *Journal of Modern African Studies* 6: 3(1968), 350.
26. Ibid., 354.
27. Quoted in Mutumba Mainga Bull, "The Barotseland Agreement 1964 in Historical Perspective. A Preliminary Study" (unpublished paper, University of Zambia, 1996), 4.
28. Quoted in Charles Allen, *Tales from the Dark Continent* (New York: St. Martin's Press, 1979), 146.
29. Letter from Jennifer Gordon Lennox, Lady-in-Waiting to H. R. H. The Queen Mother, August 20, 2001.
30. Robin J. Short, *African Sunset* (London: Johnson, 1973), 79.
31. Ibid., 89.
32. Quoted in Kevin Shillingon, *History of Africa* (New York: St. Martin's Press, 1995), 413.
33. Unidentified officer quoted in Allen, *Tales*, 139.
34. Margery Perham, *The Colonial Reckoning* (New York: Knopf, 1962), 8.
35. Margery Perham, *The Observer*, July 24, 1960, quoted in Robert Heussler, *Yesterday's Rulers: The Making of the British Colonial Service* (Syracuse: Syracuse University Press, 1963), 208.
36. Margery Perham, *The Listener*, December 10, 1964, quoted by Oliver in Alison Smith and Mary Bull, eds., *Margery Perham and British Rule in Africa* (London: Frank Cass, 1991), 25.
37. Harold Macmillan, *Pointing the Way 1959–1961* (London: Harper & Row, 1972), 118.
38. Macmillan, *Pointing the Way*, 118–19.
39. *Report of the Nyasaland Commission of Inquiry* (London: HM Stationery Office, July 1959), 16.
40. David Taylor, personal communication to the author.
41. Murray Armor, letter to the author, November 9, 1994.
42. Ibid.
43. Ibid.
44. David Taylor, personal communication to the author.
45. Quoted in Kirk-Greene, *Transfer of Power*, 14.
46. Murray Armor, letter to the author, November 9, 1994.
47. Author interview with Father Bruno, August 9, 1999.
48. Ralph Furse, *Aucuparius: Recollections of a Recruiting Officer* (London: Oxford University Press, 1962), 68
49. Quoted in Carl Van Doren, *Benjamin Franklin* (New York: Viking Press, 1938), 755.
50. Author interview with W. S. Sundano, August 8, 1999.

SOURCES

For general histories of Northern Rhodesia/Zambia, see Lewis H. Gann, *A History of Northern Rhodesia: Early Days to 1953* (London: Chatto & Windus, 1964); Lewis H. Gann and Peter Duignan, *The Rulers of British Africa 1870–1914* (Stanford: Stanford University Press, 1978); Richard Hall, *Zambia* (New York: Praeger, 1965); and Andrew Roberts, *A History of Zambia* (New York: Africana, 1979). A useful reference work is John J. Grotpeter, *Historical Dictionary of Zambia* (Metuchen, NJ: Scarecrow Press, 1979).

Introduction: Barotseland

The two most authoritative studies of pre- and early colonial Barotseland are Mutumba Mainga's *Bulozi under the Luyana Kings: Political Evolution and State Formation* (London: Longman, 1973) and Gwyn Prins, *The Hidden Hippopotamus. Reappraisal in African History: The Early Colonial Experience in Western Zambia* (Cambridge: Cambridge University Press, 1980). Mainga is herself Lozi and was one of the first Zambians to earn a Ph.D. in history. Prins departs from some of her findings, especially in his emphasis on the symbolic dimensions of early Lozi encounters with Europeans. Gerald Caplan's "Barotseland's Scramble for Protection," *Journal of African History* 10: 2(1969), 277–294, provides a useful summary of the events leading up to the Protectorate. His book, *The Elites of Barotseland, 1878–1969* (Berkeley: University of California Press, 1970) continues the story up to independence, looking at the elites through a very critical lens. Also useful are Gervas Clay, *Your Friend Lewanika: The Life and Times of Lubosi Lewanika, Litunga of Barotseland 1842 to 1916* (London: Chatto & Windus, 1968) and Eric Stokes, "Barotseland: The Survival of an African State," in Eric Stokes and Richard Brown, eds., *The Zambesian Past: Studies in Central African History* (Manchester: Manchester University Press, 1966). Unfortunately Adolphe Jalla's *History of the Barotse Nation* (Lusaka, 1921) is not available in the United States. This book was first published as *Litaba za Sicaba sa Malozi* (1909) and is based on traditions collected by Coillard's missionary colleague.

Several of Livingstone's works provide descriptions of the region: *Missionary Travels and Researches in Southern Africa* (New York: Harper, 1859 [1857]); *Livingstone's Private Journals, 1851–53,* ed. Isaac Schapera (London: Chatto & Windus, 1960); and *African Journal, 1853–1856,* ed. Isaac Schapera, 2 vol. (Berkeley: University of California Press, 1963). Other Europeans followed in his wake in the later nineteenth and early twentieth century, including F. S. Arnot, *Garenganze; or, Seven Years' Pioneer Mission Work in Central Africa* (London: Hawkins, 1889 [3rd edn.]) and idem, *Missionary Travels in Central Africa* (London: Alfred Holness, 1914); François Coillard, *On the Threshold of Central Africa,* trans. and ed. by Catherine Mackintosh (London: Hodder & Stoughton, 1902) (French original: *Sur le Haut-Zambèze* [Paris: Berger-Levrault, 1899]); E. C. Tabler, ed., *Trade and Travel in Early Barotseland: The Diaries of George*

Westbeech, 1885–1888, and Captain Norman MacLeod, 1875–1876 (Berkeley: University of California Press, 1963); Richard Sampson, *The Man with a Toothbrush in his Hat: The Story and Times of George Copp Westbeech* (Lusaka: Multimedia Publications, 1972); Emil Holub, *Seven Years in South Africa*, 2 vol. (Detroit: Negro History Press, 1971 [1881]); Frederick Selous, *Travel and Adventure in South-East Africa* (London: Rowland Ward, 1893); James Johnston M. E. D., *Reality versus Romance in South Central Africa* (Chicago: F. H. Revell, 1893); Colonel James Stevenson-Hamilton, *The Barotseland Journal of James Stevenson-Hamilton 1898–1899*, ed. J. P. R. Wallis (London: Chatto & Windus, 1953); Alfred Bertrand, *The Kingdom of the Barotse* (London: T. Fisher Unwin, 1899); Major A. St. H. Gibbons, *Africa from South to North through Marotseland* (London: John Lane, 1904); Colonel Colin Harding, *In Remotest Barotseland* (London: Hurst & Blackett, 1904) and *Far Bugles* (Croydon: H. R. Grubb, 1933); Col. J. C. B. Statham, *Through Angola, a Coming Colony* (Edinburgh: W. Blackwood, 1922). These later accounts provide fascinating glimpses of Lewanika and his court. A postscript to his visit to England for the coronation of Edward VII can be found in Nigel Watt, "Lewanika's Visit to Edinburgh. Discovery of Early Photographs," *Northern Rhodesia Journal* 2: 1(1953), 2–8, which provides a wonderful photograph of the monarch looking for all the world like a darker-hued Benjamin Disraeli.

Chapter One   Kalabo: The View from the *Boma*

Most of this chapter is based on interviews with people who lived or served in Kalabo or Barotseland in the late 1950s: Murray and Jeanne Armor, David Salmon, John Herniman, Barbro Herniman, Paul Herniman, Dick and Hazel Japp, Mike Japp, Rob and Grace Hart, Father Bruno, W. S. Sundona, Gervas and Betty Clay, and David Taylor (Sesheke early 1960s). Briefer interviews were conducted in 1999 with W. M. Mubita, *induna* of Lealui; S. M. Wendiana, principal of Kalabo Hospital; Brigid N. Mundia, assistant at the hospital; Rev. Mkuzi A. Banda, and several residents of St. Joseph Mission, Mangango. In addition, questionnaires were answered by Alec Fisher, John Herniman, David Salmon, John Housden, and Murray Armor. I have also made extensive use of David Salmon's letters to his parents, of Murray Armor's reports and unpublished reminiscences, of John Herniman's journal, and discussions with David Taylor, Philip Bowcock, and Hywel Griffiths. Both Armor and Herniman have extensive collections of photographs and slides, as well as 16 mm films by Boma Productions.

The Northern Rhodesia *African Affairs Annual Reports* provide an official overview of all administrative departments in the various provinces of the Protectorate during the 1950s, ending with independence in 1964. They are supplemented with reports from the specialized services such as education, labor, etc. These reports are available in the Public Record Office in Kew in the CO 799 and DO 123 series. I have also drawn on the voluminous Kalabo District Tour Reports for 1954–60 in the National Archives of Zambia in Lusaka (NAZ BSE 1 & 2 series).

There are also a host of published memoirs or collections of letters, the most relevant of which are: Kenneth Bradley, *Diary of a District Officer* (London: Harrap, 1953) and idem, *Once a District Officer* (New York: St. Martin's Press, 1966); Harry Franklin, *The Flag-Wagger* (London: Shepheard-Walwyn, 1974); Ralph Furse, *Aucuparius* (Oxford: Oxford University Press, 1962); R. T. Kerslake, *Time and the Hour: Nigeria, West Africa and the Second World War* (London: Radcliffe Press, 1997); Randal Sadleir, *Tanzania: Journey to Republic* (London: Radcliffe Press, 1999); Robin J. Short, *African Sunset* (London: Johnson, 1973); John Smith, *Vet in Africa: Life on the Zambezi 1913–1933*, ed. Tony Bagnall Smith (London: Radcliffe Press, 1997); D. W. Stirke, *Barotseland: Eight Years among the Barotse* (New York: Negro University Press 1969 [1922]). These are amplified by works such as Charles Allen, *Tales from the Dark Continent* (New York: St. Martin's Press, 1979); Kenneth Blackburne, *Lasting Legacy: A Story of British Colonialism* (London: Johnson, 1976); Dick Hobson, *Tales of Zambia* (London: Zambia Trust Society, 1996); Joan Alexander, ed., *Voices and Echoes: Tales from Colonial Women* (New York: Quartet, 1983); Emily Bradley, *Dearest Priscilla* (London: Max Parrish, 1950); V. W. Brelsford, *Generation of Men. The European Pioneers of Northern Rhodesia* (Salisbury: The Northern

Rhodesia Society, 1965); Helen Callaway, *Gender, Culture and Empire: European Women in Colonial Africa* (Urbana: University of Illinois Press, 1987); Joanna Trollope, *Britannia's Daughters: Women of the British Empire* (London: Hutchinson, 1983).

The pre-eminent historian of the Colonial Service is Anthony Kirk-Greene, whose extensive writings are also cited in chapter four. For this chapter the most pertinent are: "The Thin White Line: The Size of the British Colonial Service in Africa," *African Affairs* 79: 314(1980), 25–44; *On Crown Service: A History of H. M. Colonial Service and HMOCS 1837–1997* (London: I. B. Tauris, 1999); "Imperial Administration and the Athletic Imperative: The Case of the District Officer in Africa," in W. J. Baker and James A. Mangan, eds., *Sport in Africa: Essays in Social History* (New York: Africana, 1987). Other important studies include Robert Heussler, *Yesterday's Rulers: The Making of the British Colonial Service* (Syracuse: Syracuse University Press, 1963); Ralph Furse, *Aucuparius: Recollections of a Recruiting Officer* (London: Oxford University Press, 1962; Charles Jeffries, *Partners for Progress: The Men and Women of the Colonial Service* (London: Harrap, 1949); Margery Perham, *Lugard*, 2 vol. (London: Collins, 1956–60); John Lonsdale, "Kenyatta's Trial: Breaking and Making an African Nationalist," in Peter Coss, ed., *The Moral World of the Law* (Cambridge: Cambridge University Press, 2000) and idem, introduction to Terence Gavaghan, *Of Lions and Dung Beetles: A "Man in the Middle" of Colonial Administration in Kenya* (Ilfracombe, Devon: Arthur H. Stockwell, 1999).

Surprisingly little seems to have been written on the *boma* messengers, but see V. W. Brelsford, "The Boma Messenger and his Uniform," *Northern Rhodesia Journal* 2: 3(1954), 34–42, and the unpublished vignettes by David Taylor. On rural development policies there are valuable studies by John A. Hellen, *Rural Economic Development in Zambia, 1890–1964* (Munich: Weltforum Verlag, 1968); Laurel van Horn, "The Agricultural History of Barotseland, 1840–1964," in Robin Palmer and Neil Parsons, eds., *The Roots of Rural Poverty in Central and Southern Africa* (Berkeley: University of California Press, 1977); and G. Kay, "Agricultural Progress in Zambia," in M. F. Thomas and G. W. Whittington, eds., *Environment and Land Use in Africa* (London: Whittington, 1969).

Chapter Two   Libonda: The View from the *Kuta*

This chapter draws on many of the same sources, primary and published, as the introduction and chapter 1. In addition, see *Central African Territories: Comparative Survey of Native Policy* (London: HM Stationery Office, repr. 1959) and the *Calendars of the District Notebooks (Western Province), 1851–1963* (Lusaka: National Archives of Zambia, n.d.) for details of Native Administration and information on a surprising variety of subjects. On Lozi history and political structure, the works of Mainga and Caplan are particularly useful. In addition, there are a number of studies on various aspects of Barotse society by the distinguished South African anthropologist Max Gluckman: "The Lozi of Barotseland in North-Western Rhodesia," in Elizabeth Colson and Max Gluckman, eds., *Seven Tribes of British Central Africa* (London: Oxford University Press, 1951); *The Economy of the Central Barotse Plain* (Rhodes-Livingstone Papers, No. 7, Livingstone, 1941); *Essays on Lozi Land and Royal Property* (Rhodes-Livingstone Papers, No. 10, Livingstone, 1943); *The Ideas of Barotse Jurisprudence* (New Haven: Yale University Press, 1965); "Notes on the Social Background of Barotse Music," in A. M. Jones, *African Music in Northern Rhodesia and Some Other Places*, Appendix 2, (Rhodes-Livingstone Occasional Papers, No. 4, Livingstone, 1958); "The Role of the Sexes in Wiko Circumcision Ceremonies," in Meyer Fortes, ed. *Social Structure: Studies Presented to A. R. Radcliffe-Brown* (New York: Russell & Russell, 1963). A useful ethnographic summary is provided by V. W. Turner, *The Lozi Peoples of North-Western Rhodesia* (London: International African Insitute, 1952), part of the comprehensive series on Africa edited by Daryll Forde.

The work of Margery Perham on colonial administration and the role of Lord Lugard in institutionalizing indirect rule is pivotal. See in addition to her study of Lugard, her comments in *The Colonial Reckoning* (New York: Alfred Knopf, 1962). In theory, indirect rule had been superseded by the 1950s, as R. E. Robinson explains in his article, "Why 'Indirect Rule' has been replaced by 'Local

Government,' " *Journal of African Administration,* July 1950, 12–15, but in fact little changed in Barotseland.

On witchcraft, the most comprehensive study is that commissioned in the wake of the "Kaliloze gunmen" outbreak in 1957–58: Barrie Reynolds, *Magic, Divination and Witchcraft among the Barotse of Northern Rhodesia* (Berkeley: University of California Press, 1963), although Reynolds had worked primarily among the Tonga and faced severe time pressures. On agriculture and land usage, see in addition to Hellen and Van Horn, cited above, D. U. Peters, *Land Usage in Barotseland,* ed. N. Smyth (Lusaka: Rhodes-Livingstone Institute, 1960) and C. G. Trapnell and J. N. Clothier, *The Soils, Vegetation and Agricultural Systems of North-Western Rhodesia: Report of the Ecological Survey,* rev. ed. (Lusaka: Government Printer, 1957). For labor migration, I have drawn most heavily on the manuscript version of Murray Armor, "Migrant Labour in the Kalabo District of Barotseland," which was subsequently published in the *Bulletin* of the International Labour Association, and on R. Philpott, "The Mulobezi-Mongu Labour Route," *Rhodes-Livingstone Journal* 3 (1945), 50–54. The most useful look at education is provided by M. C. Mortimer, "History of the Barotse National School, 1907–1957," *Northern Rhodesia Journal* 3(1957), 303–310.

While little has been published on Lozi religion, there are several studies of royal rituals: Ernest Brown, "Drums on the Water: The Kuomboka Ceremony of the Lozi of Zambia," *African Musicology* (Nairobi), 1: 1(September 1983), 67–68; M. Yeta, "The Kuomboka Ceremony during Yeta III's Reign," *Northern Rhodesia Journal* 4(1961), 574–582; portions of C. W. Macintosh, *Yeta III, Paramount Chief of the Barotse* (London: Pickering & Inglis, 1937); and the first-hand reportage by Peter Fraenkel in *Wayaleshi* (London: Weidenfeld & Nicolson, 1959). In addition, George Hickey has made a film, "Kuomboka (To get out of water)" (1999), which traces some of the historical background but is mostly focused on the ritual in its present form. Terence Ranger provides wonderful insights into the Lozi gift for inventing tradition in "The Invention of Tradition in Colonial Africa," in Eric Hobsbawm and Terence Ranger, eds., *The Invention of Tradition* (Cambridge: Cambridge University Press, 1983). Ranger has also written an interesting essay about early religious maneuvering in Barotseland: "The 'Ethiopian' Episode in Barotseland, 1900–1905," *Rhodes-Livingstone Journal* 37(1965). Finally, see his article, "Making Northern Rhodesia Imperial: Variations on a Royal Theme, 1924–1938," *African Affairs* 79: 316(July 1980), 349–373.

C. M. N. White, *The Elements in Luvale Beliefs and Rituals,* Rhodes-Livingstone Papers, No. 32 (Manchester, 1961) shows possible northern sources for Lozi rituals. More recently, the work of Elisabeth Cameron on initiation arts in Kabompo District is also suggestive for Lozi arts because of the likelihood of cultural borrowings from Lunda. See both her article, "Women = Masks. Initiation Arts in North-Western Province, Zambia," *African Arts* 31: 2 Spring 1998, 50–61, and her paper presented at the 42nd Annual Meeting of the African Studies Association, Philadelphia, November 11–14, 1999: "Women, Art and Mukanda." Karen Milbourne has been carrying out doctoral research on the royal arts of Barotseland and her work, when completed, will be extremely valuable in filling a great gap in the literature.

Chapter Three   Salisbury: The View from the Federation

There are a number of insightful contemporary works on the Central African Federation, mostly rather critical: Cyril Dunn, *African Witness* (London: Victor Gollancz, 1959); Harry Franklin, *Unholy Wedlock: The Failure of the Central African Federation* (London: George Allen & Unwin, 1963); Boris Gussman, *Out in the Mid-day Sun* (New York: Oxford University Press, 1963); Peter Fraenkel, *Wayaleshi* (referred to earlier); Colin Leys and Cranford Pratt, eds., *A New Deal in Central Africa* (New York: Praeger, 1960); Philip Mason, *Year of Decision. Rhodesia and Nyasaland in 1960* (London: Oxford University Press, 1960); Anthony St. John Wood, *Northern Rhodesia: The Human Background* (London: Pall Mall, 1961). Doris Lessing's *Going Home* (London: Michael Joseph, 1957) provides a dispiriting picture of her visit to the land of her birth in 1956, just before Welensky became federal prime minister.

Sir Roy Welensky's *Welensky's 4000 Days: The Life and Death of the Federation of Rhodesia and Nyasaland* (London: Collins, 1964) is an unabashed *apologia pro vita sua,* portraying its author as an apostle of enlightened multi-racialism, brought down by the devious politicians of Whitehall. Garry Allighan's *The Welensky Story* (Cape Town: Durnell, 1962) and Lewis Gann and Michael Gelfand's *Huggins of Rhodesia. The Man and his Country* (London: George Allen & Unwin, 1964) also present the two leaders in a largely favorable light. Hugh Macmillan and Frank Shapiro, *Zion in Africa: The Jews of Zambia* (London: I. B. Tauris) includes a shorter entry on Welensky but within the very rich context of the Jewish community in southern Africa. Robert Rotberg, *Black Heart: Gore-Browne and the Politics of Multiracial Zambia* (Berkeley: University of California Press, 1977) is an exhaustively researched biography of this idiosyncratic figure and his influential role in shaping the politics of Northern Rhodesia up to independence. Useful although less directly relevant to this chapter is Alan Megahey, *Humphrey Gibbs, Beleagured Governor: Southern Rhodesia, 1929–69* (Basingstoke: Macmillan, 1998).

On nationalist politics, there are first of all the writings of Kenneth Kaunda himself: "Rider and Horse in Northern Rhodesia," *Africa South* 3(July–September 1959) 52–56; *Zambia Shall Be Free: An Autobiography* (New York: Praeger, 1963) and *Black Government?* (Lusaka: United Society for Christian Literature, 1960), written with Colin Morris. Kaunda is also the subject of two very sympathetic biographies: Fergus Macpherson, *Kenneth Kaunda of Zambia: The Times and the Man* (Lusaka: Oxford University Press, 1974) and John Charles Hatch, *Two African Statesmen: Kaunda of Zambia and Nyerere of Tanzania* (Chicago: Regnery, 1976). More generally, see David C. Mulford, *Zambia: The Politics of Independence 1957–1964* (London: Oxford University Press, 1967); Robert Rotberg, *The Rise of Nationalism in Central Africa: The Making of Malawi and Zambia 1873–1964* (Cambridge: Harvard University Press, 1965); and Ian Henderson, "The Origins of Nationalism in East and Central Africa: The Zambian Case," *Journal of African History* 11: 4(1970), 591–603. What is surprising is the dearth of more recent studies of the period except for brief treatments in general works on decolonization and the transfer of power (see below, chapter 4).

There are several contemporary accounts of the Kariba Dam project and its immediate consequences. The most authoritative is that of the eminent anthropologist, Elizabeth Colson: *The Social Consequences of Resettlement: The Impact of the Kariba Resettlement upon the Gwembe Tonga* (Manchester: Manchester University Press, 1971). Professor Colson also kindly provided answers to my queries. More journalistic in approach are the reports by David Howarth, *The Shadow of the Dam* (London: Collins, 1961) and Frank Clements, *Kariba: The Struggle with the River God* (New York: Putnam, 1960). On the vampire scare, see in addition to Fraenkel, W.V. Brelsford, "The 'Banyama' Myth." *NADA* 9: 4(1967), 49–68; and the recent book by Luise White, *Speaking with Vampires: Rumor and History in Colonial Africa* (Berkeley: University of California Press, 2000). The Capricorn Society and its guiding spirit, Colonel David Stirling, await a proper study, but a start has been made by Bizcek Jube Phiri, "The Capricorn Africa Society Revisited," *International Journal of African Historical Studies* 24: 1(1991), 65–83. Although not directly relevant to Barotseland, Hortense Powdermaker's classic work, *Copper Town: Changing Africa. The Human Situation on the Rhodesian Copperbelt* (New York: Harper & Row, 1962), offers keen insights into the social ramifications of federation policies and attitudes.

Chapter Four   London: The View from Whitehall

Anthony Sampson's *Anatomy of Britain* (London: Hodder and Stoughton, 1962) provides a superb dissection of official and establishment Britain for the time period in question. Sir Nikolaus Pevsner complements this architecturally in the first volume of his *London* (Harmondsworth: Penguin, 1973), which covers Whitehall and Westminster. There are several works by Whitehall insiders: Sir Cosmo Parkinson, *The Colonial Office from Within* (London: Faber and Faber, 1947) and Sir Charles Jeffries, *Whitehall and the Colonial Service: An Administrative Memoir, 1939–1956* (London: The Athlone Press, 1972). Nothing, however, matches the publications of Anthony Kirk-Greene on the role and character of the colonial service, especially *Britain's Imperial Administrators, 1858–1966* (London: Macmillan, 2000); *On Crown Service* (see above), and *The Transfer of Power: The Colonial Administrator in the Age of Decolonisation* (University of Oxford Inter-Faculty Committee for African Studies, 1979), the edited proceedings of the symposium he organized in 1978 at St. Antony's College, Oxford, which brought together for the last time a range of people intimately involved at all levels in the colonial enterprise. Appropriately, Kirk-Greene also penned the chapter, "A Historiographical Perspective on the Transfer of Power in British Colonial Africa: A Bibliographical Essay" in *The Transfer of Power in Africa,* edited by Prosser Gifford and Wm. Roger Louis (New Haven: Yale University Press, 1982). Finally, he co-edited with Douglas Rimmer *The British Intellectual Engagement with Africa in the Twentieth Century* (London: Macmillan, 2000).

Many of Margery Perham's shorter writings have been conveniently collected in the two-volume *Colonial Sequence, 1949–1969: A Chronological Commentary upon British Colonial Policy in Africa* (London: Methuen, 1970). I have also drawn on her novel *Major Dane's Garden* (New York: Africana, 1971), originally published in 1926, and on her biography of Lugard (see above). A biography of Perham herself is announced but has not yet appeared; in the interim there is an extremely valuable collection of essays devoted to her life and work edited by Alison Smith and Mary Bull, *Margery Perham and British Rule in Africa* (London: Frank Cass, 1991).

For Perham and her contemporaries, the *Dictionary of National Biography* of course provides an indispensable point of entry. Creech Jones's views can be found in his *New Fabian Colonial Essays* (London: Hogarth Press, 1959) and "British Colonial Policy, with Particular Reference to Africa," *International Affairs* 27(1951), 176–83. Sir Andrew Cohen's 1958 lectures at Northwestern have been published as *British Policy in Changing Africa* (London: Routledge and Kegan Paul, 1959). I have also drawn on two studies of Cohen by Ronald Robinson: "Sir Andrew Cohen: Proconsul of African Nationalism (1909–1968)," in L. H. Gann and Peter Duignan, eds., *African Proconsuls: European Governors in Africa* (New York: Free Press, 1978), and "Andrew Cohen and the Transfer of Power in Tropical Africa, 1940–1951," in W. H. Morris-Jones and Georges Fischer, eds., *Decolonisation and After: The British and French Experiences* (London: Frank Cass, 1980).

The literature on late colonialism, decolonization, and the transfer of power is hyperabundant. Among the most accessible are James Morris, *Farewell the Trumpets: An Imperial Retreat* (New York: Harcourt, Brace Jovanovich, 1978); Lawrence James, *The Rise and Fall of the British Empire* (London: Little Brown, 1994); and Brian Lapping, *End of Empire* (London: Granada, 1985), which accompanied a television series of the same name. *The Oxford History of the British Empire: The Twentieth Century,* edited by Judith Brown and Wm. Roger Louis (Oxford: Oxford University Press, 1999), reflects the most recent scholarship, but since it covers the entire empire, Africa is not the only focus. The same is true of P. J. Cain and A. G. Hopkins, *British Imperialism: Crisis and Deconstruction, 1914–1990* (London: Longman, 1993), which emphasizes the role of economic factors in imperialism and its decline. Two other useful general works are Kenneth Robinson and Frederick Madden, eds., *Essays in Imperial Government* (Oxford: Blackwell, 1963) and D. K. Fieldhouse, *The West and the Third World: Trade, Colonialism, Dependence and Development* (Oxford: Blackwell, 1999).

On Africa more specifically, I have drawn on Penelope Hetherington, *British Paternalism and Africa, 1920–1940* (London: Frank Cass, 1978); Crawford Young, *The African Colonial State in Comparative Perspective* (New Haven: Yale University Press, 1994); Prosser Gifford, "Misconceived Dominion: The Creation and Disintegration of Federation in British Central Africa," in Prosser Gifford and Wm. Roger Louis, eds. *The Transfer of Power in Africa: Decolonization, 1940–1960* (New Haven: Yale University Press, 1982), and in the same volume, Cranford Pratt, "Colonial Governments and the Transfer of Power in East Africa." There are several fascinating studies that track the twists and turns of British colonial policy more broadly, including R. D. Pearce, *The Turning Point in Africa: British Colonial Policy, 1938–1948* (London: Frank Cass, 1982) and David Goldsworthy, *Colonial Issues in British Politics 1945–1961* (Oxford: Clarendon Press, 1971). However, because of the 30-year rule, many government documents for the period under study were not available for these works. Among the first to fully exploit them once they were unsealed was Philip Murphy in his

Party Politics and Decolonization: The Conservative Party and British Colonial Policy in Tropical Africa, 1951–1964 (Oxford: Oxford University Press, 1995). Similarly, John Hargreaves has incorporated new material in the second edition of his classic *Decolonization in Africa* (London: Longman, 1996) and in his "Approaches to Decolonization," in Rimmer and Kirk-Greene, eds. *The British Intellectual Engagement with Africa* (see above).

Murphy's *Alan Lennox-Boyd: A Biography* (London: I. B. Tauris, 1999) also exploits both Colonial Office and Conservative Party records, but his argument that Lennox-Boyd's policies were headed in the same direction as those adopted by his successor, Iain Macleod, seems debatable. Macleod died before writing his own memoirs. One of his few published writings is the much-quoted leader, "Trouble in Africa." *The Spectator,* January 31, 1964. He is the subject, however, of two biographies: Nigel Fisher, *Iain Macleod* (London: Deutsch, 1973) and Robert Shepherd, *Iain Macleod* (London: Hutchinson, 1994). Harold Macmillan made sure that his own version of events would be heard by publishing his multi-volumed memoirs soon after his retirement. Volume Four, *Pointing the Way 1959–1961* (London: Harper & Row, 1972) details his views and actions concerning African policy in this period. A talk on his African trip in early 1960 was published in abridged form as "Africa" in *African Affairs* 59(1960), 191–200. The authorized biography of Macmillan is that of Alistair Horne: *Harold Macmillan,* 2 vol. (Harmondsworth: Penguin, 1989). Horne had access to Macmillan's diary and generally presents a sympathetic portrait of the prime minister. There are other biographies, including Anthony Sampson, *Macmillan: A Study in Ambiguity* (London: Allen Lane, 1967), Nigel Fisher, *Harold Macmillan* (New York: St. Martin's Press, 1982), and Richard Lamb, *The Macmillan Years 1957–1963: The Emerging Truth* (London: John Murray, 1995). The last of these, as the title suggests, is the most critical of Macmillan and uses the now open sources to demonstrate how unreliable Macmillan's own account is. An interesting gloss is provided by Tony Hopkins, "Macmillan's Audit of Empire, 1957," in Peter Clarke and Clive Treblicock, eds., *Understanding Decline: Perceptions and Realities of British Economic Performance* (Cambridge: Cambridge University Press, 1997).

Several works joining the debate about empire itself have been useful. On the pro side, there is Sir Alan Burns, *In Defence of Colonies* (London: George Allen & Unwin, 1957), while critiques can be found in J. E. Flint, "Macmillan as a Critic of Empire," in Hugh Macmillan and Shula Marks, eds., *Africa and Empire: W. M. Macmillan, Historian and Social Critic* (London: Temple Smith, 1989); Mona Macmillan, "Macmillan, Indirect Rule and *Africa Emergent,*" Ibid.; Leonard Barnes, *Empire or Democracy? A Study of the Colonial Question* (London: Victor Gollancz, 1939) and *The Duty of Empire* (London: Victor Gollancz, 1935); and the various writings of Dr. Rita Hinden, longtime secretary of the Fabian Colonial Bureau, such as *Empire and After* (London: Essential Books, 1949). See also essays in Rimmer and Kirk-Greene, cited above.

Finally, the Devlin Report, published officially as the *Report of the Nyasaland Commission of Inquiry,* Cmd. 814 (London: HM Stationery Office, July 1959), is a remarkable document, as is the rejoinder forced upon the hapless Governor Armitage: *Nyasaland Despatch by the Governor relating to the Report of the Nyasaland Commission of Inquiry,* Cmd. 815 (London: HM Stationery Office, July 1959).

Epilogue

The epilogue draws largely on sources already cited for evolving British policy, the end of the Federation, nationalist politics, and the transfer of power in Zambia. A key document, however, is the *Report of the Advisory Commission on the Review of the Constitution of Rhodesia and Nyasaland,* Cmd. 1148 (London: HM Stationery Office, October 1960), the report of the Monckton Commission, which spelled the demise of the Federation and anticipated the constitutional changes that preceded independence in the two northern territories. The *Memoirs* of Reginald Maudling (London: Sidgwick and Jackson, 1978), Macleod's successor as colonial secretary, include a brief chapter devoted to Africa, as does Lord Butler's *The Art of the Possible* (Boston: Gambit, 1972). The final volume of Harold Macmillan's memoirs, *At the End of the Day 1961–1963* (New York: Harper & Row, 1973), covers the events leading up to independence from the perspective of Downing Street. On a more local level, the concluding chapter of Allen's *Tales of the Dark Continent* (cited above) puts the transfer of power in human terms—how individual colonial officers reacted when the flags came down. A searching examination on a more theoretical level can be found in Dennis Austin, "The Transfer of Power: Why and How," in W. H. Morris-Jones and Georges Fischer, eds., *Decolonization and After: The British and French Experiences* (London: Frank Cass, 1980).

Politics in Zambia, edited by William Tordoff (Berkeley: University of California Press, 1974), serves as a sequel to Mulford, examining the first post-independence decade. Both Mulford and Hall deal with the early secessionist movement in Barotseland, but two articles by Gerald L. Caplan provide more details and carry the story further: "Barotseland: The Secessionist Challenge to Zambia," *Journal of Modern African Studies* 6: 3(1968), 343–60 and "Zambia, Barotseland, and the Liberation of Southern Africa," *Africa Today* 16: 4(1969). See also Dr. Mutumba Mainga Bull, "The Barotseland Agreement 1964 in Historical Perspective. A Preliminary Study," an unpublished paper prepared for a Joint History Seminar of The History Department and The Institute for African Studies Seminar Programme, September 4, 1996, University of Zambia, and anon., "Zambia: The Lozi Challenge," *Africa Confidential,* November 9, 1990. The attempted coup of 1999 in the eastern Caprivi Strip was reported in the *New York Times,* August 6, 1999, under the somewhat misleading title, "Tangled War in Congo Now Snares Namibians." Better perspective is provided by an unsigned article, "The Lozi Lost," in *The Economist,* September 4, 1999.

ACKNOWLEDGMENTS

This book had its genesis on a bright summer Sunday in Nottinghamshire, England, although I had no idea of it at the time. Some years and several visits to Orchard House later, I realized that there was a story to be told, in fact several stories. My greatest debt, therefore, is to Murray and Jeanne Armor who planted the seeds of these stories and have continued to sustain them with truly memorable hospitality and a treasure trove of material. Unfortunately, Murray died early in 1998, but not before we had recorded several hours of conversation and he had put me in touch with a number of his friends and former associates. Murray was *sui generis.* I can only offer this book as a small memorial to our friendship and my gratitude.

I am very grateful as well to David and Liz Salmon, John Herniman, Dick and Hazel Japp, Mike Japp, Rob and Grace Hart, Father Bruno, Gervas and Betty Clay, and David Taylor for graciously providing information, letters, journals, photographs, various ephemera, and, on occasion, welcome hospitality. Barbro Herniman, Paul Herniman, Alec Fisher, John Housden, Philip Bowcock, and Hywel Griffiths also supplied helpful information and insights. In Zambia, I thank Dr. Mutumba Mainga Bull, W. S. Sundona, W. M. Mubita, S. M. Wendiana, Brigid N. Mundia, Reverend Mkuzi A. Banda, John Hudson, and the residents of St. Joseph Mission, Mangango. Matthew and Sally Durdy kindly received us in Lusaka, and their help along with that of Rhoda Chama was invaluable in organizing and carrying out our trip to Barotseland. Later Professor Walima Kalusa and his students, Leonard Chinda and Chilelu Kakanwa, provided a mountain of source material from the National Archives of Zambia. I thank Bryan Callahan for facilitating this.

Many years ago Anthony Kirk-Greene welcomed me to St. Antony's College, Oxford, and to the symposium on the transfer of power that he organized in the spring of 1978. Little did I know then how valuable that experience would turn out to be. I am grateful for his encouragement more recently as I have begun to labor in the vineyard that he has cultivated so fruitfully for many years. The Interlibrary Loan Department of the Mount Holyoke College library has once more performed magnificently. I would also like to thank the staffs of the Public Record Office and Rhodes House library.

A number of friends and family offered helpful comments on portions of the manuscript: the late Peter Warren, Alan and Martha Armstrong, Antonia Woods, Richard and Sandra Lauderdale Graham, Zoë Strother, Joe Ellis, David Apter, Gren Lucas, Pat Cody, and Ellie Weld. Ellie has played a very special role in this book since she accompanied me on my first trip to Nottinghamshire, and she and David London have offered me a warm home away from home on many trips to England. Others to whom I am indebted include H. R. H. the Queen Mother, Elizabeth Colson, Bob Schwartz, Fred LeBlanc, Tom Millette, Magdélena Dohnalovà, Karen Milbourne, Awam Ampka, and Diana Wylie.

As always, my family has been a treasured source of happiness and a reminder that human relations are the heart of history. My husband, Bob, is my surest reader and my staunchest supporter, and has borne my trips to Africa over the years with stoic equanimity.

INDEX